To God.

Contents

Acknowledgments

1 Building Better Web Pages: Who, What, How   1

Here Are Some of the Things This Book Can Show You How to Do   *2*
Who This Book Is For   *3*
A Word About Standards and Webbons of Choice   *5*
    What Standard HTML?   *5*
    This Standard   *7*
    Save Money!   *7*
    Browser Wars   *8*
How This Book Is Set Up   *10*

2 Page Elements, Layout, and Navigation   11

Get the Look   *11*
    No Web Weenies   *12*
    "One" Wins   *14*
    Free Page Elements, for Example   *27*
    Free Total Looks and Fantastic Stuff   *29*
    Dangerous Backgrounds   *30*
    Embossed Backgrounds   *36*
    Margin Backgrounds   *39*
    Gradient Backgrounds   *41*
    Shaded Borders, Scallops, Etc.   *41*
    Hidden Message to Pseudo Luddites   *42*
    For the Star Tech Enterprise   *42*
Fancy Initial Caps   *42*

Sew on Buttons Seamlessly   *45*

Button Makers   *47*

Text and Fonts   *48*

    ASCII Graphic Letters with Figlet Utility   *51*

Layout and Space   *51*

    Put Objects in Their Place—Precisely   *52*

    Quick-and-Dirty Clean Space Margins   *53*

Layout with Tables   *55*

    Refresher: Basic Tables   *57*

    Spanning Single Cells over Multiple Rows or Columns   *58*

    New Summary Attribute in HTML 4.0   *59*

    Keep Column Headers Handy   *60*

Table-Based Page Layout   *60*

    Example Page Layout with Invisible Table   *62*

Frames: Traditional, None, and Inline   *66*

    Refresher: Basic Frames   *66*

    There's More to "No Frames" Than <NOFRAMES>   *72*

    New Inline Frames in HTML 4.0   *72*

Intuitive Navigation   *73*

    The Right Logical Structure   *74*

Other Navigational Tools   *76*

    Never Never Land   *77*

    Downloadable Java Link Applet   *80*

    Necessary Ways to Say "We Care"   *80*

    Avoid Navigational Nightmares   *80*

    Absolute vs Relative Links   *81*

    Meta Moving/Forwarding   *81*

Help Others Get With the Program   *82*

    Templates   *82*

The "Look" Is Free—the "Feel" Costs Extra   *83*

Finishing Touch—Webmaster's Contact   *86*

3 Objects Part 1: Images   89

Putting It All In   *89*

Covering Bases, Hedging Bets   *91*

Images   *92*

The Right Graphic for the Job: Bitmap, Vector, or Metafile   93
    Bitmaps   93
    Vector Images   94
    Metafiles   95
    Use GIF and JPG Bitmaps Whenever Possible   95
    Refresher: The IMG Tag   96
    Choose between GIF and JPG for Each Individual Image   97
GIFs   98
    GIFs and Color Palettes   98
Transparent, Interlaced, and Animated GIFs   100
    Transparent GIFs   100
    Interlaced GIFs   103
    Animated GIFs   105
JPEG, JPG, and JPE   118
    JPG Wins as Big Loser   119
    Converting to JPG to Save Space   120
    Progressive JPGs   120
PNG Files   121
Good Things, Small Packages   122
    The Golden Rule(r)   123
    Decreasing Byte Count   123
    Split It Up   127
    Space-saving Illusions   128
Grabbing Graphics   131
    Free Clip Art   131
    Screen Capture   131
    Artistic License(ing)   135
    Video Capture   136
    Digital Still Camera   136
    Scanners   137
    Film Development on Disk or E-mail   138
    Graphical ASCII Text Banners   139
Special Effects   141
Drop Shadows   149
Spectacular Cast Shadows   155
Easy Drop-Cast Shadows for Text in Paint Shop Pro   155
Special "Framing" Looks   156
    Other Framing Effects   158

Page-Top 3-D Text   *158*
Morphing   *160*
Figure Modeling   *160*
Virtual Reality   *161*
Special Symbols   *163*
Art, Copyright, and Licensing Issues   *164*
  Comment Lines in Animated GIFs   *164*
  Watermarks   *164*
  Steganography   *165*
  For More Information   *165*
  Copyright Notice   *165*

4 Objects Part 2: Sound   *167*

  <EMBED>, <BGSOUND>, <APPLET>, or <OBJECT> Tag?   *170*
Sources for Sound   *171*
Sound Quality and File Size   *172*
  Channels   *172*
  Sampling Rate   *173*
  Bit Depth   *173*
  Lossiness   *173*
  Clip Length   *173*
File Formats   *173*
Streaming Audio—Now with No Media Server Required   *174*
  When to Stream   *176*
  How to Stream RealAudio from Your Page   *176*
Editing Sound (Effects)   *177*
Sound Alternatives   *179*

5 Objects Part 3: Ready-Made Drop-Ins: Java Applets, JavaScript, Active X, and Plug-Ins   *181*

  Adding Java Applets to Your Page   *182*
Netscape Plug-Ins (and Active X and Java Counterparts)   *185*

6 Web Marketing and Press Coverage for Grownups 201

Marketing Your Site 201
    Search Engine Tips and Tricks 202
    Other Venues 204
    Talk "Dot Com" Everywhere 208
    Educate Your Spokespeople! 208
Get Press Attention 209
    How to Lure the Press to Your Site 212
    What to Put in Your Announcement 212
    Get Help When You Need It 215
    Money Saving Grace 215
    E-mail Wires 216
Sending Announcements by E-mail 217
    More Tips for Sending E-mail to the Press 219
    Mistakes Everyone Makes with Mailed URLs 221
    Clueful People Standing By 222
Once the Press Arrives: Your On-line Press Page 222

7 Toy Box: FAQs, Counters, Tricks, and Tools 225

Magic Trick: The Great Frame Escape 225
Put Some Class into "File Not Found" 227
Hands-Free Update Notifications 228
Put a Proper and Useful FAQ on Your Web Site 229
    Formatting Your FAQ 232
Pop-In Visitor Counter 237
Free Guest Book Offers Visitor Info 238
Add a Topical Search Engine 238
Let Visitors Search Your Web Site 239
Put Up a Clock 240
If You Offer Downloads 240
The Socially Conscious Thing 240
Easy and Interesting Content 240
    Check Your Provider's Attic Trunk for Treasures 241
    Glorious Things 241

Puzzles   *241*
Off-Site On-Topic FAQ   *242*
History Page   *242*
Testimonials   *243*

8 Hiding in Plain Site: Cloak-n-Dagger Web Pages   245

Steganography—Hide Files Within Files   *247*
Steganography Programs   *249*
More Sneak for Your Stego   *255*
Stego/Crypto Resources   *255*
Miniaturization—Hide Boulders in the Twinkle of an Eye   *257*
Miniaturization Tips   *258*
Miniaturization Resources for Netscape and Microsoft Browsers   *261*
Zero Links   *261*
Password Access to Web Pages (for UNIX, Windows, and Other Platforms)   *264*
Non-CGI Password with NCSA HTTPd   *264*
Password Protection without a UNIX Machine   *265*
Password Protection without Your Own Server!   *265*
Choosing Passwords for Web Pages and Stego Objects   *265*
Bonus Tricklet   *266*

Appendixes

A Basic Structure of an HTML Page   267

B HTML Tags   269

Index   281

Acknowledgments

I owe a great debt to the following cast of characters, without whom this book would be less than it is:

Thanks to Robert Dinse, owner and SysOp of Eskimo North (www.eskimo.com), for putting up the BBS I've been dialing into since 1990, when it ran on a TRS-80 and got its News via UUCP. Over the years, Robert has made full Internet access affordable for many thousands of people and provided shell access that hatched many careers in programming, system administration, Web design, Internet journalism, and more. Robert has given me many interviews for magazine articles and answered lots of questions behind the scenes for articles and for this book. Robert's background puts him in the Golden Rolodex for combined expertise in UNIX, telecommunications, and Earth-to-Media reality about the Internet.

Thanks to the three brave Webmasters who read this manuscript and offered critiques: Robert Lunday, SysOp and Webmaster of Hemp Net (www.hemp.net), Michael D'Antoni, LAN Analyst/Webmaster of Overlake Hospital (www.overlakehospital.org), and Brett Jones, owner and Webmaster of Escargot.com (www.escargot.com). Special above-and-beyond thanks to Robert Lunday for writing pages of helpful suggestions and offering valuable links to resources for our Linux readers.

Thanks to Mike Nadeau, now Senior Analyst at Mainspring (www.mainspring.com), for recommending me to AP Professional for this book. As an editor, Mike was the one who always made me wish I'd said it the way he edited it. He demands objectivity from his writers and gives them back work they can be proud to have their names on.

Thanks to AP Professional's Jeff Pepper for giving me the shot, and Thomas Stone and Thomas Park for their patience and kindness—and for what I suspect will be a very good product. Special thanks to intuitive and inventive AP production editor Shawn Brown, who has been great with tricky things.

Thanks to Carol Keller for her elegant interior book design and page layouts.

Thanks to the folks who tested some of the pages I created while trying out techniques for this book, mostly on other platforms and browsers. They include Tom Rohan, Esther Schindler, James Michael Edwards, Jim Brass, Robert Dinse, and Brett Jones.

Thanks to Tom Rohan for believing in me and for his many years of merciless support. (He made me say that.)

God care for Father Andy (Rev. Andrew Bullwinkel) 1943–1997.

Art Credits/Copyrights

Thanks to Nicholas W. Plummer, Ph.D., (http://www-personal.umich.edu/ ~nplummer) for growing and photographing *Cattleya walkeriana*—the beautiful orchid in Chapter 3—then letting me do all kinds of weird things to the photo to demonstrate graphic special effects. Go see the orchid in color at Nick's Website, along with his aquatic and carnivorous plants.

Thanks to my daughter, Marcia, for granting the use and weirdification of her photo in several pictures in this book.

Thanks to Maximillian "Max" the cat for the use of his photo, as well as fur-and-purr therapy.

Thanks to Debi Hobbs, photographer and adopted mom of featured pooches Mochi and Lilly.

Thanks to John Faherty, Webmaster (www.ultranet.com/~fahertys), for permission to reproduce his byte-saving "house siding" art and screen shots from his site.

Thanks to Joan Stark, ASCII Artist and Webmaster (www.geocities.com/ SoHo/7373/), for permission to use screen shots of her ASCII art.

Thanks to "Bimsan," Brith-Marie Wärn, Page and Graphic Designer, for permission to use several shots of her fabulous free Web graphics (www.bimsan.net/).

Thanks to Lola Wärn, Graphic Artist of the magical Porenn's Button Gallery (www.geocities.com/Athens/Acropolis/5041/geobutt.html), for permission to use screen shots of her site.

Thanks to Dan Evans, Content Master, Rent Com, Inc. (www.rent com.com), for permission to use the screen shot showing the embossed background.

Thanks to Ronn Wiehler, Director of Marketing, InterCAP Graphics Systems, Inc. (www.intercap.com), for permission to use screen shots of the zoom capabilities of the InterCAP Inline Plug-in.

Thanks to David M. Wilson, Publisher, DanceArt.com (www.dance art.com), for permission to use screen shots of downloadable dance clip-art from the site.

Thanks to Mario Cascio, President, WebProMotion, Inc. (www.web promotion.com), for permission to use a screen shot of its downloadable GIF animations.

Thanks to Marwan Aridi, master designer, Aridi Computer Graphics, Inc., for use of a screen from www.aridi.com showing beautiful initial caps.

Thanks to Bill Hagen, Manager, IEEE Copyrights, IEEE Service Center, for use of screen shots of http://computer.org/, which demonstrate a hidden message for folks with primitive browsers.

Thanks to Ray Everett-Church, J.D., Co-Founder & Congressional Liaison, Coalition Against Unsolicited Commercial Email (CAUCE) (www.cauce.org), for permission to use a screen shot of the CAUCE page.

Thanks to Scott Hazen Mueller, creator, "Fight Spam on the Internet" page (http://spam.abuse.net/spam), for permission to use a screen shot of that site.

Thanks to J.D. Falk, charter member and Webmaster, Internet Press Guild (www.netpress.org), which hosts the "Care and Feeding of the Press" page, for permission to use a screen shot of that page at www.netpress.org/ careandfeeding.html.

Thanks to Esther Schindler, OS/2 Goddess, The Bit Ranch (www.bit ranch.com), and consolidator of the "Care and Feeding of the Press" page at www.netpress.org/careandfeeding.html.

Thanks to Steve Leon, President, Technopolis® Communications Inc. (www.technopolis.com/), for permission to use a screen shot of his PR site.

Thanks to Excite (www.excite.com), for the screen shot of its EWS page. Excite, and the Excite Logo are trademarks of Excite, Inc. and may be registered in various jurisdictions. Excite screen display copyright © 1995–1997 Excite, Inc.

Thanks to Artville (www.artville.com, 800-631-7808, 608-243-1215) for the scissors photograph used to illustrate interlaced and noninterlaced GIFs in Chapter 3.

Image of crucifix copyright © 1997 PhotoDisc, Inc., www.photo disc.com. Used under license agreement.

Image "Portrait. TIF" copyright © Lifetouch Portrait Studios Inc. (www.lifetouch.com/Other/NH14.html and www.JCPportraits.com). Used with permission.

Legal Stuff

The Internet is the Wild West of the 90s, and the author, editor, and publisher of this book obviously have no way of guaranteeing addresses will be working or that they will have what we found when we visited; that downloadable items will still be available or still be freeware or shareware; that you will not be offended by things you find at any sites; that programs, downloadable art, applets, and other materials are the original work of the people who run the sites; that things you download from the Internet (or buy at the mall, for that matter) will interact with your hardware or software without breaking them; or that instructions in this book, whether applied or misapplied, will interact well or badly with your hardware or software, your business, or your life.

I'm also not a lawyer, doctor, pharmacist, accountant, stock broker, chef, professional hairdresser, or astrologer, and nothing in this book is intended as advice in those areas.

Take responsibility for what you do. Use your head, back up your hard drive, store some copies off-site, and know that we aren't going to pay for any misfortunes you get into. I have been a highly underpaid writer for so long that anything I made on this book was already owed and will be on its way to paying debts before your eyes hit the cover. I try to be very responsible with what I say, but I can't anticipate everything that can go wrong out in the world, including, but not limited to, system problems, angry customers, paper cuts, hair loss, and bad dreams. That said, I sincerely hope this book helps you transform your site into the best it can be. I've been advocating for the user as a reviewer and computer/Internet journalist since 1988.

Building Better Web Pages
Rebecca Frances Rohan

CHAPTER 1

Building Better Web Pages: Who, What, How

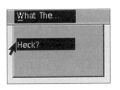

You're already a Webmaster. You taught yourself the skills by shamelessly hoisting up other people's pages and staring at their bare HTML, checking out on-line references, talking with colleagues, asking around Usenet, reading books, and experimenting with HTML editors. You know the basics. You already have a Web presence that's a lot more than a "Welcome to ACME Anvils" with an ACME_CRATE.GIF and a dynamite-with-fuse divider bar. Now you're ready to take the next step. You want your site to look completely professional, carry out more business functions, work quickly throughout, and perform for everyone who visits your site, no matter what browser they ride in on. You want your site to have the sparkle of the top 1% of all Websites—the sparkle of doing things professionally instead of tossing glitter on an average site.

Maybe you're at that moment of truth when you compare your pages to the best of the best, and see something a little too hodgepodge or patchwork. Maybe your site has an aesthetically professional look, but doesn't deliver what visitors are looking for in an organized, complete, and speedy way. This book will help you make better pages and better sites—*without* learning to program or write scripts. Everything in this book can be done without learning a stitch of CGI, JavaScript, Perl, or anything that requires a pocket-protector.

Here Are Some of the Things
This Book Can Show You How to Do

- Deliver multiple content formats with one set of HTML tags so every browser gets the best view it can
- Make users feel safe buying from your site
- Place objects on the page precisely where you want them—to the pixel point
- Ease updates with templates
- Ease maintenance with downloadable link-checkers
- Boost visitor satisfaction by helping them find what they want right away
- Boost speed by reducing file size for images, sounds, and animations
- Create a unified, professional look that's inviting, accessible, and fast
- Create embossed backgrounds, margin backgrounds, and gradient backgrounds
- Work with initial caps, create 3-D buttons, and work with indents and outlines
- Lose the ugly borders around hot-graphics
- Take a practical approach to fonts
- Get a hex number for any color—not just the few you see in charts
- Re-color clip art to match your site
- Automatically update links connecting all the pages at your site
- Get thousands of free objects for your pages
- Download programs to do the work for you
- Forward traffic to your new site with the <META> tag
- Grab whole pages of graphics instantly, without the "Save" routine
- Make your domain name do more for your business
- Auto-respond to visitor queries
- Format FAQs correctly for perfect navigation
- Make transparent GIFs to show the page background around shaped images
- Smooth image "jaggies"
- Learn when to choose a GIF and when to choose a JPEG for the best image and fastest download time
- Traditional frames, new inline frames, and the great frame escape
- Layout with invisible tables
- When to choose interlaced/non-interlaced GIFs and progressive/static JPEGs

- Offset frames and global color palettes for smaller animated GIFs
- Make streaming RealAudio and add it to a site free
- Legacy document solution: complex format conversions
- Turn movies and videos into fast streaming video or animated GIFs
- Balance non-streaming sound quality and download time
- Special effects for sound
- Special effects for images
- Drop-shadows and cast shadows
- Feathery inset "frames" for photos
- Download programs that create math and chem symbols
- Hide signatures in your original work
- Hide information in plain sight for colleagues and customer contests, and to update field forces privately
- Attract search engine spiders
- Create a page that helps the press cover you instead of your competition
- Password-protect selected pages
- Add free update notification, guest book, or clock
- Much more!

There's a tremendous amount you can do with basic Web skills and/or downloadable programs that let you drag, drop, and decree your way to a truly great Web site. And when you've got the perfect site, turn to Chapter 6 to find some ways to promote it, how to get the press interested in reviewing or mentioning it, and what to have waiting for the press when we get there. (In addition to writing how-to's about the Web and news about the Net for magazines from *Web Developer* to *Internet World*, I've chosen, reviewed, rated, and ranked Web sites for magazines from *NetGuide* to *The I-Way 500*.)

Who This Book Is For

Though this *isn't* a beginner's book, Appendix A shows a skeletal HTML page with brief explanations, and Appendix B is a chart of ratified HTML 4.0 tags. In addition, there are short refreshers of tags throughout the book to go along with the projects that call for them. For example, the section on improving images includes a quick reminder of how to use the <IMG> tag. But the focus of this book is making better Web pages—not making a first page. The chapter on images, for example, is about more sophisticated images, faster images, special effects, drop shadows, feathered frames, transparency, the right format for the type of image, integrating the image into your site's overall look, creating smaller animated GIFs, and so on.

Beginning, intermediate, and advanced Webmasters can all get useful things from this book, though the target is the intermediate Webmaster who knows the basics and wants more professional pages without becoming a programmer. Beginners should stop and download a good HTML editor that automatically creates a skeletal Web page and allows direct editing of the plain text code, so they can get used to the basics of generating pages. A good example is Brooklyn North's HTML Assistant Pro 97, and a fully functioning 30-day trial version for Windows 95 and NT 4.0 is available for download at www.brooknorth.com. Not using Windows? Chapter 2 has a table of editors for several platforms. Once a beginner generates code automatically within an HTML editor, looks at the code, and toggles between the HTML and the result in a browser, it will become obvious what the HTML does. With a little playing around, that beginner will have enough of a handle on the basics to move on to topics in this book such as frames, tables, graphical special effects, and streaming multimedia.

Intermediate Webmasters will get the most out of this book. The middle-master has experience with basic topics. This often self-taught person knows enough to become the Webmaster at work, or have a good personal page or a nice page for a club or organization. The intermediate Webmaster is the most likely to be actively pestering friends and acquaintances for some of the very information between these pages, and probably needs, or will soon need, the techniques in this book. I know this audience because I wrote this book with real people in mind, remembering the questions they asked, and seeing other things that would improve already good sites. They're heroes—systems administrators and others who may find themselves solely responsible for the work that should belong to a team made up of both technical and artistic people. They have succeeded in putting up respectable sites. Now they want great sites.

Advanced users will also find useful information here—from details about improving their pages in specific areas to promoting their sites to the press. However, people who describe themselves as "advanced" are likely to be looking for instruction in scripting and applet programming, or even help with specific scripting languages for database-to-Web applications. This book doesn't go there—it offers pointers to applets and scripts that anyone can download and drop into their pages, describes how to put them in, and suggests downloading an eval copy of a program such as Allaire Corp's Cold Fusion for database applications.

A Word about
Standards and Webbons of Choice

This book offers practical solutions that will reach the largest number of visitors to your site. That means using standard HTML tags with exciting and useful content that visitors with most browsers on most platforms can experience, and offering alternatives to those with simpler browsers. After all, why would anyone download and fire up a different browser or download and install a new plug-in just to see something on your page? Unless you have a captive audience, where you issue everyone's gear like a supply sergeant—or you have the only footage of the second coming of Elvis—visitors will move on to a site that they can take advantage of with their browser of choice.

What Standard HTML?

Before most of us ever heard of the World Wide Web, we were dialing into BBSs with communications programs like ProComm and Crosstalk, joining conferences limited to our own provider's customers instead of the universal Internet Relay Chat (IRC), and engaging in ANSI shooting wars—creating blinking, colored words and pictures in front of fellow conferees as if we were in some sort of electronic belching contest. (Well, maybe not *most* of us.) It didn't escape us that all that ANSI stuff we made didn't appear on anyone's monitor unless they happened to have the file ANSI.SYS loaded (on a PC), and a supporting terminal emulation, such as ANSI BBS, chosen in their communications program, *even though ANSI stands for "American National Standards Institute."* We were just amazed that Macs, PCs, C64s, and Amigas could all type to each other on the local UNIX BBS, through the miracle of ASCII (American *Standard* Code for Information Interchange) text. But we soon discovered that plain text files weren't quite the same on DOS and UNIX machines. In spite of the foreshadowing, we were still a little naive about standards at the time the graphical Web appeared.

Soon after the rise of the graphical Web, we learned through programs like SoftQuad's Panorama that HTML (HyperText Markup Language) itself was a tiny subset of the huge SGML (Standard Generalized Markup Language). A lot more of SGML could conceivably be a part of HTML—not to mention other inventions, if browser vendors had their say. Notices sprang up on Web pages telling visitors they should have Netscape Navigator to see everything at a given site. Microsoft, ever desirous of . . . well . . . everything, developed its own proprietary tags, and buttons appeared declaring that visitors needed Internet Explorer to experience other sites. By the time Netscape and Microsoft spit out their respective version 4 browsers, both were eager to appear to embrace "standards" in the form of recommendations by the World Wide Web Consortium (W3C), a body that set out to help tame the evolving two-headed dragon.

By that time, application developers had created plug-ins for Netscape Navigator so visitors could see content developed with very off-Web authoring tools, and Microsoft pushed its own Active X as an alternative to plug-ins. Sun and others developed Java—a cross-platform tool for delivering virtually any kind of content, including just-in-time executable applets—mini applications that download to the visitor's browser and execute on the spot. But when Microsoft put Java in Internet Explorer, the result was apparently deviate enough to spark a lawsuit from Sun. Don't worry too much—just test your Java applets in both Netscape's and Microsoft's version 4.0 browsers. You were going to test anyway, weren't you?

To complicate things a little further, different platforms converging on the Web brought different formats for content such as images, sounds, and video. The early file format winners were often cross-platform solutions, such as the CompuServe GIF image file, or the most bandwidth-friendly solution, such as streaming Real-Audio, or simply a survivor of early telephony standards, such as AU sound files. Some things change when popular and practical—like making room for Windows WAV sound files next to the sometimes hissy AU sound format that's been around the Web a lot longer. But no matter how many Windows users are familiar with BMP image files, the unwieldy BMP format won't bump the practical, bandwidth-conservative GIF or JPEG graphics formats. An even more Web-efficient format, the PNG (Portable Network Graphics) file, hasn't caught on because the format doesn't have enough built-in support in older browsers.

Most Webmasters are aware by now that the real-world Web is an unfortunate mishmash of tags and tools from competing vendors, but they may not understand the distinction between various stages of "real" HTML and ad hoc "extensions" to HTML. The W3C's "draft proposals" are a snapshot of what may or may not become a recommendation. The "recommendation" is the official HTML standard. "Extensions" to HTML are unofficial tags, often developed unilaterally by a browser publisher, that may or may not catch on with the public, other browser makers, and the W3C itself. Netscape frames only became a part of HTML with HTML 4.0, ratified December 18, 1997, even though frames were supported by Microsoft and Netscape and utilized widely well before that. The HTML 4.0 recommendation includes advances such as inline frames that weren't part of original Netscape frames.

Even when a tag is part of a W3C recommendation, that doesn't mean that browser publishers will implement it, or implement it uniformly. That's why the same HTML page appears differently in different browsers. Another problem is over-hasty action on W3C draft proposals by browser vendors and other developers. The public criticized the W3C for being too slow to recommend changes to HTML during those early days when Netscape charged ahead with new tags that caught on as de facto standards for many. W3C still takes some time to publish full-fledged recommendations, but they've also instituted a rule that they must publish draft proposals within 3 months of considering them. Vendors and Webmasters have the unfortunate habit of locking onto those draft proposals as though they were solid recommendations, when in fact they are meant for discussion, and are subject to change and sudden death. In fact, things changed so much while HTML 3.0 was under consideration that HTML 3.0 never became a recommendation at all. The W3C scrapped HTML 3.0 and proposed and recommended HTML 3.2, and then 4.0.

This Standard

One important mission of this book is to help you cut to the "most standard," and therefore most universal, solution for anything you want to present on the Web, and create it and get it out there for the widest possible audience quickly, easily, and inexpensively. There are tools to do just about everything in the most standard format with the most standard tags—most of them free for the downloading. That goes for all the tools on your side of the glass—not just the ones that create HTML—because we work on content itself for most of the book. You'll find tables of downloadable tools for creating content throughout the chapters here, whether you're marketing from Maui with Windows 95/NT, waging corporate warfare from Atlanta on UNIX, minding the store from the den on a Mac, presiding over The OS/2 Bit Ranch (www.bitranch.com) in Arizona, or staging a world takeover from a hardened undersea multiplex on Linux. Even though the examples of working with art, sound, video, and HTML throughout this book are done with Windows programs, I've included tables of downloadable tools for other platforms.

Save Money!

This book should save you money by helping you keep an eye on migration from platform to platform and from business needs to business needs—you can't afford to invest in tools, training, or human resources with dead-end technologies. This book will help you learn to watch your back, as well as the road ahead—helping you get other departments to bring their technologies into line with the possible coming integration of all your company data into a browser-based environment. If you're the person the company is likely to call on when they want a centralized database serving the Web, an intranet, customer service, and sales—or when they want other departments to have templates for publishing their results in a browser-readable format—today isn't a minute too early to start making them make it easy for you to do that. The formats and styles people are using in other departments today are your legacy conversion nightmares or rewards of tomorrow.

Consistency of documents from everyone contributing to your Website will make the difference between being able to use tools to search and replace content at your site automatically and doing updates by hand. Standardization must enter into everything you do in, on, or around your Website and your entire company if you want to breeze through content changes or simply hold up during inevitable technological changes. None of us need know what those changes will be to appreciate the role of standards in making the changes less painful. This book will help you prepare.

Browser Wars

There is one more topic under standards that is so important you should consider it all by itself. I've alluded to the fact that different browsers handle tags differently, and that only the most egomaniacal Webmaster—or one who has a captive audience on an intranet or in an organization where he can issue his browser of choice—would demand that people go download another browser just to experience his content.

Web visitors and people with personal pages can afford to play "holy war" with browsers, but businesses can't. It doesn't matter how you feel about Netscape or Microsoft—what matters is what your visitors are using. And they aren't all using the same browser. They aren't even all using one of the Big Two. For a nonscientific sampling of what browsers are checking into iWORLD's Browser Watch page, check out http://browserwatch.inter net.com/stats/stats.html. Browser Watch notes what horse its visitors ride in on, but the author is careful to describe its visitors as software developers and editorial types who must have the latest and greatest browser. Another place to check is the research firm Computer Intelligence—go to www.ci.zd.com and run a search on the term "browser AND market."

Even with Microsoft putting free browsers in every clothes dryer and box of cereal, the stats I get from research companies while doing news stories for Net magazines still put Netscape ahead, with Microsoft gaining. All other browsers combined still have 2 or 3 percent market share, and the plain text browser Lynx is a significant piece of that. There are also lots of folks out there counted under graphical browsers who've actually turned off graphics, Java, JavaScript, and other nonessentials so they can get to information faster. If prominent Internet author and speaker Daniel Dern pays a visit to your site, it's likely to be from a text-based browser, or with all the bells and whistles turned off for his graphical browser, even though he has a cable-modem connection. One of several reasons this fellow-member of the Internet Press Guild cites is "no danger to my computer from hostile (or inept) Java, ActiveX, etc." In fact, Dern has a Web page devoted to his "Works JUST FINE With Any Browser" Policy at www.dern.com/justfine.html. The site includes collected logos such as "Best Viewed With a Budgie" and "This Web page is Lynx Friendly!"—as well as resources on text-based browsing and related accessibility issues.

Your visitors will likely represent the gamut of browsers, but HTML 4.0 and very little elbow grease will eventually help with that. For now, it's important to test every page on a variety of browsers, including those written long before HTML 4.0 was ratified. Many people sensibly hang on to a browser that works for them, especially after a newer version of a browser crashes their system, or after a botched un-install necessitates a disk reformat to put things right.

Although this book explains solutions that offer visitors drill-down choices to the objects their browser can handle, there is a limit to your company's resources for delivering different content formats. This book will help you see how much you can do without any kind of applet, plug-in, or Active X control. In fact, many of the things done out on the Web with those technologies could have been done with standard Web content formats and plain HTML. If you do have to choose something more complex, cross-platform, cross-browser Java makes a lot of sense for many—or look for a technology supported both by a plug-in that's already built into Netscape and an Active X control. (Remember that even Netscape 4.0 users can't see Active X.) Before you choose a technology that requires visitors to download an additional browser plug-in, consider this: There were 176 plug-ins available for download as of January 7, 1998. How many of those have you downloaded and installed? Think carefully before asking visitors to go to all that trouble to experience your stuff.

As for the competing Netscape and Microsoft versions of dynamic HTML, at the time HTML 4.0 was ratified, the World Wide Web Consortium (W3C) site said it clearly: "Dynamic HTML is still in its infancy and current implementations are experimental." If someone expects you to indulge in dynamic HTML before its time, get help from tools that build for both Microsoft's and Netscape's versions. Tools that do both—and have free trials—include Pictorius iNET Developer (www.pictorius.com), mBED Interactor (www.mbed.com), and Astound Dynamite (www.astound.com).

Armed with knowledge of these issues surrounding standards, you'll better understand why this book nudges you toward certain choices as you create content, pages, and sites throughout.

How This Book Is Set Up

Chapter 2 helps beef up site structure, page layout, and navigation, and create a professional "look." The next three chapters concentrate on objects—creating, improving, and installing content. Chapters 3 objects are images, Chapter 4 objects are sound, and Chapter 5 goes into drop-in objects such as Java and plug-in content. Chapter 6 helps you market your site professionally and get positive press attention. Chapter 7 is a toy box full of things you can add to your site. Chapter 8 is a unique journey into the secret side of Web pages—how to conceal things at your site at those times you need to get sights and sounds to people in the field right under the noses of unsuspecting surfers. Appendix A is a bare-bones HTML page, and Appendix B is a concise reference list of HTML 4.0 tags. All told, this book should take your site to the next level.

Thank you for choosing this book—may its techniques save you time and money, and your results exceed your goals.

Here's to your Better Web Pages, and to you!

Rebecca Frances Rohan

CHAPTER 2

Page Elements, Layout, and Navigation

Synchronize your watch with your future as "Master of the Web," because it's time to:

- Create or upgrade to a professional site design
- Gain absolute power over placement of objects, including images
- Make your Webspace more navigable and user-*useful*.

We'll also touch on some oft-overlooked features of standard HTML, and add original touches that put your site in a league of its own.

We'll start with what most people think of as a site's "look"—the color scheme, background, buttons, and so forth. Of course, everything about a site contributes to its look—including spacing of elements, cutting off a page in the right place, text layout, and more. The more you think of *everything* at your site as an important contributor to the "look," the more professional your site will be.

As you pick up techniques in this book, you'll want an image-editing program to help carry them out. You'll find the location of downloadable image editors in Table 2–1.

Get the Look

We've all seen top-honors Websites—those crème de la crème pages that are indisputably great. As a Net reviewer, I've chosen sites and determined star ratings for *NetGuide's* CyberGuide, and selected sites for whole

TABLE 2-1 *Downloadable Image Editors*

Image Editor	Platform	The Deal	URL
Jasc Paint Shop Pro 4.14	Windows 3.1/NT 3.51 or 95/NT 4.0	30-day trial	www.jasc.com
The GIMP (GNU Image Manipulation Program)	Linux (ELF / a.out), FreeBSD-2.1 / FreeBSD-2.2, HP-UX, Solaris 2.4 / SunOS 4.1.x IRIX (tardist)	Free distribution	www.XCF.Berkeley.edu/ ~gimp/gimp.html
PM View 1.0	OS/2	Unknown	www.os2bbs.com
NIH Image	Mac 68000 or Power PC	Unknown	http://rsb.info.nih.gov/ nih-image/download.html

categories of *The I-Way 500*, but the sites I'm talking about now would never have only 3 stars, or take the Number 10 slot in a category. These sites would be number 1, 2, or 3 out of hundreds or thousands in a category. When they appear on your screen they're so right you expect white clouds to roll out from under your monitor. That's the look we're after. You may not consciously know what it is that makes a site so fine, but you know it when you see it—and so do others. We're going to get very specific throughout this book, so you can build a site so splendid you'll feel like wiping your feet before you go into it.

No Web Weenies

I'm sure you've seen enough from the HTML hot-dogs who put "everything on it." Pthththt! That's just nasty! "Everything on it" pages give visitors aesthetic indigestion. Companies might as well hold formal evening recitals where their children play Chopsticks with one finger on each hand.

In fact, does your site look as if it were thrown together by a fourth-grader? Take the test:

1. Does your site have a sign at the top that begins "Welcome to . . ."?
2. Does your site play a sound when people reach it just because you know how to make it happen? (In fact, is there *anything* on your site that's there *only* because you know how to do it?)
3. Do you have dark, rectangular photos hanging heavily on a light, plain background?

4. Do you have any rectangular photos hanging without some kind of framing effect?

5. Do images with transparent backgrounds look not only as if the images are part of the page, but as if they *should be* part of the page?

6. Does your site have a full-screen background texture with a strong pattern—whether it's easy to read text over it or not? We're talking wood grain, cloth, a starry night, marble, etc.—anything but the most delicately embossed light-on-white or subtly etched pearl-gray-on-paler-gray image that has absolute relevance to your site. (If your company is called The Star Tech Enterprise, and your "look" is the bridge of a starship facing out a viewscreen, then you might get away with a night filled with tiny stars, but if you're going to go for that kind of background, be prepared to run a very tight starship, indeed.)

7. Do you have a background texture that you've seen at other sites?

8. Does your site have a strong background *color*? We're talking pumpkin, mustard, toilet bowl cleaner, key lime, leaf (in any season), walnut, wine, fire truck, or Easter candy? (Not margin color, mind you, but full-window background color.)

9. Are there divider bars or buttons on your page that you thought looked neat and decided to download, even if they weren't designed to go together? Do any elements, such as buttons and bars—whether they match *each other* or not—look as if they weren't created specifically for your site?

10. Is art jammed up against the side or ceiling of your site—or sitting awkwardly in a line of text where it pushes other lines of text out of even spacing, because you don't know how to place objects where you want them or wrap text the way you can in a desktop publishing program?

11. Do you have hot-links on every word that has a possible related URL— for example, a professional writer with a link to the front door of every magazine he mentions writing for? (One exception: Professional Web designers show-casing the sites they've designed for clients who paid them lots of money for their work. If that's you, you probably don't need this book anymore.)

12. Does your site have broken graphic links and outdated URLs—the electronic equivalent of a run-down trailer with a yard full of broken down cars? Do people pass your virtual real estate and whisper, "Byte trash?"

If you answered "yes" to even one of these items, don't just scrape the relish and ketchup off; put the whole hot dog down the disposal and *really* start over—with a clean plate and a heapin' helpin' of neighborly advice, provided ahead. After all, you're not really throwing anything away—just opening a brand new file and creating a new work of wonder. If you still want anything from your old site once you've been through Auntie Rebecca's Web Charm School, then put your overalls on and haul it back in. But I think you'll like what you produce from now on a lot better.

"One" Wins

The best sites don't have several looks, or three looks, or two looks. They have one look, and only one look. I'm not talking about limiting alternative pages—you should have plain text alternatives—and if you choose to write specifically for two or three browsers, that's your choice, too, because you can set it up so any one visitor sees only the content that applies to him. But whichever page you're on, the look should be singular, and it should be unmistakably yours.

Dying to Match   Everything on your site should belong—aesthetically as well as logically. That means you start with actual color and design choices. Your colors should belong together. You'll use those colors for page accents like a margin down the side, for navigation bars and their text, for image maps, shadows, and buttons, for recoloring clip art to match your site, for divider bars (if you think you need them), and for icons. At least one of those colors will probably be a big part of your company logo—so you'd better take a good long look at that logo and fall in line with it, if not in love with it. These colors will even be what you strive to bring photos in line with, however subtly—by slightly adjusting their hue, saturation, and other tweakles.

Your basic page color, under the items you paint with your scheme, should almost always be white, and the text used for actual content—not button text—black. Other colors should be as few as you can get away with—the main two (and a third for backup) should actually be the same color with different luminescence. We'll get to luminescence, along with hue and saturation, in a moment. The fourth (and fifth for backup) colors should be different from the first three—these will be your accent colors. They must look great with the original three variants of one color. We'll discuss choosing accent colors. Those five colors are all most Web sites need—and it's easy to get the right ones. Your software will help you do the getting—you don't have to be a graphics artist to accomplish any task in this book.

Note: When you use the three variants of one color correctly, the Web visitor will be aware of one predominant color, and perhaps realize the color is shown in "two" shades that are in some inexplicable harmony. The one or two accent colors, when seen, will seem like a designer's choice. The "reading areas" with black text on white "paper" won't detract either—and they'll make visitors comfortable staying and absorbing your message.

Choosing Colors. First you'll need a utility or program that allows you to select colors from a full palette or color picker—at least 16-bit high color, which is 65,536 colors. Color bit-depth or bit resolution is the number of bits per pixel on the screen. Since more bits per pixel allows for greater distinction for each color, it allows for a greater number of colors to be distinguished, like so:

Bit Depth	Binary 2 (off/on) ^{x}	Number of Colors
1-bit	2^1	2 (usually black and white)
4-bit	2^4	16
8-bit	2^8	256
16-bit ("High Color")	2^{16}	65,536
24-bit ("True Color")	2^{24}	16,777,216
32-bit	2^{32}	4,294,967,296 (Windows treats as 24-bit)
64-bit	2^{64}	1.844674407e+19 (Windows treats as 24-bit)

Your video card, driver, and monitor have to support the color depth you want to draw colors from. If you have a 24-bit video card, but only see 16 colors or 256 colors, you either don't have the right driver configured, or you don't have the right driver installed. See your video card documentation. You may also have an outdated or substandard program that doesn't support more than 16 or 256 colors. Another distinct possibility: your video card or monitor doesn't support the number of colors you want at a high screen resolution—the options for High Color (65,536-color) or True Color (16,777,216-color) drivers may appear only with a 640 × 480 or 800 × 600 display setting, not 1024 × 768 or higher. Most systems sold today have 24-bit color video cards and are relatively easy to configure. Windows 95 users can check Control Panel's Display/Settings option. To get there, hit the START button, then Settings/Control Panel/Display/Settings/Color Palette.

The utility or program with a high-color color picker should also let you see information about Hue, Saturation, and Luminescence for a selected color. This information may appear in a status bar at the bottom of the program screen, or near the area that shows which color is chosen, or in the dialogue box where you choose the color. You probably have a basic paint program that does this—if not, you can download an image editor from the Net. Windows 95 users will find a color picker in the Control Panel Display settings.

Hit the START button, then Settings/Control Panel/Display/Appearance.

Click on one of the representations of a windows element that offers a color choice, such as Desktop, Window, or Active Title Bar.

Click on the Color bar. A small color palette of 20 color squares, plus "Other..." appears.

Choose "Other." A Color dialog window appears with a palette of color squares on the left, a large multi-colored area to the right of that, a thin strip of colors with an arrow pointing in toward it to the right and, below—information about Hue, Saturation, Luminescence, and RGB (Red, Green Blue). Figure 2–1 shows this standard Windows 95 Color dialog, which you'll see in image editors and paint programs, as well. (Note: Use "Cancel" to avoid changing colors in your Windows interface.)

Windows 3.1 users can open Windows Paint and double click a color in the palette. An Edit Colors dialog appears—click the bar that says "Define

FIGURE 2-1   *The standard Windows 95 Color picker*

Custom Colors" to get to the color picker. Consult the help files for programs downloaded for Mac, OS/2, UNIX, and other operating systems.

Pick Three of a Kind, Plus Two. For the moment, let's assume you're starting with no colors that you have to match—no corporate logo, no warehouse full of letterhead, and no swatch the boss bought in from a favorite couch at home. You just want to choose a good color scheme. So we'll do a little color scheming at the meta-message level, then come back to our color picker for the technical details.

Mission: Think about what your enterprise does—its mission, its product, its service, its image. Some enterprises lend themselves to certain general color families. For example, you might want to associate a coffee company with the brown family, baby dolls with comforting light blues, Victorian articles with beige, mauve, and maroon, or pale apricot and beige, and a church with something gold and glorious.

Tone: Think about the tone you want to take with color as carefully as you choose a tone of voice to speak with your enterprise's customers or clients. Most businesses don't purposely yell, whine, or yodel at people who step into their offices, and the entryway at most organizations is as tasteful as the organization can afford within its mission parameters. For many organizations, a Webmaster can choose colors safely by asking, "Would I see this color in an upscale dentist's office? A high-end bank?"

Go into your color picker program. It's actually a good idea to do this in a paint or image-editing program, rather than just an area that checks video display colors, etc., so you can dip your brush into the selections and paint with them. (*Hint:* Windows 95 users who upgraded over Windows 3.1 may still find Windows Paint in their Windows directory, depending on the options they chose.) Sticking with our demo in the Windows 95 color picker, click different points on the large multicolored area near the right of the window. A surprisingly large variation of colors show up individually as you click different points of similar-looking color in the color picker. You'll notice that the color bar on the far right of the screen changes to reflect a band of color close to the one you clicked on. Zero-in on your perfect color using any combination of clicks in the big window and moving the arrow up and down along the thin color bar on the right. When you get that perfect color, immediately write down the exact Hue, Saturation, and Luminescence numbers, and the exact Red, Green, and Blue (RGB) numbers.

If your program also shows a hex number, write that down, too—it will save you some steps later. If not, don't worry—you can get the hex number several ways, which we'll go into later in this chapter. Some graphics programs don't show the correct Hex number. If you record the Hex number and it doesn't show the same color in your browser, follow the directions later in this chapter for finding the correct Hex number.

Hint: Your program might let you "Add To Custom Colors," as the Windows Color Picker does. Unfortunately, it's way too easy to overwrite one custom color with the next one in Windows. Always write each color down the moment you have it. An example for one color's info would be:

Hue/Sat/Lum	RGB	Hexadecimal
Hue 136	Red 152	Hex 98D4FF
Sat 225	Green 212	
Lum 191	Blue 255	

Once you've written down your Hue/Sat/Lum and RGB numbers for the first color you chose, it's time to pick two more colors that are the same as the first, but considerably darker or lighter. You'll find those colors by simply moving the arrow up and down on the thin strip on the right side of the window, or by changing the numbers in Luminescence (only). You're looking for two variations on the first color that, together with that first color, give you light, medium, and dark versions of the same color. The results will be beautifully matched! If you wish to add extreme light and extreme dark variants for future reference, then you might as well grab them while you're doing all this. They may come in handy.

Now you have your "three of a kind" (if not five) main color variants, and you need two contrasting, different, accent colors. These might be colors you just feel right about—go into your image editor, such as Jasc's downloadable trial of Paint Shop Pro (www.jasc.com) and actually see what colors look good with your first three. Don't guess without looking—ignore the "rules" in your head about what goes with what. Just dip your brush in many different colors and try them one at a time beside the colors you have so far.

If you want to be more scientific, look at a color wheel, as shown in Figure 2–2. Red, yellow, and blue—the primary colors—are in three pieces in a six-color pie, and between them are the colors they create together. Between red and yellow is orange, between yellow and blue is green, and between blue and red is violet. Starting with red, you have Red, Orange, Yellow, Green, Blue and Violet, or the famous mnemonic fellow "Roy G. Bv." A color's complement is opposite it on the wheel, and may be a nice accent

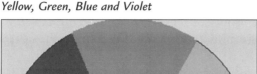

FIGURE 2-2   *The color wheel—Red, Orange, Yellow, Green, Blue and Violet*

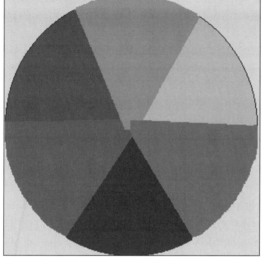

color, but that's not a lot of help, unless you want a blue site with orange accents, or violet with yellow. In this case it's usually best to ditch science and go steal from the professionals. They've done the work for you—and it's everywhere.

Start by checking out the templates and color scheme builders that came with your presentation (electronic slides) program. If you don't have a copy of a presentation program on your disk, knock on some doors down the hall and ask for Microsoft Power Point (in Microsoft Office 97 Professional Edition www.microsoft.com), SPC ASAP Word Power or Harvard Graphics (www.spco.com), Lotus Freelance Graphics (www.lotus.com), or the like. This is an easy way to take advantage of work done by people with an eye for color—there will be complete color schemes on templates, and there may be walk-throughs that begin with your first color and let you choose colors to go with it from a selection that narrows with every choice you make.

Most business presentation programs are designed for people like us—geeks, not graphics artists, who need a professional look. Don't have a presentation program? Download a trial version, get a CD trial, or go to a shareware site. If a presentation graphics publisher doesn't offer a demo version, it may offer free templates and a run-time player to see them with.

Hint: When looking at a presentation program, don't be put off by the fact that your starting color, which may be medium or dark, is the background color on the "slide" the program is designing. You won't be using that color as a background at your site. Remember that the Web is about daylight backgrounds, while slides have to show up in the dark. You're just using the presentation program to collect colors that work together. (Templates for overhead transparencies, as opposed to slides, are usually dark-on-white (clear), which works well for the Web.)

✪ *Danger:* Don't use accent colors in equal amounts with main colors. The ratio of accent color to main color should reflect the intensity of the accent color: the more intense the color, the less to use.

Check out color templates for "special paper" if you have them installed in your desktop publishing program or word processor. While they generally use fewer colors than presentation color schemes, they may give you an idea for the right accent colors. You'll need accent colors—if not for hot-links or active links (the links as they appear when you're stepping on them with the mouse), then for text on navigational buttons or something else. Paper Direct has paper catalogs that show all their multicolor paper designs. (Home businesses and small businesses that do extremely small print runs should consider using these predesigned papers—especially if they have a laser printer instead of a high-end color printer.)

Hint: Don't use an accent color for visited links. Visited links should look "done," not active. Think charcoal gray, muted navy blue, dark chalkboard green, etc., to signify links the visitor has already been to.

Walk through an upscale department store and study the colors put together on each female mannequin wearing a suit, blouse, and scarf, and each male mannequin wearing a suit, shirt, and tie. Even the colors within a single subtle tie can be a clue about accent colors. Again, professionals have already selected colors that work well together. Let them sweat while you window shop.

Hint: Remember a Website is more likely to look good in the colors you find in a women's department than men's, because they're generally brighter and lighter. Dark colors must be restricted to very small areas of your site. For example, a wide margin down the left side of the page must be a medium or fairly light variant of your main color—not dark. A dark margin should be narrower. Too much dark—such as a wide band of navy blue—won't accent your page; it will chop off the dark section completely in the mind's eye. It can work, especially if you want to make the page seem narrow, but you need to be aware of the effect. But if you're doing original graphics and not simply using safe standbys like margins, you can control the proportion of dark color beautifully and have a very elegant site.

Q&A: Why choose colors and make note of their color numbers for margins, when margins are usually done with a graphics file instead of with hex numbers in the HTML file? Because you'll create new graphics or bring graphics files in line with the actual color choices so *everything* matches perfectly. See "recoloring" later in this chapter.

If You Have a Color to Start With   What if you have a starting color or two? Maybe the Web color scheme has to play off the blue and white corporate logo, or one of your main responsibilities is to display paraphernalia for the Girl Goblins—most of it two shades of green. The trouble is, you don't have the numbers for those colors. What you really need is a copy of anything digital in that color that's required at the site, such as an image of the Girl Goblins' logo. If that's not available, then start scanning—but if something is already in digital format that you must use, it's imperative to start with that, because of the differences in monitors and real world color. If Image Zero—the digitized logo approved by your company—doesn't look right over a variety of displays on different platforms, get a green light to change it before you get started, then make your color selections from the improved version. Depending on your corporate culture, adjustments to the image of the logo may be a big deal—so do bring it up at the very beginning.

Once you have a good digital image—or the one you have to use as is—you can find the color's RGB numbers by opening a copy (never the original) and using your image-editing program's eye dropper tool, selecting the colors you want and recording their values as they appear on screen. If the image isn't in a graphics file format by itself, or isn't in a file format you know how to work with, take a screen capture of the image with a program like SnagIt for Windows 95, which you can download for a free trial at www.techsmith.com, then save the image to a graphics format your image editor can use. Table 3–6 (in Chapter 3) shows downloadable screen capture programs for Windows, Mac, and UNIX. See Table 2–1 (in this chapter) for downloadable image editors for several platforms.

Finalize Color Scheme and Make It Handy   Create an HTML page that calls each of your colors for use as HEAD 1 text, and also as individual graphics files, like so:

```
<HTML>
<HEAD>
<TITLE>Big Macho Machine Co.--Color Swatches</TITLE>
</HEAD>
<BODY BGCOLOR="FFFFFF" TEXT="000000" LINK="000000"
```

```
VLINK="000000" ALINK="000000">
<FONT COLOR="809F8C"><H1>MAIN COLOR—MEDIUM TRUCK
GREEN</H1></FONT>
HUE 95
SAT 33
LUM 135
R 128
G 159
B 140
Hex 809F8C
<IMG SRC="truckmed.gif" HEIGHT=50 WIDTH=100>

<P>Of course, you'll fill in the numbers for these, too:</P>

<H1>VARIANT LIGHT TRUCK GREEN</H1>
<IMG SRC="trucklit.gif" HEIGHT=50 WIDTH=100>
<H1>VARIANT DARK TRUCK GREEN</H1>
<IMG SRC="truckdrk.gif" HEIGHT=50 WIDTH=100>
<H1>ACCENT 1 </H1>
<IMG SRC="accent01.gif" HEIGHT=50 WIDTH=100>
<H1>ACCENT 2</H1>
<IMG SRC="accent02.gif" HEIGHT=50 WIDTH=100>
```

Don't forget to make the actual GIF color files for each color (at 100 pixels wide × 50 pixels high each).

```
</BODY>
</HTML>
```

Check how the file looks in various browsers—make sure the results are great with different browsers on different platforms.

Next, create a directory for your colors and templates and put the HTML file and color GIFs you just created into it. You'll want to get to your colors whether you're in your browser, an HTML editor, your image editor, or a text editor, so you need to make a couple more files.

Use your GIF editing program to create a GIF file with generous swatches of all your colors, and use the text tool in that image-editing program to write Hue, Saturation, Luminescence, Red, Green, Blue, and Hex values beside the colors. (See Table 3–3 in Chapter 3 to download a GIF editor for your platform).

Finally, create a plain text file with the colors' numeric values by descriptions of the colors. (This will come in handy when you're editing pages out of a plain text editor, word processor, or HTML editor, and need to use font colors by matching their descriptions to hex numbers.)

TECHNIQUE

How to Get a Hex Number for a Color

Use one of these methods to grab a color's hexadecimal number for use in backgrounds, fonts, links, tables, and other HTML tags that accept color values in hex. It's important to use the hex number instead of color names such as "red" in your HTML, so that more browsers can read the colors and present them the way you expect them to appear. Not everyone has Netscape Navigator or Microsoft's Internet Explorer.

1. Have the graphics file with the color you want ready—if it's not in a graphics file that your image editor reads, take a screen shot. Windows 95 users can get screen shots using Alt + Print Screen (a key in the top row on the keyboard) to copy the active Window to the Clipboard, then paste the image to an image-editing program with the Edit Paste command. You can also download free (and free trial) screen capture programs for various platforms. (See Table 3–6 in Chapter 3.) Capture programs often offer more control over what part of the screen to snap, and how to activate the capture (sometimes via hot-keys from within the target program, and sometimes via a countdown, which works best when trying to capture images from screen savers and other screens that disappear when you touch a key).

2. Open or paste the captured image into an image-editing program such as Paint Shop Pro (available for a 30-day free trial from Jasc at www.jasc.com). If your image-editing program requires that you open a new file before pasting an image, make sure you select the maximum number of colors necessary to accommodate your color—usually 24-bit or 16 million colors. In Paint Shop Pro, just choose Edit without any files open, and the "Paste As New Image" default will be fine.

3. Select the color you want from the image file. In Paint Shop Pro and many other programs, you do this by selecting the eyedropper tool and clicking on the color. In Paint Shop Pro, once you've clicked on the color with the eye dropper tool, move the dropper to the foreground color box beneath Paint Shop Pro's multicolored color selector on the right side of the program. (See Figure 2–3.) The RGB values—a set of three numbers written after the letters R, G, and B—appear beneath the color boxes. Note that if you move the eyedropper cursor off the foreground color box in Paint Shop Pro, the RGB values will change to those the dropper is passing over. Simply return the dropper to the foreground color box, and record your RGB color values.

(continued)

4. Now you have choices:

Choice 1   Windows users download a 30-day trial of Luckman's WebEdit (www.luckman.com) and choose Insert/Hexadecimal Color Value. A color picker pops up—choose "Define Custom Colors" and copy the Red, Green, and Blue (RGB) values of the color you grabbed from the image editor into the RGB boxes and click OK. The hex number will appear in the WebEdit window. See Figure 2–4.

Choice 2   If your calculator program has a hex function, just type in each RGB number, one number at a time. For example, if you kept the old Windows 3.1 Calculator, switch it to Scientific View, and click the radio button for DEC (decimal view). Type in the first of the three R, G, and B color numbers. If the color is pure red, it will be R 255, G 0, B 0. Type in 255 and click the radio button for HEX. "FF" appears where the 255 was. Repeat for the green and blue values, one at a time. Note that the 0 in DEC appears as 0 in HEX, even though you're going to need six digits for your color. Simply use a second zero. You get FF0000, the correct hex value for pure red.

Choice 3   If you'd rather geek out, go to www.escape.ca/~skinner/colortag/colrtag.html and learn how to do the math for the R, the G, and the B. Basically you'll divide each of the three values by 16 and multiply its decimal remainder by 16, then convert the resulting number to hex by consulting this chart:

Number	Hex Value	Number	Hex Value	Number	Hex Value
0	0	6	6	12	C
1	1	7	7	13	D
2	2	8	8	14	E
3	3	9	9	15	F
4	4	10	A		
5	5	11	B		

Example:
A color we'll label "Loudest Lavender" has RGB numbers Red 247, Green 102, and Blue 255. Start with Red and divide 247 by 16 to get 15.4375. Put the 15 aside and multiply the .4375 times 16 to get 7. That gives you a 15 and a 7 for Red—and the chart translates that to F7. The same process turns the Green to 66 and the Blue to FF. Be sure to keep the results in RGB order—and our Loudest Lavender hex number is F766FF. Plug your result in as a <BODY BGCOLOR> to check your math by eyeballing the color.

Time-Saver: 255 will always turn out to be FF and 0 will always be 00.

FIGURE 2-3 *In Paint Shop Pro, the RGB values appear beneath the color boxes on the right.*

FIGURE 2-4 *Luckman's WebEdit gives an instant Hex value for any color.*

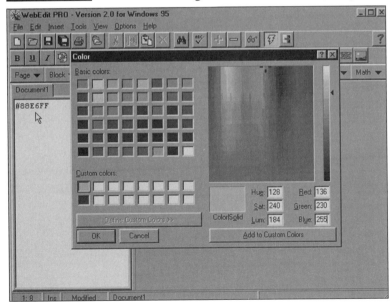

TECHNIQUE

Re-coloring Clip Art

Here's a place to use some of those carefully selected colors in your grand scheme. If you see a neat drawing of three golf tees that would be perfect if the tee colors matched your site's colors, you have a couple of options. You can open the picture in an image editor (remember you can take a screen shot to get it in a workable format) and use one of the following common art tools:

- **Color Eraser**   To exchange a patch of identical color for another, your image editor's color eraser will let you specify which color to trade for another. Usually a color eraser must be "rubbed" across a specific area of the image to make a change under the cursor, but sometimes there's also an option to double-click to exchange all of Color A for Color B at once. *Hint:* To make the "rub" type of erasure go faster, use a larger brush. Most image editors allow you to configure a brush shape (such as circular or square) and select a size, from one pixel to many.

- **Fill Bucket**   Another tool that works on patches of identical color usually looks like a bucket tipping and pouring. This time you're simply applying Foreground Color A to an area of Color B, as you would with the paintbrush, except you cover the entire continuous area of Color B, regardless of its shape. Simply dip you cursor into a foreground color, hit the bucket tool, and zap the unwanted color with a single click on it.

- **Paint Brush with Zoom**   If your patch of "continuous single color" is actually many different, albeit similar, colors (which always happens with photos and scanned images), you'll need to recolor each pixel. Use the image editor's Zoom tool (usually on a View menu) to jack up the picture to a size that makes it comfortable to re-color everything precisely.

Note: If you want the background behind the golf tees to disappear, don't color it to match your background, which may change. Instead, make the background transparent, so you can use the image on any page without redoing the background. See Chapter 3, Images, for instruction on "Transparent GIFs."

If you happen to have the presentation program Microsoft PowerPoint, you can use its Re-color Picture tool. Create a slide and add your piece of art. Earlier versions have a recoloring option on a menu, but PowerPoint '97 automatically brings up a Picture toolbar when you add and click on a piece of clip art. The Re-color Picture tool looks like a bucket with a painting. Click it and get a dialog with a check list of colors on the left and, beside each color, a drop-down list of colors. Check the box of the color you want to change on the left, and select the color you want to change it to from the

(continued)

drop-down list on the right. The new color can be one from your current colors or any color. You can change all instances of a color in the picture, or just a fill color (and not line color).

Hint: If you have a photo with many colors, you can use the Recoloring Tool, but the tool's dialog will list only the first 64 colors, so it may pay to create files of small areas, bring them in for recoloring, and paste them back over a copy of the original file.

TECHNIQUE

Tinting Photos

Your image-editing program allows you to adjust the color of photos to bring them into line with the overall tones of the site. There are many tools for doing that within image-editing programs, since it's one of the software category's prime tasks. Make a backup copy of your image, then play with these menu settings: Hue and Saturation, Level, Tone Map, and Color Balance. Be sure to look at your handiwork on a couple of different displays (video card and monitor) before putting it on-line.

Free Page Elements, for Example

Now that you know how to re-color art, it's a little safer to consider some of the downloadable page elements, such as buttons and bars, that you'll find on-line. (See Table 2–2.) Before you go to these types of sites, consider what you've learned about tasteful, professional looks, and remember what not to do as well as what to do. Always look at downloadable art with an eye to completely customizing it for your site. Ask yourself especially if you've ever seen a beautiful corporate site use the downloaded red balls you see at all the button factories. Consider whether the pros use downloaded divider bars at all. Are the top professionally designed sites more likely to use the <HR> command with 3-D to mark off small sections? (You get the 3-D effect with a command like

    <HR SIZE=4>

where "4" is the thickness of the line.)

Professional Web designers are even more likely to divide the actual pages so well that they don't need to cut them with divider lines. (Many

TABLE 2-2 *Free Page Elements*

Name	Free Web Bullets, Icons, Dividers, Background Textures, and Coordinated Web Looks*	URL
Abed's Icons, Buttons, Lines, etc.	Buttons, balls, icons, and lines.	http://darkwing.uoregon.edu/ ~alquds/icons.html
Anthony's Icon Library	Icons in several categories	www.sct.gu.edu.au/~anthony/ icons/index.html
Backgrounds Archive	Stucco, exotic, etc.	http://the-tech.mit.edu/KPT/ bgs.html
Ball Boutique	Spheres large and small, ovals, cubes, buttons, words, and alphabets.	www.octagamm.com/ boutique/mainball.htm
Disturbing Patterns	The "twisted textures" of Jeffrey Zeldman. Disturbing backgrounds—really. The ad men *do* know how to get to us. . . .	www.zeldman.com/ patterns.html
Fay Studio Free Graphics	Nice backgrounds, bars, and such. "Colorful Corporate," "River Rhythms," etc.	www.proaxis.com/ ~fayn/free_graphics.html
Free Art for HTML (Harlan Wallach)	Mostly initial caps: Victorian, 3-D red, 3-D blue, animated block letters, and more. Some downright thrilling gold buttons and bars, plus Vomitone (don't ask).	www.mcs.net/~wallach/ freeart/buttons.html
Graphx Kingdom	2400 icons: automobile, baseball, basketball, birds, book, cartoon, college, computer, document . . . you get the idea without traversing the entire alphabet.	www.trailerpark.com/phase2/ immortal/index.html
HTML Goodies Domain	Good text descriptions save you time when getting to the right ball, line, button, icon, or arrow at this site containing over 400 items.	www.htmlgoodies.com/
Jelane's	Lots of original HTML graphics—many abstracts and neons.	www.erinet.com/jelane/ families/
Leo's Icon Archive	Illustrator icons, caps, lines, markers, butterflies, Mozilla icons, arrows, buttons, construction signs, and more.	www.silverpoint.com/leo/lia/
Music	Music-related backgrounds, dividers, and icons.	http://members.aol.com/ skaiser2/music/images/ index.htm
NCSA	Forty backgrounds. See all in iconic form on one fast-loading page, then click to see as background with sample text.	www.ncsa.uiuc.edu/SDG/ Software/mosaic-w/coolstuff/ Backgrnd/index.html

Name	Free Web Bullets, Icons, Dividers, Background Textures, and Coordinated Web Looks*	URL
Neferchichi's Egypt Clip Art & Backgrounds	Backgrounds include papyrus, gods, bricks, etchings, and statues. See Clip Art table in Chapter 3 for description of other art.	http://members.aol.com/ crakkrjack/egypt.html
Netscape	Background textures: paper, raindrops, fabric, marble, and other familiar fare.	www.netscape.com/assist/ net_sites/bg/back grounds.html
Pardon My Icons (Jeffrey Zeldman)	Incredible work from ad man Jeffrey Zeldman—weird icons of pop icons or, as the man himself phrases it, "32 x 32 images from a Rotarian's nightmare."	www.zeldman.com/icon.html
Realm Graphics	Over 330 background textures, 380 bullets, 130 buttons, 150 icons and lines, and 3 total design sets.	www.ender-design.com/ rg/index.html

*__Note:__ Just because we don't mention limitations on use, doesn't mean there aren't any. Look around and ask the Webmaster or artist if you're not sure.

people don't scroll down from the first screenful anyway.) The short pages you find at pro sites are part of excellent navigational schemes that help people get right to what they're after. (See navigational schemes later in this chapter.) Besides, the quality of a 3-D effect with rules varies on different background colors. If your page colors change, the effect might be disappointing.

Some of the items in Table 2–2 are genuinely marvelous, and would be the Ming vase that perfectly finishes a designer's dream site, but there's bad in with the good, and what perfectly finishes one designer dream can simply finish another. Pay attention to the limitations on use—some of the art is only free to noncommercial sites. Whether your site is commercial or not, the bottom line question is, does it look professional? Choose wisely, and "use with spare."

Free Total Looks and Fantastic Stuff

The are some very cool things in Table 2–2, but Table 2–3 takes it into orbit. There's a family of incredible artists in Sweden that includes two

TABLE 2-3	*Free Total Looks and Fantastic Stuff*	
Bimsan's Web Graphics	Utterly amazingly beautiful total looks for your Web site. Every element is superb, including graphics, icons, lettering, texture, and HTML-appointed colors. Themes include Gear, Fairy, Golden Cat, Water, Dragon, Rose, Train, Sea, and many more.	www.bimsan.net
Bimsan's Web Graphics II	A few more sets from the wonderful Bimsan, including Children's and Professional themes.	http://bimsan.modernz.net/
Porenn's Place	Charming art buttons by a sister of Bimsan, above. Tons of tiny 1K graphics make the page long to load, but worth the wait. Some pages appear to be just gorgeous icons, but lead to whole sets of matching graphics.	www.geocities.com/Athens/ Acropolis/5041/ geobutt.html

sisters known as Bimsan and Porenn, and they've created and offered some of the most breathtaking button sets and total "looks" for Websites that you'll ever see. I have their permission to include the screen-shots in Figures 2–5 to Figure 2–11. Even if you can't use the designs shown, you can at least learn a certain style that's appropriate in some settings. You can also commission the art you need from these talented people if you have a budget for art.

✪ *Tip:* Want all the buttons you see? Don't download them individually if you're in a hurry—especially if they have nondescript names. Just grab the whole screenful at a time with a screen capture program, and cut out and name what you need as you need it. This is an even better idea when you consider that pages on the Web are often here today and gone tomorrow. Most screen capture programs only catch one visible screen at a time, but SnagIt (www.techsmith.com) can scroll and capture at the same time, grabbing entire long pages.

Dangerous Backgrounds

It's important to consider what people see while loading your page—especially the people with 14,400 bps modems. I have a 28.8 myself, which is plenty slow enough to show a lot of Webmasters with their pants down—and I don't mean at the X-rated sites. Most people don't test their sites over a modem and, if they do, they don't flush their disk cache and RAM cache between tests and restart their browser to get the picture real visitors get. If

FIGURE 2-5 *Bimsan's downloadable train theme from www.bimsan.net shows pieces that look as if they were made to go together. (They aren't all meant for the same page.)*

FIGURE 2-6 *Bimsan's downloadable panda theme from www.bimsan.net*

FIGURE 2-7   *Bimsan's downloadable angel theme from*
http://bimsan.modernz.net/

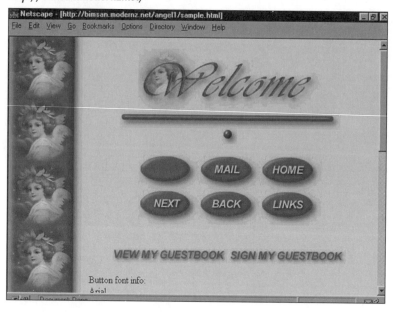

FIGURE 2-8   *Bimsan's downloadable clown theme from*
http://bimsan.modernz.net/

FIGURE 2-9 *Collection of downloadable themes by Bimsan from www.bimsan.net*

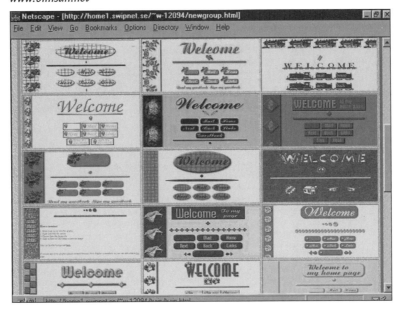

FIGURE 2-10 *Another collection of downloadable themes by Bimsan from www.bimsan.net*

FIGURE 2-11 *Some of Porren's amazing downloadable buttons from www.geocities.com/Athens/Acropolis/5041/geobutt.html*

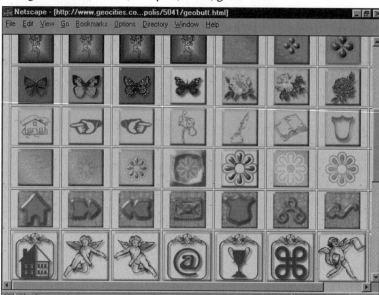

they did, there would be fewer sites that use the following recipe for annoyance:

1. White background color
2. White or yellow text
3. Black or navy image file background that loads after the background color and text, if at all. (Remember, some people turn off images to speed things up. Most of us just wonder what kind of nut puts yellow text on a white page and if a dark background will come along before we bail.)

One reason Webmasters keep doing this is that their browser came with a dark gray default page color. Others have set their own browser to always show a dark background and light text, and forgotten the rest of the world doesn't see it that way. But there are many folks like me who've set our default background to white. We haven't set up our browsers to *override* the Webmaster's background color—just to have a nice clean, white page as a default *when the Webmaster doesn't specify a <BODY BGCOLOR>.*

The fix, of course, is to always specify a <BODY BGCOLOR> in your HTML, and to always make it one that shows your chosen text colors while visitors wait for the background image to load. There's no need to worry about most of the folks who *override* a Webmaster's colors, because those folks generally pick a background *and text colors* that are quite readable wherever they go. It is important, though, for you to specify all such things as text, link, active link, and visited link colors *in the <BODY> tag* when you specify a background color. You can always override colors in select areas with the <FONT></FONTS> tags as needed. Offer a full set of <BODY> colors, and make them show up with each other, and you stand a much better chance of getting your message across. Let me help you out with a quick refresher of the color setup.

```
<HTML>
<HEAD>
<TITLE>Background, Text, and Link Color Samples</TITLE>
</HEAD>
<BODY BGCOLOR="FFFFFF" TEXT="000000" LINK="0000FF"
VLINK="8A8A8A" ALINK="FF0000">

<P>The Background Color of this page is white.</P>
<P>This is Text. It is black.</P>
<P><FONT COLOR="0000FF">This is Text, but it's 0000FF (blue)
instead of black because it is surrounded by Font tags that
override the Text="000000" (black) color in the BODY
tag.</FONT></P>
<P><A HREF="http://www.whitehouse.gov">This is a visited link,
and it's gray. You'll have to click me so I can actually become
a visited link and turn gray.</A></P>
<P><A HREF="http://www.whitehouse.gov">This will show an Active
Link, which is red, when you click and hold me.</A></P>
<P><A HREF="http://nowhere.man">This is a plain, unvisited link,
and it is blue.</A></P>
</BODY>
</HTML>
```

Table 2–4 identifies a few hex numbers to substitute for the "=XXXXXX" in case you're in a rush to test something and haven't worked out your color scheme yet. This *isn't* a color scheme, and most of these colors would "hex" your page with ghoulish backgrounds if you used them.

Hint: Always use hex numbers instead of color names, because color names aren't supported by all browsers. (The following aren't all official names, anyway.)

If you're looking for new colors and want to see how they'll work together, the best way I know is with Brooklyn North's HTML Assistant Pro 97, which you can download from www.brooknorth.com for a free trial.

HTML Assistant Pro 97 not only is a clean and powerful HTML editor, but its built-in WYSIWYG Background Assistant gives you a split screen with a real-time preview of a mock HTML page on the left and color selectors on the right, as seen in Figure 2–12. You can run the slider bars back and forth to adjust the Red, Green, and Blue values, or click the Color Picker bar to bring up the color picker. Your choices for Background, Text, Link, Visited Link, and Active link show up together as they would on a real page. You can even call in a graphical background image and see how your text plays against that. And yes—Background Assistant shows hex values for colors, too.

Embossed Backgrounds

If you haven't seen embossed backgrounds, check out the beautiful example at Rent Com Inc. (www.rentcom.com). See Figure 2–13 and note that the effect is used on the top (index) page, where visitors have to read only heavy rendered letters and a small amount of heavy text—not thin "reading text." Other pages have plain white backgrounds. Note, too, the use of the same pattern in the large graphic. The repetition works well.

TABLE 2-4 *Hex Colors for Test Purposes Only—Do Not Ingest.*

Color	Hex Number
Black	000000
White	FFFFFF
Red	FF0000
Bright Green	00FF00
Royal Blue	0000FF
Marigold	FFFF00
Cyan (Light Blue)	00FFFF
Violet (Reddish Purple)	FF00FF
Olive Green	909090
Dark Blue	3232A7
Seafoam Green	32D8D8
Rain Gray	DCDCDC
Burnt Orange	DC8888
Brown	8C4100

FIGURE 2-12 *Download HTML Assistant Pro 97 and try colors together in its "Background Assistant."*

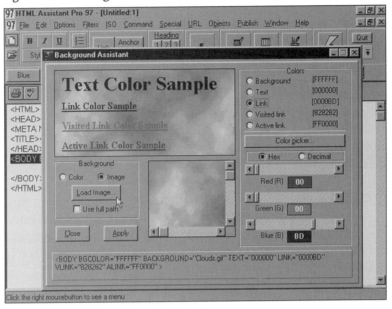

FIGURE 2-13 *Rent Com Inc. (www.rentcom.com) uses an embossed background behind heavy text, and repeats the embossed motif in a graphic.*

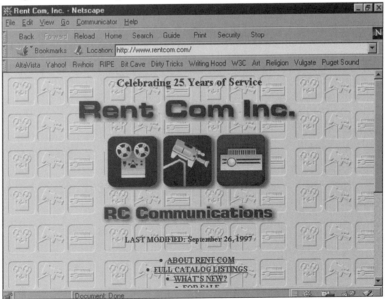

To create an embossed background, draw or locate your icon or icons, and arrange them horizontally in a single graphics file. (To use special effects filters, you may have to work with a 24-bit color file, which calls for increasing color depth until you have your effect, then decreasing the number of colors so you can create the final GIF file. See Chapter 3, "Images," for great detail on this.) The space around each icon should be equal in all directions, because the pattern will repeat to fill the background. Make the backgrounds a uniform color and add square lines around each icon now if you plan to at all. From there you simply use your image-editing program's Emboss filter, then tweak the results with the contrast and brightness settings. You'll see examples of programs with special effects filters in Chapter 3, "Images," along with a discussion of special effects and places to download image editors that offer them.

Figure 2–14 shows a larger image run through the embossing process so you can see how simple it is. I started with Photoshop and a picture of my daughter's head (taken more than 20 years ago). I'd already isolated the image on a white background pixel-by-pixel during prior tests for Chapter 3. In the series of images in Figure 2–14 you see that:

- The first image is in color, which you may not be able to tell from the grayscale picture in this book.

FIGURE 2-14   *Series 1–4 from color to gray to embossing to brightening for use in a background.*

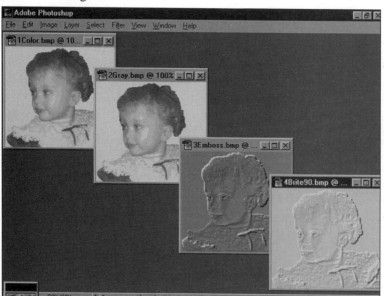

- In the second frame, I've changed the image to grayscale with the menu commands Image/Mode/Grayscale.
- The third picture shows the effect of Filter/Stylize/Emboss (using the Emboss defaults). Note that changing the angle of light can really change the mood of the subject, which I didn't do.
- The fourth picture shows the effect of Image/Adjust/Brightness&Contrast/Brightness 90. I didn't change the Contrast setting because I didn't like the effect on this particular picture. Your picture may call for a different balance of brightness and contrast. You can preview the effects of both Contrast and Brightness together within the dialog box—and on the actual picture if you move the dialog box out of the way.
- Figure 2–15 shows Marcia's head "SmartSaved" to GIF format from Ulead's PhotoImpact, then tiled on a Web page, with the original (color) photo on top, with and without a frame.

Margin Backgrounds

Margin graphics down the left side of a page are a popular and often elegant way to accent a page—as long as you observe two necessities:

Make the non-margin side of the background graphic wide enough to not repeat the margin part on the right side of the page, no matter what

FIGURE 2-15 *Finished embossed picture tiled on a Web page, with the original photo on top (with and without a frame).*

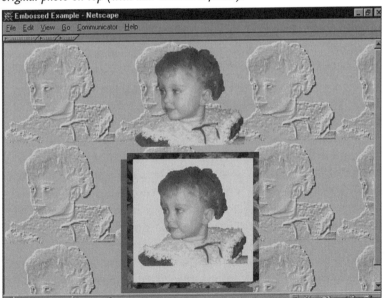

resolution it's viewed in. Even though you're designing for a 640 × 480 pixel resolution, the background graphic itself should be 1280 pixels wide. Unlike other (non-background) graphics, this will look fine at 640 × 480, 800 × 600, 1024 × 768, and 1280 × 1024. Any graphics *other than* the <BODY BACKGROUND> must still be *less than* 640 pixels wide, to fit within the screen and vertical scrollbar. Your visitors at 640 × 480 must never have to scroll *horizontally* to see your page. But get a mental picture of your beautiful margin background with text over the light side of the page as it would look if the dark margin repeats across that page. The 1280-pixel-wide margin will prevent that for most people. If the sample is short enough—say, 3 to 5 pixels high—the file won't take too long to download.

Keep text and other objects that don't belong on the margin itself from creeping onto it. (If you want menu bars or other items there, see the section on Navigation later in this chapter.)

The way to keep text and other items off those margins is to create an invisible table the entire width of your page and section off the first column the width of the margin plus the space you want between the margin and the main area of your page. To make the invisible table itself, see "Table-Based Page Layout" later in this chapter.

The remaining columns contain everything else on your page. The width of the remaining column, *together with the width of the first column,* totals 600 pixels. (Always design for 640 × 480 screens, so people don't have to scroll left and right as well as up and down in order to see the page. Part of the 640-pixel-wide screen is taken up by the browser's vertical scroll bar, so the safe parameter for the entire table is 600 pixels. It won't matter if the table or actual graphic is short of the monitor's width, since your solid color in the background of the graphic is also called precisely by hex number for the background color of your page. Yes—you can and *should* use a body background color along with your body background graphic. The two together prevent a lot of gaffes that only your visitors would know about. See "Dangerous Backgrounds," earlier in this section, for more information.)

To make the actual margin background file, create a short, wide file, shaped like a horizontal strip across the width of the monitor. Simply make the whole background the main page color (preferably white), and put a color or pattern on the left side of the screen, about 125 pixels wide. As the browser repeats the horizontal strip down the page, the vertical pattern repeats and creates a vertical file with a long margin strip down the left side of the page.

Here's what it all looks like in HTML, using a 1280 × 5 pixel margin file called margin.gif (the gradient type margin described in the next section):

```
<HTML>
<HEAD>
<TITLE>Margin Down Left of Neat & Tidy Page</TITLE>
</HEAD>
<BODY BGCOLOR="FFFFFF" BACKGROUND="MARGIN.GIF" TEXT="000000"
LINK="0000FF" VLINK="848484" ALINK="FF0000">

<TABLE BORDER="0" WIDTH="100%">
  <TR>
    <TD ALIGN="LEFT" VALIGN="TOP" WIDTH="125">
    <IMG BORDER="0" SRC="SPACER.GIF" WIDTH="125" HEIGHT="5">
    </TD>
    <TD ALIGN="LEFT" VALIGN="TOP" WIDTH="475">
    THIS IS WHERE ALL THE REST OF YOUR CONTENT GOES
    </TD>
  </TR>
</TABLE>

</BODY>
</HTML>
```

Gradient Backgrounds

You could create a gradient background by making a small, thin horizontal strip using the left-to-right gradient fill tools in your paint program, but spreading a rainbow all the way across your page is a real fashion risk unless you're a daycare center or a Jerry Garcia fan club. A more subtle use: create a small strip of gradient fill between two shades of one color, such as a gradient from dark blue to white. For example, in Ulead's PhotoImpact (www.ulead.com), create a pure white (R 255, G 255, B 255) strip 1280 pixels wide by 5 pixels high. Drag your blue-to-white gradient fill bucket from the left edge inward, but only the distance of a normal background margin—about 125 pixels—not the width of the page. Be sure to observe the rules in the previous section for keeping text and other objects from creeping onto your margins.

Shaded Borders, Scallops, Etc.

Strong borders with a shadow to the right, gently scalloped borders, and patterned borders can be wonderful—and make a bolder impression than a gradient fill. Get over to Chapter 3, Images, and see some of the things you can do with little effort once you download a capable image editor.

Hidden Message to Pseudo Luddites

"Best viewed with" signs aren't cool because people should write so that all browsers can get a decent view, and many people have a browser that reads at least HTML 2.0. But if you feel the need to proselytize, you can use color to send a semi-private message to visitors with graphical browsers who don't see your background colors, as follows:

Specify a hex background color number, and, somewhere on the page, use text with fonts in the same hex color to put up a little sign. That's it. You can see an example at the IEEE Computer Society page at http://computer.org. Slowly, slowly, glide your mouse over the area between the last text on the page and the bottom of the page. When your mouse cursor changes, you'll see where the "hidden" text is. If you select that area by clicking and dragging before and after it, you'll highlight the hidden text and see the "secret" message. (See Figures 2–16 and 2–17.) For much more sophisticated Dick Tracy stuff, see Chapter 8, "Hiding In Plain Site: Build Cloak and Dagger Web Pages." There *are* real business reasons to put up files that only your clued-in colleagues are likely to see or hear, as you'll see in Chapter 8.

For the Star Tech Enterprise

If you're going for a high-tech, sci-fi ambiance and want a quick "Trik" that costs few bytes, nail up that black background and put up a panel of blinking lights made of:

- a single-cell table
- a row of periods in a techno-green font with <BLINK> </BLINK> tags
- the ^ character (Shift + 6 on your keyboard) in a red font
- other characters, colors, and states of <BLINK>ing that make your eyebrows point up.

Place a few asterisks (Shift + 8 on your keyboard) around the page—some white and some cyan, some blinking and some not—for stars.

Think of other ways to use low-tech tricks to make high-tech looks. If you prefer actual higher tech tricks, see later chapters on drop-in Java and easy animated GIFs.

Fancy Initial Caps

Initial caps go back at least as far as the illuminated manuscripts of old—when monks laboriously copied books by hand and added a fancy first capital letter to the beginning of a large section. Initial caps are still a nice

FIGURE 2-16   *The suggestion to upgrade is hidden near the pointer.*

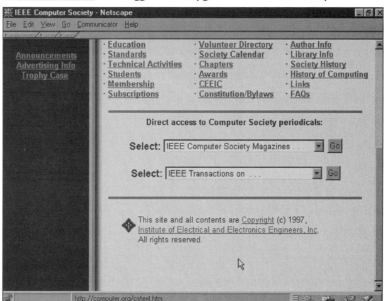

FIGURE 2-17   *The suggestion revealed by highlighting the words will show without any action to the people who don't have browsers set up to support the colors specified by Webmasters.*

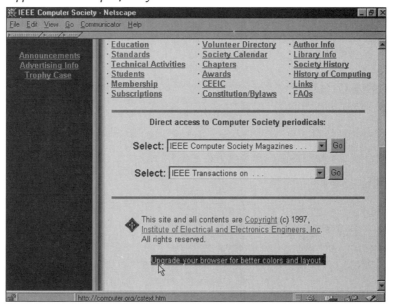

way to add an elegant touch to text, even in the days of the Web. An ornate capital is often all the graphic you need—it certainly won't do to run an ornate initial cap in the same screen with most other illustrations, or on top of a textured or patterned background. It can look lovely to pick up a color from your initial cap and make it your background color with the <BODY BGCOLOR="XXXXXX"> option in the <BODY> tag and the correct hex number for the color. (See "Technique: How to Get a Hex Number for a Color," earlier in this chapter.)

You know to always use plain text alternatives with image files, using the "ALT=Blah blah blah" option with the <IMG> tag, but it's even more important when using initial caps, as seen here:

```
<IMG SRC="Z_letter.gif" ALT="Z">.
```

so your word or meaning doesn't appear ridiculous to people as they wait for the initial cap graphic to download. Imagine how an on-line pub named "Sass" would look if people didn't see an alternative text "S" while they waited for the "S" to download! "Amoral" would become "moral" (and we just can't have that). On the other hand "Agnostic" with a slow "A" would make a believer out of any Webmaster.

The image height and width options will help the plain HTML text that follows the image become visible faster. Here's the 2-second refresher on that:

```
<IMG SRC="Z.gif" width=45 height=65 ALT="Z">.
```

Cut the wait time further by letting the air out of the graphic. There's plenty of help with that in Chapter 3, "Images."

Hint: Put your <H1> </H1> (header-size font) tags around the entire graphic and plain text combo, as shown:

Example A

```
<H1><IMG SRC="S.gif" WIDTH=45 HEIGHT=65 ALT="S">WORD FIGHT KILLS
TWO</H1>
```

rather than just around the plain text, as shown:

Example B

```
<IMG SRC="S.gif" width=45 height=65 ALT="S"><H1>WORD FIGHT KILLS
TWO</H1>
```

Otherwise, the <H1> tag after the graphic will force a new line to start.

The result for Example A will look like this:

SWORD FIGHT KILLS TWO.

The result for Example B will look like this:

S

WORD FIGHT KILLS TWO.

You can download initial caps from the Web (Table 2–5), which are often free if you supply an artist credit and link back to the artist's site. Sometimes this applies only to noncommercial use—always check policies at the site.

I'm not one to hawk for-pay products in this book unless they're truly exceptional. Aridi's professional initial caps *are*. Check them out at www.aridi.com if you want something truly outstanding. See Figure 2–18 for a peek at some ARIDI caps at their site, and Figure 2–19 for what you can do with them. Be sure to see the caps at the site, in color, too.

Finally, don't overlook the initial caps in some of those collections of 50 million pieces of clip-art you get with drawing programs. You may have a letter that suits you to a "T".

Sew On Buttons Seamlessly

You may have gone to a lot of trouble to put transparent backgrounds on nonrectangular buttons like basketballs, gears, airplanes, lipsticks, or doll heads. (If not, see Transparent GIFs in Chapter 3, "Images.") But if you create a link from the button to another page or object, a border appears

TABLE 2-5 *Downloadable Initial Caps*

Free Art for HTML by Harlan Wallach of The Arthole Gallery	Initial caps: Victorian, 3-D red, 3-D blue, and jazzy animated block letters. Includes a downright thrilling gold lamé-look divider.	www.mcs.net/~wallach/freeart/buttons.html
Briar Press Ornaments	Letterpress cuts of nostalgic design. Also whole words, borders and holiday Mac graphics. Postscript line art in .hqx format.	www.westnet.com/~bpress/bpress.html
Ball Boutique	"Alphabet Aisle" is just one section in this offering of all kinds of Web graphics. Letter types include stencil, metal, raised, etc.	www.octagamm.com/boutique/mainball.htm
Andy's Art Attack	3-D gold on green marble letters, and dripping blue fright alphabet	www.andyart.com/f_letters.htm
Leo's CAPS Archive	Nine different designs, including "Cats Caps" by Talyce, featuring felines crawling through and rubbing up against the capital letters.	www.silverpoint.com/leo/lia/

FIGURE 2-18   *Some wonderful initial caps by ARIDI at www.aridi.com.*

FIGURE 2-19   *An ARIDI initial cap in use. Be sure to see the caps at the site, in color.*

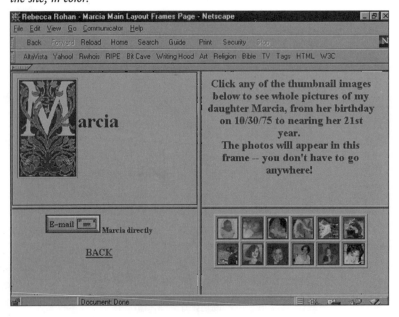

around the graphic that you may find objectionable. If that border is the only cue that the picture is a hot link, then it's best to just suck it up and let the border hack up your perfect page. But I believe in you—I believe you've planned your page so nobody will doubt they're supposed to click the picture to get the link, because:

a. the alternate text flag flies out to say "Click to go to the zowie page."

and

b. the graphical buttons are lined up precisely beside short lines of menu-style text.

So how do you break the picture out of the box? With the BORDER option set to zero. Try it like this:

```
<CENTER> Now Showing </CENTER>

<A HREF="HTTP://www.cinema1.com"><IMG SRC="boomers.gif"
ALT="Laid Back Boomers" ALIGN="MIDDLE" HEIGHT=44 WIDTH=39
BORDER=0></A> Cinema 1: "The Big Pill"

<BR>

<A HREF="HTTP://www.cinema2.com"><IMG SRC="umpire.gif"
ALT="Umpire Talking" ALIGN="MIDDLE" HEIGHT=44 WIDTH=39
BORDER=0></A> Cinema 2: "Interview With The Umpire"

<BR>

<A HREF="HTTP://www.cinema3.com"><IMG SRC="babybear.gif"
ALT="Baby Bear Eating" ALIGN="MIDDLE" HEIGHT=44 WIDTH=39
BORDER=0></A> Cinema 3: "The Breakfast Cub"

<BR>

<A HREF="HTTP://www.cinema4.com"><IMG SRC="storestockroom.gif"
ALT="Grocery Store Stock Room" ALIGN="MIDDLE" HEIGHT=44 WIDTH=39
BORDER=0></A> Cinema 4: "Men In Back"
```

Button Makers

You don't have pretty buttons yet? No topical icons? Download a free trial of Ulead's PhotoImpact from www.ulead.com. With the selection tool highlighted, select a button-size piece of a photo or other image, go to the menu marked "Web," and choose "Button Designer," then "Rectangular." You'll get a nifty place to try different button styles on the image before choosing the one that makes you want to go "click" all over. See the instant button creation playground in Figure 2–20. The Button Designer feature in PhotoImpact includes "pressed" and "unpressed" button looks ("inward" and "outward"), and the new version 4.0 lets you make buttons of any shape, as well as rectangular. (You can download free trials of various components of PhotoImpact to use as Photoshop plug-ins, too.)

Text and Fonts

Most Webmasters have a good basic idea of how to make text look nice using header tags such as <H1></H1> through <H5></H5>, and regular (default), italic <I></I>, and bold <B></B> text tags. Others use the <FONT></FONT> tags to specify a preferred font face (and alternatives) along with size and color, like so:

```
<FONT SIZE=12 COLOR="#000000" FACE="CLOISTERBLACK
BT,BIGTOP,INCISED901 ND BT,ARIAL,V2 LUCIDA SANS BOLD">Here's the
message, finally.</FONT>
```

Obviously this example is just for show, since the string of fonts are supposed to be a list of preferences, from best to worst, that might be

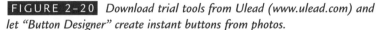

FIGURE 2-20 *Download trial tools from Ulead (www.ulead.com) and let "Button Designer" create instant buttons from photos.*

found on the visitor's computer, and the fonts named are hardly good substitutes for one another. If you do specify typefaces, such as Arial, Courier New, and Times New Roman, it's important to recognize that not everyone will even have one of them, and some people will override them anyway. Don't make anything you design depend on visitors seeing those fonts.

If you're working with something that absolutely requires a certain typeface over a tiny area, use a GIF of the word. If you're trying to format a significant amount of "reading text," and the fonts are the most important thing in your world, use Adobe Acrobat (see the sidebar for a review of Acrobat) or arrange to send or transfer formatted Word files with embedded fonts. Both measures are extreme as Web measures go, and you should have a phenomenally good reason for demanding specific fonts, such as the need to send printable forms or demonstrate something related to fonts. Absolutely requiring specific fonts just to make things look the way you like them is totally incompatible with both the technology and philosophy of HTML (and there are better uses for Acrobat, as you'll see in the review).

Most Web professionals have caught on that readability is the most important issue of all. If you bought this book, you probably aren't one of the perpetrators of the blinky stinky neon sites with BIG PRINT cyan on black backgrounds, and you're not especially likely to have come to the Web from the print publishing industry. Folks from the publishing world drag a mixed blessing along: They know what looks good in print, so they're not from the "Ransom Note School of Web Design," but they often can't come to terms with using Web-appropriate tools like HTML—and they make deals with the devil to force their fonts of choice on visitors. Publishing types are most likely to succumb to the worst ideas—like making visitors see all of every page in a weird and crashy implementation of Java, just so they can control the fonts and layout people see. I beg you, even if your background is in publishing, to resist that urge, because your visitors will. Many people turn off Java for security reasons or just because they don't have time to wait for blinking lights or somebody's choice of typeface—and entire site pages that are invisible without Java are just dumb. It will eventually be acceptable to use large areas of Java that show off your typefaces if you use the HTML 4.0 <OBJECT> tag to specify one or more alternatives, the last of which should be plain text. (See the Object Overview at the beginning of Chapter 3.) But that time isn't here today, because many of your visitors are still using older browsers which don't support the <OBJECT> tag.

When you're tempted to pay too much attention to fonts, remember that people may be seeking text at your site because they came for

Adobe Acrobat 3.0

If you want absolute control over the appearance of your pages, so you can specify how everything looks—and actually publish documents exactly as they appeared in the programs that created them—consider buying Adobe Acrobat 3.0 (the program that creates Acrobat files, not just the free downloadable reader or reader plug-in). The catch is that you will be creating PDF (Portable Document Format) documents, not HTML. The good news is that people can either download and view your PDF documents in a free Acrobat Reader or view them inline on the Web with an Acrobat Netscape plug-in. It is a solution that goes against everything this book is about for general Web pages—but it is a perfect solution for intranets and for captive Web audiences such as a membership that agrees to outfit itself with Netscape and the Adobe plug-in.

Several characteristics of Acrobat make it outstanding if you do have that committed audience. First, you can print files to PDF format from any program that has a print command. That means you can take pages from Word, Excel, Power Point, Paint, Eudora, or whatever, turn them into PDF pages with the Print command, and put them together as individual pages within one PDF file.

The file sizes are extremely small, which makes it a great choice for viewing on-line. My first test file for version 3.0, a 5-page color newsletter with a graphic and a whole movie file inside it, was only 71K! (It supports QuickTime movies.) Text remains text, not a mere image of text, so that it is searchable. You can also instantly drag hyperlinks around words without ever learning HTML, for things like linking items in a table of contents to its target pages, or linking questions and answers on a quiz. That makes it great for training over an intranet. Acrobat 3.0 even supports forms. Adobe Systems Incorporated, Windows/Mac/UNIX, $295. Free betas, readers, and Netscape plug-ins available from www.adobe.com.

meaning—content over form. The Web is not a magazine. Special typefaces on the Web are like special typefaces on TV: It's nice in the main title, but then it's over and on with the real performance.

Cascading Style Sheets (CSS), which offer control of many visual elements of the page, just haven't caught on—at least not yet—but there is support for many of their features in both Netscape Navigator 4 and Internet Explorer 4—despite wildly inaccurate talk to the contrary about Netscape. Cascading Style Sheets let you designate global rules for certain page elements. For example, you can dictate that all <H1></H1> header text be blue throughout the page. Still, users can override your style sheets if they choose to.

The HTML 4.0 recommendation ratified December 18, 1997, "deprecates" many of the manual formatting tags, such as <FONT>, to encourage Webmasters to use CSS to specify such things. However, you can still use deprecated fonts, and should, until you're sure the whole graphical audience you're writing for has at least Netscape's Version 4 or Microsoft's Version 3 browsers. Lots of people stay with earlier browsers because they work just fine, or they've had a problem with a later one.

Specifying various presentation attributes with style sheets really does make sense—especially if you have a large site with lots of updates to do. When the installed base of CSS-enabled visitors merits the change, embrace the time-saving CSS technology with open arms. In the mean time, find out more about CSS at the World Wide Web Consortium (W3C) Style Sheet page at www.w3.org/Style.

ASCII Graphic Letters with Figlet Utility

Working on a completely separate text-alternative page? There are such things as ASCII banner fonts—letters built up of groups of plain text characters to draw each character in a particular style—and places on the Web you can go (and utilities you can download) to have such "fonts" applied to a word. The words are big, and probably beneath the dignity of DTPers and halfway sophisticated Web visitors. They will also drive speech synthesizers crazy because none of the characters building up a letter is necessarily the letter being built. But ASCII fonts do carry particular styles—and carry them to folks with tools as simple as Lynx, as well as to folks with high-end graphical browsers. See images of Figlet fonts and find out more—including where to get your text Figlet-ized—in Chapter 3, "Images." Hey, it's *character-building*.

Speaking of being a good character, if you choose to use ASCII banners (or ASCII pictures, discussed in Chapter 3), put a quick note *above* the graphic warning folks with speech synthesizers that an ASCII graphic is up next, and give them an idea of how many characters and how many lines the graphic takes so they can move past it.

Layout and Space

You don't have to study Zen art to recognize that layout is at least as important as color, and that space is as much or more an element to use as other kinds of content. Space says you're wandering in wonder on the flight deck of an aircraft carrier instead of sitting in a wet rowboat. Space says luxury, security, and trustworthiness. You can use space like a river to make visitors' attention flow where you want it to go. Make space direct their gaze as if you were standing beside them and gesturing. Space suggests, directs, connects, focuses and cues. And the more space you use—yes, white space—the more your site will look like a Robin Leach living room than a convenience store after an earthquake. Remember, you're not paying for paper—you're not paying for postage—and you're only using itsy bitsy bytes of disk space to indicate where to show nothing.

Using lots of space doesn't mean extending the length of a page. Keep pages to two or three screenfuls or less at 640 × 480 resolution. Simply use less content per page, and make sure people get to almost everything directly from the top page of your site by doing excellent site planning and making navigation logical, consistent, and descriptive. Most important, set up to offer things the way the users think.

Related Topic Alert: In Chapter 3, "Images," you'll find tips for keeping images small unless someone chooses large images from thumbnails, plus how to create thumbnails, and guidelines for keeping the number of thumbnails per page at an inviting level.

Put Objects in Their Place—Precisely

To master space and objects, you obviously need to have control over where they go. Too many Webmasters imprison their artwork within a table in the middle of the page because they know how to center tables with the <CENTER> command, or they just let the image get sucked into a corner by default alignment. *Your* pictures don't have to go through life with their noses pressed against the left, right, or center of a Web page, with text jammed up beside or below them. And you *don't* have to manually nest tables within tables to get objects exactly where you want them—you just drag and drop with a mouse, and position objects exactly where you want them, right down to the pixel level!

No, I haven't gone over to the dark side—you won't need to introduce Java, plug-ins, or Active-X just to make your stuff go where you want it to. It's done with a complex set of plain HTML tables, *but you don't do the work.* NetObjects Fusion does. Download a free 30-day trial of Fusion at the NetObjects, Inc. site at www.netobjects.com, for Windows 95/NT 4.0 or the Power PC with Mac OS 7.1.2 and drag-and-drop your way to complete control over space and objects. (At least on your Web site.) You'll like the site management features, too, that let you not only provide a consistent look throughout your site, but update links automatically throughout your site as you add, remove, or move pages.

Quick-and-Dirty Clean Space Margins

Another way to create space is with indents, and you know all too well that you don't get indents in HTML by hitting the TAB key, or by hitting the space bar multiple times. What you *can* do, if you don't want to fool around with tables, or spend your life creating a series of

```
     
```

(non-breaking space) escape sequences, is to put the line or paragraph to be indented inside <UL> </UL> (Unordered List) or <OL> </OL> (Ordered List) tags, *without* the <LI> (List Item) tags in front of each item. The LI tags before each item would create numbers in ordered lists and bullets in un-ordered lists. Another thing the <LI> tags are responsible for is keeping each list item on a separate line. If you're indenting something that you want to keep list style, use a
 (line break) tag after each item in the list to keep them from jumping up into a horizontal string of words. Don't use the <P> (paragraph) tags instead—they introduce too much space between lines. If you're indenting paragraphs, you won't need the <BR> tags—the words will wrap to accommodate the indents.

You can nest indents (up to a point) with this technique—for example:

```
<CENTER> Fur-balls I Have Loved </CENTER>

Smokey<BR>
Snoopy<BR>
Yoko<BR>
Gozer<BR>
Max<BR>

<UL>
Smokey<BR>
Snoopy<BR>
Yoko<BR>
Gozer<BR>
Max<BR>
</UL>

<UL>
<UL>
Smokey<BR>
Snoopy<BR>
Yoko<BR>
Gozer<BR>
Max<BR>
</UL>
</UL>
```

```
<UL>
<UL>
<UL>
Smokey<BR>
Snoopy<BR>
Yoko<BR>
Gozer<BR>
Max<BR>
</UL>
</UL>
</UL>

<UL>
<UL>
<UL>
<UL>
Smokey<BR>
Snoopy<BR>
Yoko<BR>
Gozer<BR>
Max<BR>
</UL>
</UL>
</UL>
</UL>
```

made nice, progressive indents. And this:

```
<UL>
Smokey<BR>
Snoopy<BR>
<UL>
Yoko<BR>
</UL>
Gozer<BR>
Max<BR>
</UL>
```

indented "Yoko" within the indented list, leaving the cats' names before and after flush with each other to the left. Use the technique to show materials in outline form, or to simply move all your text over to create white space—or space to show a colored margin—without tables or frames.

Block Quote Twist: To indent whole paragraphs or lines from both the left and right margins, you can use <BLOCKQUOTE></BLOCKQUOTE> tags, which won't alter your fonts. But if you nest block quotes, the successive paragraphs will continue to narrow from both left and right, so the <BLOCKQUOTE></BLOCKQUOTE> tags aren't useful for creating outlines. See Quick-and-Dirty Clean Space Margins, earlier in this section, for a better technique for successive indents.

Warning: Spacing Out PRE-Danger: The <PRE></PRE> tags allow Webmasters to create text that more accurately represents the number of spaces typed in the HTML document. If you type three spaces before or between words within the <PRE> </PRE> tags, three spaces will appear. But <PRE> </PRE> tags also alter the overall appearance (font size and normal character spacing) of the text in some browsers, and not in others, giving unpredictable results. The results are different in Netscape Navigator and Microsoft Internet Explorer.

Layout with Tables

You're probably well aware that tables are a popular and practical way to control layout—of a page in general, of columnar data within pages, and even of graphics and other objects on a page. Now it's easier than ever to get that precise control in your pages with HTML editors like these, which you can download for a free trial:

- Luckman's WebEdit Pro lets you type data into a spreadsheet-like form to create instant tables, complete with push-button attributes. See this wonderful table tool in Figure 2–21, and download a trial of WebEdit Pro from www.luckman.com.
- NetObjects Fusion lets you place objects such as images anywhere on the page with the mouse, and make them stick there exactly—to the pixel point—by generating complex nested tables to hold them there. Figure 2–22 shows images of stamps dragged to arbitrary positions in the Fusion editor, and Figure 2–23 shows the stamps still in place in the Netscape browser. Get a free trial of Fusion at www.netobjects.com.
- Many Web page editors offer professional layout templates that use invisible tables to divide and conquer the page. These table-based layouts can give a page a sharp, professional look while delivering a lot of varied information.

Despite all the easy graphical tools available, you'll probably want to create small tables by hand, tweak others, and remember your way around if you need to update data in tables manually. Here's a refresher in basic tables, followed by an example of tables used for an attractive page layout.

FIGURE 2-21 *The "Table Builder" from Luckman's WebEdit Pro (www.luckman.com) works like an easy, helpful spreadsheet. Download a trial.*

FIGURE 2-22 *NetObjects (www.netobjects.com) Fusion lets you drag images anywhere on the page with the mouse.*

FIGURE 2-23   *The pictures dragged in NetObjects Fusion hold their positions perfectly in the browser shown. Download a trial from www.netobjects.com.*

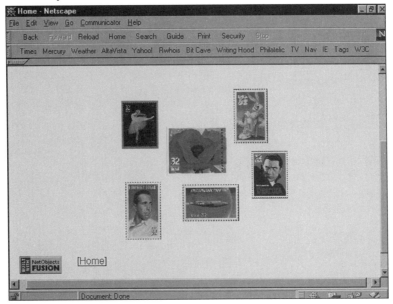

Refresher: Basic Tables

The following page with a simple table contains the necessary <TABLE> </TABLE> tags surrounding the whole business, an optional BORDER attribute (in this case 1 pixel wide), optional <CAPTION></CAPTION> tags, optional <TH></TH> Table Header tags to make header cells with bold and centered text, <TR></TR> Table Row tags to begin and end each row, and <TD></TD> Table Data tags to create the columnar data. The <TD></TD> data tags go between the <TR></TR> row tags.

```
<HTML>
<HEAD>
<TITLE>Basic Table</TITLE>
</HEAD>
<BODY>

<TABLE BORDER=1>
<CAPTION>Animals</CAPTION>
  <TR>
    <TH>Cats</TH>
    <TH>Dogs</TH>
    <TH>Birds</TH>
```

```
      </TR>
      <TR>
        <TD>American Curl</TD>
        <TD>Afghan</TD>
        <TD>Amazon</TD>
      </TR>
      <TR>
        <TD>Burmese</TD>
        <TD>Basset</TD>
        <TD>Budgie</TD>
      </TR>
      <TR>
        <TD>Siamese</TD>
        <TD>Scottie</TD>
        <TD>Sparrow</TD>
      </TR>
    </TABLE>

  </BODY>
  </HTML>
```

There are a number of standard things you can do to tart up your tables. Of course, you'll want to dress your tables carefully, complementing the rest of your page and your site, as discussed in earlier sections of this chapter, such as "Dying to Match," and "Choosing Colors." The complete list of table elements and attributes is in Appendix B, but some of the most effective tools to dress up tables are:

- bgcolor=hex# The cell color, e.g., <TD BGCOLOR="#FF80FF">Blue Jay</TD>
- cellpadding=# (of pixels) The space between cell contents and cell walls
- cellspacing=# (of pixels) The space between cells

Spanning Single Cells over Multiple Rows or Columns

You can change the table layout for a different look, and even make single cells span several rows or columns to break up a table-based page that's too blocky, or to accommodate odd-sized data within a regular table on a page. Just use the rowspan and colspan attributes with the table's <TD> (Table Data) element, or with the <TH> (optional Table Header) element. In this example, we make the second cell down in Column 2 span down Rows 2 and 3. See the results in Figure 2–24.

FIGURE 2-24 *The HTML code in the large image shows the spanned columns in the smaller image.*

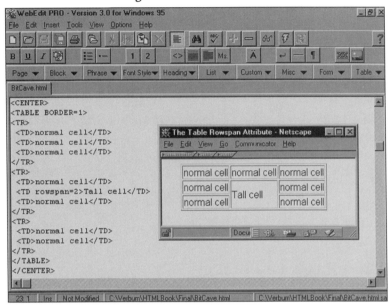

```
<TABLE BORDER=1>
   <TR>
      <TD>normal cell</TD>
      <TD>normal cell</TD>
      <TD>normal cell</TD>
   </TR>
   <TR>
      <TD>normal cell</TD>
      <TD rowspan=2>Tall cell</TD>
      <TD>normal cell</TD>
   </TR>
   <TR>
      <TD>normal cell</TD>
      <TD>normal cell</TD>
   </TR>
</TABLE>
```

New Summary Attribute in HTML 4.0

It's also a good idea to make generous use of the summary attribute, which tells nonvisual browsers, including Braille readers and speech synthesizers, what's going on in the table. The summary text won't show in graphical browsers. Example:

```
<TABLE summary="This table compares test scores of male and
female monkeys tested for speed and agility on the tasks of
climbing a ladder and descending a ladder. Females scored . . .
etc.">
```

Keep Column Headers Handy

Whenever necessary, break up your tables, repeating header and footer information for each screenful of data. I deleted material on making fixed headers and footers with the HTML 4.0 THEAD, TFOOT, and TBODY tags after finding inadequate support in both Netscape's and Microsoft's version 4.0 browsers. You should avoid those tags, too, until they are supported not only in the latest browsers, but in the browsers the majority of visitors use.

Table-Based Page Layout

If you want a layout that's as well-divided as a frames page without using frames, an invisible table is a wonderful choice. Like frames, tables allow you to specify a percentage of the available screen for table width and column width, which makes tables a useful tool for visitors with various display resolutions. Do make sure your design is readable horizontally without using the browser's scrollbars at 640 × 480 resolution. If so, users at higher resolutions will be able to see it, too. Don't actually make the table 640 pixels wide, because there are pieces of the browser interface that take up some of that space. Try a table 600 pixels wide <TABLE width=600>, or 100% of available space <TABLE WIDTH=100%>, making sure that visitors at 640 × 480 don't have to scroll left and right to read.

Up and down scrolling is fine—just don't make your whole page more than two to three screenfuls long at the very most. It's a good idea to make the tables start and stop within a screenful, too. In fact, the more professional your site, the more likely it is that every page will be no longer than one screen, with only administrivia—such as the Webmaster contact mailto:address—beyond that first eyeful. If you do have a longer page, let tables help keep them neat.

Remember to set the table's border to zero <TABLE border=0> so you won't visually chop up the page with the normal table grid. Don't merely eliminate the border attribute, or other elements may not work—actually specify <TABLE border=0>. Set cell padding (the area between cell contents and cell walls) and/or cell spacing (the area between cells) high enough to give the various objects on your page generous breathing room—for example, <TABLE cellpadding=15>. Strung together with width and border attributes, your table might start with <TABLE width=100% border=0 cellpadding=15>.

You don't have to make a table column for a decorative left-hand margin. Remember a visual margin is usually created with a thin horizontal—not vertical—strip across the page that has a color to the far left and white across the rest of the way to the right and repeating it down the page automatically using <BODY BACKGROUND="FILENAME.GIF">, rather than adding a vertical colored graphic to the left side of the page. See "Margin Backgrounds" earlier in this chapter for how to create a margin graphic. However, as part of an invisible table layout, the left margin graphic can be a wonderful visual cue that things are organized in columns—and the invisible table can help keep content off the margin graphic, even though it's actually part of the <BODY BACKGROUND> GIF. You can add still more vertical support with table rules or with a super-thin column the width of a super-thin divider—colored, of course, to complement your page. You'll see it pulled together in the example ahead.

Determine the width of columns by specifying percents of available width in the <TD> elements. You should usually specify width as a percent, rather than number of pixels, so the table will show if the browser is resized. Using percent instead of pixels also means you don't have to worry so much about various screen resolutions—but do design and test at 640 × 480 first and foremost, unless you know your closed audience is running at a higher resolution.

Watch how the following code makes a table fit across a browser screen, then shrink to fit a resized browser, all in Figure 2–25. Note that the border attribute is set to "1" so you can actually see what's going on. (You'll turn the border to "0" for real layout tables.)

```
<HTML>
<HEAD>
<TITLE>Resized Table Works Due to WIDTH=PERCENT</TITLE>
</HEAD>
<BODY>
<TABLE width=100% border=1 cellpadding=15>
  <TR>
    <TD bgcolor="#00FFFF" width=10%>cat</TD>
    <TD bgcolor="#00FFFF" width=80%>bat</TD>
    <TD bgcolor="#00FFFF" width=10%>hat</TD>
  </TR>
</TABLE>
</BODY>
</HTML>
```

FIGURE 2-25 *The large image shows the code for a table with its width set in percent of the available screen. The smaller image, on top, shows the resulting table in a browser. The smallest image shows the same table, automatically resized when the browser screen is resized.*

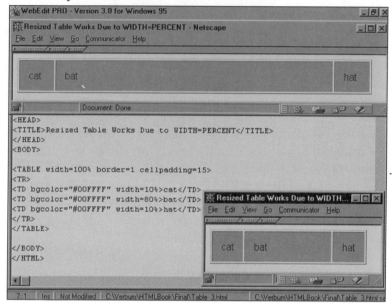

Bear in mind that the actual width of the column will expand to fit the widest object or non-breaking text it contains.

Use pixel-based column widths such as <TD width=10> (with no percent sign) when you want to make the cell fit an object precisely and not resize when a visitor resizes her browser. Be sure to adjust the cell padding, eliminate it, or figure in the cell-padding pixels, too, to get the precise fit you're looking for. You can even set the cell padding to zero, but be cautious about doing so. Even the default 1 pixel of padding you get without using the cell-padding attribute can help "unjam" a table's look.

Example Page Layout with Invisible Table

Here's the code for a table-based layout, but keep in mind that infinite variations are possible. You can see how the finished product looks in Figures 2–26 and 2–27. Figure 2–27 has telltale borders so you can see where the actual table cells were before they disappeared with the <TABLE border=0> attribute. The table follows a centered graphic banner that's not in a table. The table has four cells in one row. Note that the colored margin down the

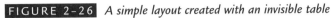

FIGURE 2-26 *A simple layout created with an invisible table*

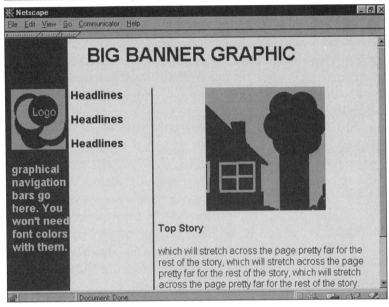

FIGURE 2-27 *The layout from Figure 2-26, showing table lines to illustrate where they are.*

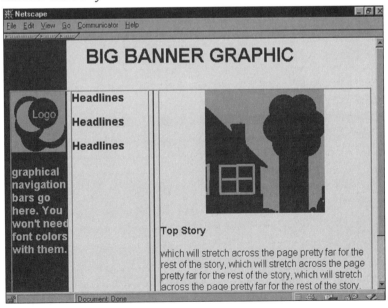

left side of the page is part of the page <BODY bgcolor>, not an inline image, since that would take too much bandwidth. That band of color isn't held there with a column, though using a set pixel width for the first column helps keeps stuff from the second and third columns from creeping onto it. The logo graphic at the upper left is what really keeps things from creeping onto the margin when the browser is resized. If you don't want to use a logo graphic, you can use a transparent GIF one pixel high by the appropriate number of pixels wide. (See Chapter 3, "Images" for the how—and why—of creating transparent GIFs.) But you'll probably add graphical navigation buttons beneath the logo, and those would also help keep the first column free of object-creep.

The second column holds the series of headlines in the example. The third column holds the thin vertical line near the center of the page. The line is a graphic only two pixels wide, but the column that holds it is set to width=50, so the text in adjacent cells won't jam up against it. The fourth column gives the remaining space to bigger stories and pictures.

To make the page work, as it does in Figure 2–26, you'll need to create graphics in these sizes and with these names:

Margin Background	1024 pixels wide × 1 high; color first 105 pixels	marginbg.gif
Logo at upper left	91 pixels wide × 98 high	logo.gif
Thin Line in Cell 3	2 pixels wide × 400 high	thinline.gif
Large Picture in Cell 4	200 pixels wide × 200 high	picture.gif

Here's the page code:

```
HTML>
<HEAD>
<TITLE></TITLE>
</HEAD>
<BODY BGCOLOR="FFFFFF" BACKGROUND="marginbg.gif" TEXT="000000"
LINK="0000FF" VLINK="00B9FF" ALINK="0000A7">

<CENTER><H1>BIG BANNER GRAPHIC</H1></CENTER>
<BR>

<TABLE BORDER=0 CELLPADDING=0 CELLSPACING=0>
  <TR>
    <TD width=100 valign=top>
    <IMG SRC="logo.gif">
    <BR>
```

```
    <H3><FONT COLOR="80FFFF">graphical <BR> navigation <BR> bars
    go <BR> here. You won't need font colors with
    them.</FONT></H3>
    </TD>

    <TD width=150 valign=top>
    <H3>Headlines</H3><H3>Headlines</H3><H3>Headlines</H3>
    </TD>

    <TD width=50>
    <CENTER><IMG SRC="thinline.gif"></CENTER>
    </TD>

    <TD valign=top>
    <CENTER><IMG SRC="picture.gif"></CENTER>
    <H4>Top Story</H4> which will stretch across the page pretty
    far for the rest of the story, which will stretch across the
    page pretty far for the rest of the story, which will
    stretch across the page pretty far for the rest of the
    story.
    </TD>
  </TR>
</TABLE>

</BODY>
</HTML>
```

Details Explained   There are a few more things you may have noticed—and they're all part of the attributes of HTML elements available in Appendix B. Here's what you saw:

- Valign (vertical alignment) tells the contents of a cell to rise to the top of that cell, rather than stay in the middle. The contents of these cells wanted to align themselves with the middle of the long thin line in the third cell, so we had to nudge them up. You can use the align= attribute for horizontal alignment.
- The good old generic <CENTER> tag was used with the thin vertical line in the third cell, as well as with the picture in the fourth column, to keep those things horizontally centered within the cell.
- In the first cell, colored text is standing in for graphical navigation buttons (preferably neat and tidy graphical bars stacked in a column). In real life you would definitely want to make those nav bars and not use the light text on the dark margin graphic, because the default page is white behind it. See "Dangerous Backgrounds" earlier in this chapter.

That's it—one table layout among infinite possibilities. Now that you know the basics, check out layouts you see on-line and peek at layout templates that come with your HTML editor. Think about the kind of site you're building and the layout that would be ideal for its purpose. With what you know about tables, you should have no trouble making just the layout you need.

Frames: Traditional, None, and Inline

"Netscape frames" could hardly be a topic for this book when they were ad hoc inventions of Netscape, rather than official HTML, but the World Wide Web Consortium (W3C) finally ratified frames as part of HTML 4.0 on December 18, 1997. Netscape frames had already become an important de facto standard since Microsoft adopted the Netscape Navigator 2.0 tags for Internet Explorer, but it's the W3C's HTML 4.0 ratification that makes frames legit for this book.

Refresher: Basic Frames

You can create different frames layouts by visually choosing an example in a good HTML editor like Brooklyn North's HTML Assistant Pro 97, which generates the code for you (see Figure 2–28), or Luckman's WebEdit, which lets you place frame edges with the mouse (see Figure 2–29). (You can download a free trial copy of HTML Assistant Pro from www.brook north.com and WebEdit from www.luckman.com.) But here's a quick how-to refresher so you can make frames from scratch and edit them with ease, even if you don't have a great HTML editor.

One of the most useful frames layouts is a fixed banner on top, a columnar menu of topics down the left, and a content area in a wide, downward-scrollable, right-hand frame. (See Figure 2–30.) Clicking a topic on the menu at left makes the appropriate content page appear in the right-hand frame. Even though the contents of each frame is a separate document, there's no need for a visitor to have a sense of leaving a page, going to another, then coming back to the original to leave again—at least when you do frames right. (For most situations, sending visitors to a whole new browser window, rather than changing the content in place, is doing frames wrong.) Letting users go down the menu at left, clicking different content into the same viewing area at right, makes this frames layout nice for:

- Magazine sites with illustrated articles popping into the main frame
- Catalogs with product descriptions and pictures in the main frame
- Photo albums with individual photos popping up

FIGURE 2-28 *Choose a frames layout in HTML Assistant Pro by example. Download a trial from www.brooknorth.com.*

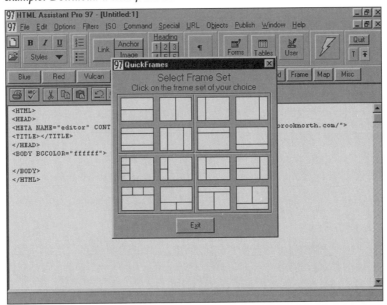

FIGURE 2-29 *Create a frames layout by clicking a vertical or horizontal bar button and clicking where you want it to go in Luckman's WebEdit Pro. Download a trial from www.luckman.com.*

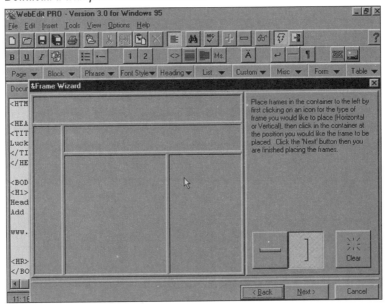

FIGURE 2-30 *Create this frames page with the code example in this chapter.*

   The documents you make for the frames are regular HTML documents, but you have to make them look good at the size of their intended frames, so visitors aren't scrolling in either direction to see a picture, nor scrolling horizontally to read text—and that must be true for visitors at 640 × 480 resolution. The pages intended for frames must also look as if they belong with the banner above and the menu to the left—the whole set of frames has to look great, no matter what page is loaded. See the exact color matching techniques elsewhere in this chapter.

   It will take one or more layout documents to tie all the frames pages together. The first layout document is what loads first—it specifies the first two frames, where to put them, how big they should be, and what documents to display in them. If you want three frames, you start by specifying two, then make one of the two frames into two more, and so on. You can assign names to frames so it will be easy later to "target" a particular frame to display a document when the user clicks on a hot-link for that document.

   To start with the first two frames, create the following file and name it MAINPAGE.HTM—note that there are no <BODY> tags—just <FRAMESET> tags:

```
<HTML>
<HEAD>
<TITLE>Postage Stamps, Main Layout Page</TITLE>
</HEAD>
<FRAMESET rows=70,*>
  <frame src=banner.htm scrolling=no>
  <frame src=twomore.htm>
</FRAMESET>
<NOFRAMES><CENTER><H3>This is a frames document, viewable only
from a frames-enabled browser such as Netscape Navigator 2.0 or
higher.<BR>
You can see a <A
HREF="http://www.nonexistent.com/nfstamps.html">non-frames
version<A> of this page now, or you can download <A
HREF="http://home.netscape.com/comprod/mirror/index.html">Net
scape's browser</A>now.</H3></CENTER>
</NOFRAMES>
</HTML>
```

The "70" and "*" above are each rows. The top row (the banner) is 70 pixels high, and the second row takes up the remaining space. We specified file names to load for the top and bottom documents, and said not to allow the scrollbars in the banner row. If the document in the bottom window is larger than the frame, the browser will automatically display scrollbars, because we didn't specify "scrolling=no."

The <NOFRAMES> tags offer a message to people who don't have a frames-capable browser, including a link to a non-frames alternative page and a link to Netscape, where visitors can download the browser if they choose to. Only the message in the <NOFRAMES> tags will appear to these people—and the message won't appear to the frames users.

Next step—Create the following TWOMORE.HTM file, and put it in the same directory as MAINPAGE.HTM, noting that this is another layout file, with <FRAMESET> tags instead of <BODY> tags:

```
<HTML>
<HEAD>
<TITLE>Two More Frames to Divide Bottom Frame into
Columns</title>
</HEAD>
<FRAMESET cols =30%,70%>
  <frame src=stmplist.htm name=list>
  <frame src=stmpfoto.htm name=photos>
</FRAMESET>
</HTML>
```

Now you've divided the bottom frame into two columns that take 30% of the window width in the left-hand column and 70% on the right. (You could have specified widths in pixels by using numbers without percent signs.)

Now create the following BANNER.HTM file, and put it in the same directory as MAINPAGE.HTM, noting that it is a normal content HTML file with <BODY> tags:

```
<HTML>
<HEAD>
<TITLE>Postage Stamps, Banner Page</TITLE>
<BODY>
<CENTER><H1>Postage Stamps</H1></CENTER>
</BODY>
</HTML>
```

Your banner could also be a graphic of the title.

Next, create STMPLIST.HTM, another regular HTML file that uses <BODY> tags instead of <FRAMESET> tags. The new wrinkle here is the "target=" directive, which tells the browser which frame to open photos in. When you created TWOMORE.HTM, you named the right-side frame "photos," and "photos" will be the target frame.

```
<HTML>
<HEAD>
<TITLE>Postage Stamps, List</TITLE>
</HEAD>
<BODY>

<H4>Legends of Hollywood Series</H4>

<UL>
<LI><A HREF="monroe.htm" TARGET="photos">Marilyn Monroe</A>
<LI><A HREF="dean.htm" TARGET="photos">James Dean</A>
<LI><A HREF="bogart.htm" TARGET="photos">Humphry Bogart</A>
<LI><A HREF="hitch.htm" TARGET="photos">Alfred Hitchcock</A>
</UL>

<H4>Classic Movie Monster Stamps</H4>
<UL>
<LI><A HREF="dracula.htm" TARGET="photos">Dracula</A>
<LI><A HREF="mummy.htm" TARGET="photos">The Mummy</A>
<LI><A HREF="wolfman.htm" TARGET="photos">The Wolf Man</A>
<LI><A HREF="frankie.htm" TARGET="photos">Frankenstein's
Monster</A>
<LI><A HREF="phantom.htm" TARGET="photos">The Phantom of the
Opera</A>
```

```
</UL>
<H4>Lunar New Year Series</H4>
<UL>
<LI><A HREF="rooster.htm" TARGET="photos">Year of the Rooster -
1993</A>
<LI><A HREF="dog.htm" TARGET="photos">Year of the Dog - 1994</A>
<LI><A HREF="boar.htm" TARGET="photos">Year of the Boar -
1995</A>
<LI><A HREF="rat.htm" TARGET="photos">Year of the Rat - 1996</A>
<LI><A HREF="ox.htm" TARGET="photos">Year of the Ox - 1997</A>
<LI><A HREF="tiger.htm" TARGET="photos">Year of the Tiger -
1998</A>
</UL>
</BODY>
</HTML>
```

You can come back later and fine-tune the formatting—especially replacing the menu list in the left-hand column with a smart little menu made of individual small bars with graphical text on their faces and text alternatives written into each <IMG> tag.

Next, create STMPFOTO.HTM, which will have this content:

```
<HTML>
<HEAD>
<TITLE>Postage Stamps, Photo Frame</TITLE>
</HEAD>
<BODY>
<CENTER><H3>Click a link at left to display a stamp photo
here.</H3></CENTER>
</BODY>
</HTML>
```

Finally, create the actual photo pages, such as monroe.htm and dracula.htm, which will show in the right-side frame when visitors click the links at left. In this case, each file will be a simple HTML page with an inline image of the stamp and some information centered on the page. Here's hitch.htm—you can do the others the same way:

```
<HTML>
<HEAD>
<TITLE>Legends Of Hollywood Series: Alfred Hitchcock</TITLE>
</HEAD>
<BODY>
<CENTER><IMG SRC="hitch.jpg" ALT="Alfred Hitchcock
Stamp."></CENTER>
```

```
<CENTER><H2>Alfred Hitchcock</H2></CENTER>
<CENTER><H3>Legends of Hollywood Series, Stamp #4</CENTER>
</BODY>
</HTML>
```

The images are from the U.S. Postal Service site at www.usps.gov.

Open MAINPAGE.HTM in your browser. You should see what's in Figure 2–30.

There's More to "No Frames" Than <NOFRAMES>

You can use frames and address non-frames-capable browsers easily through the <NOFRAMES> </NOFRAMES> tags. Anything that goes between the <NOFRAMES> tags will show up in a browser that reads plain text—you can even put a URL to a non-frames page between them. The best plan, however, is to have a true non-frames INDEX.HTML page that offers a choice between frames and non-frames pages.

Some Web authors use a script to detect a visitor's browser, then serve up what it views as the appropriate page, but some people who have frames-capable browsers don't *like* frames. Those people find it annoying to be shoved into frames without being asked. Others may not mind frames on principle, but arrive with a 640 × 480 screen and have to deal with frames designed for a higher resolution. Constantly scrolling back and forth horizontally to read the contents of a frame gets old very fast, which is why the non-framed INDEX page is the best plan.

Since some people wind up on a frames page by coming in through a search engine or a link from someone else's site, add links to non-frames pages to every framed page. Even if you don't use framed pages, people who follow a link to your page from poorly designed frame sites may still be trapped in a frame when they arrive. You can help those people escape with Chapter 7's "Magic Trick: The Great Frame Escape."

New Inline Frames in HTML 4.0

HTML 4.0 did more than adopt Netscape frames—it gave us inline frames with <IFRAME> </IFRAME> tags. Inline frames let you add an inline subwindow to your page—a framed page popped into a page—without creating the traditional sets of framed pages. A page that's otherwise accessible to all browsers can have one little frame that certain browsers don't interpret, but those browsers will read the text alternative. Notice how simply the alternate text is treated in the example below, in contrast with the <NOFRAMES> tags:

```
<HTML>
<HEAD>
<TITLE> IFRAME (Inline Frames) </TITLE>
</HEAD>
<BODY BGCOLOR="29E9FF" TEXT="000000" LINK="0000FF"
VLINK="8A8AFF" ALINK="000000">

<IFRAME src="hitch.htm" width="200" height="400"
scrolling="auto" frameborder="1"> [Your browser either doesn't
support inline frames or you have that feature disabled. Use
this link to see the <A href="hitch.htm">Hitchcock Stamp.</A>]
</IFRAME>
<p>
```

Here's another version of the message to visitors without IFRAME viewing capabilities. This time the message draws less attention to the fact that the visitor is missing something:

```
<p>
<IFRAME src="hitch.htm" width="200" height="400"
scrolling="auto" frameborder="1"> [<A href="hitch.htm">Hitchcock
Stamp</A>] </IFRAME>

</BODY>
</HTML>
```

The <IFRAME> tags weren't implemented in Netscape Navigator 4.0, but are a part of Internet Explorer 3 and 4. Although the second example of offering an alternative message:

```
<IFRAME src="hitch.htm" width="200" height="400"
scrolling="auto" frameborder="1"> [<A href="hitch.htm">Hitchcock
Stamp</A>] </IFRAME>
```

is nicely low-key, it may be best to wait for implementation in Netscape's browser before designing with <IFRAME> tags. Another HTML 4.0 tag to look forward to when the big browsers implement it and most people have those debut versions (and higher) of those browsers, is the <OBJECT> </OBJECT> tag set, which you'll see more about in Chapter 3. The <OBJECT> tags will also let you plant HTML documents within other documents—but will go further.

Intuitive Navigation

Busy people—the people who make and spend money—don't want to have a "new experience" on the Web—they want the same experience, so they know where everything is when they come in the door. That's why people eat at the Golden Arches in strange cities, and why they like shopping in the same grocery store. It's why people "frequent" favorite places. But a lot of Webmasters don't get that. So people go to their site and find a "unique" organizational scheme, based on the company's departmental breakdown, or where a Webmaster could just pop something in on a page he happened to be updating, or any number of harebrained plans or non-plans that miss the One True Way: the way the customer thinks.

Couple bad logical divisions in a site with poor navigational cues—like graphics that make you guess where they're sending you—and visitors will click around aimlessly, muttering unkind things about your company, your kith and kin, and your camel. They're likely to exit and go elsewhere, since the door out of your site is always clearly marked in their browser tools, and offers a sense of control in a land-of-the-lost environment. It may take longer for people to realize they're being jacked around when things are hard to find than when images take too long to load, but when they realize how much time they've wasted digging for bones, they'll be twice as annoyed with your company. At least with slow graphics, they knew *something* was coming.

The good news is that it's easy to be a hero and make customers and potential customers happy. If you're delivering content to your own people on an intranet or extranet, the time you save the users is money that stays in the company sugar bowl, making your project a real asset.

The Right Logical Structure

The customer doesn't know—or want to learn—whose responsibility, whose department, whose division, or whose territory something is. They get enough of that on the telephone with companies, from waitpeople in restaurants, and from bureaucrats, where arguments can actually be made for going to the right person. But on a Web page—where there is no person involved—all issues of departmental responsibility must be invisible to the visitor/user/customer/person you're trying to reach.

What you can do to make sure you're setting things up the way the visitor thinks, is to approach the company like a visitor. What do you want to do?

- Look for a specific product
- Browse products, with every single item text-linked as well as photographed, alphabetically *and* by catalog number or other ordering system meaningful to the customer
- Check prices, including shipping and "hidden" costs, before wasting time
- Find out how long it will take to get the product in their hands

- Check the return policy or warranty
- Get help with a problem—customer service or tech support
- Find out who to talk to—contact information
- Get right to the press contact info (see Chapter 6, "Web Marketing and Press Coverage for Grownups")
- Whatever else your organization's potential friends might want or need

On the Web, Everybody's from Missouri   When I was asked to participate in *Internet World Magazine's* "The Kantor Group," on the subject of on-line shopping, the most important part of my contribution was on the absolute importance of what I call "comfort information"—the information people require before they'll part with their money. A lot of it is the information that TV infomercials throw into the "Call Now" box on the final screen—not just the price and shipping and handling charges, but the money-back guarantee, and other reassuring facts.

Consider that when you view an infomercial, you can call an 800 number and get a live operator who may have additional comfort info, such as how long it will take to receive the item, how you would go about returning it, how much refills cost, etc. On the Web, people need to see that information up front, too. They need it even more than when they're shopping from TV, because any 14-year-old can toss up a Web site and ask for your credit card number, as can companies that are technically legitimate, but have substandard policies.

As you design your Website's major areas to coincide with the needs and wants of the people who (you hope!) will use it, here are some things to consider thoughtfully as options.

With text links (not images), divide products into the most intuitive groupings, of a reasonable size, but also have an "all" page, where they can browse everything without jumping back and forth to a main page. One of the most irritating schemes on the Web makes you shuttle back and forth between an index with an alphabet and individual pages for items beginning with each letter. It would be far better to have all items named or described very briefly on one page, with links to detailed descriptions on another page. The result will allow visitors to navigate very quickly to what they want specifically, yet allow them to browse more of your items without the back-and-forth hassle.

Now add the visuals—but not on the two text pages we just described. On the more detailed page, add a plain text link to a photo for each item. Don't add thumbnail photos to a product page of any length—say, more than five products. Use plain <A HREF></A> tags to send visitors who select an item to a new page that has a photo and gives detailed information from the plain text page they just came from.

Give every bit of product information available—size, weight, color, what other products match it or work with it, how long it takes to assemble, what the user will need to have on hand, and more. Describing color is extremely important on the Web, since monitors don't all display color alike, and a dark monitor can turn navy blue to black, etc.

Give detailed policies for guarantees, warranties, and returns, including who pays shipping on returns, how to obtain an RMA number, what actions void the warranty, and how (and how soon) a customer's money will be returned if they're not satisfied. Run these things by your legal department—don't guess.

Never assume a customer will e-mail or call for more information in order to make a buying decision. Most would rather walk away than send an e-mail out with no clue as to when they'll get an answer. Tell them everything they could possibly think to ask about the products, your business, and your policies, prices, shipping and handling costs, and just about everything else they could conceivably want to know. They'll only click on the information they want to read—it can only hurt you to leave it out.

Never ask for a credit card number, address, or identifying information of any kind from a customer until they're ready to buy. If they can't see shipping costs, etc., before placing products in their shopping cart, then you're asking them to give up a piece of themselves just to shop. You wouldn't give a credit card number to get into a store and look around or turn over a price tag, so why would anyone do it on the Web?

Other Navigational Tools

Besides the basic links between hot words and destinations, and the links between hot images and destinations, there are navigation bars, graphical menus, and image maps. They all have a different flavor, but they are all images with hot areas, and they're easy to create with image map tools in good HTML editors such as Luckman's Web Edit (www.luckman.com) or HTML Assistant Pro (www.brooknorth.com). Both programs allow you to load an image and define areas of the graphic as hotlinks using the mouse. See Table 2–6 for HTML editors for various platforms.

Note: Every Website should offer a simple, consistent, plain-text menu on every page—usually right below a centered image map at the top of the page, or at the tip-top or bottom of a page with a side-margin image-map. (A side-margin image map is a tidy little patch of "menu" made of a graphic that includes small, styled fonts as part of the graphic. The image

TABLE 2-6 *HTML Editors*

HTML Editor	Platform	The Deal	URL
Luckman's WebEdit Pro 2.03	Windows 95/NT	30-day trial	www.luckman.com
HTML Assistant Pro 97	Windows95/NT 4.0	30-day trial	www.brooknorth.com
HTML Assistant Pro 3	Windows 3.x	30-day trial	www.brooknorth.com
NetObjects Fusion 2.0	Windows 95/NT 4.0	30-day trial	www.netobjects.com
NetObjects Fusion 2.0	Power PC with MacOS	30-day trial	www.netobjects.com
HTML Studio	OS/2	45-day trial	www.program.com/panacea
asWedit	AIX 3.2.5, Digital UNIX/OSF1 V3.x, HP-UX 9.x, IRIX 5.x/6.x, Linux 1.2.x SCO, SCO OpenServer 5, SunOS 4.1.3/5.3/5.4/5.5	Free for students and staff in education, charitable nonprofit organizations (non-commercial use only), evaluation by individuals and commercial organizations	www.advasoft.com/asWedit.html
The Emacs Package "hm--html-menus"	XEmacs (formerly called lemacs or Lucid Emacs) and the Emacs 19	Free	www.tnt.uni-hannover.de/~muenkel/software/own/hm--html-menus
tkHTML	Linux x86 and m68k ELF and a.out, Solaris 2.4 Sparc, SunOS 4.1.3, Irix 5.3, OSF1 3.2	Free for non-commercial use	www.cobaltgroup.com/~roland/tkHTML

map graphic fits within a graphical margin down the left side of the screen, which is created with the BACKGROUND=filename.gif attribute of the <BODY> tag. (See "Margin Backgrounds" earlier in this chapter.)

Never Never Land

Pictures *aren't* always worth a thousand words. Never create a pictorial image map without text painted right on it to show the destination of click

Luckman's WebEdit Pro 2.03 for Windows 95/NT

Remember Kenn Nesbitt's WebEdit with its many features and many tool-bars? Now it's Luckman's WebEdit, and you'll feel lucky to have it when you see the increased power and clean new interface. WebEdit combines the freedom and accessibility of plain-text editing with buttons, wizards, and builders to make everything from bare-bones HTML pages to forms, tables, multimedia pages, drag-and-drop image maps, and mouse-designed sets of frames pages. There's even an HTML validator you can set to the level of HTML you decide to use, and a download-time estimator to help gauge the speed of transferring your pages at various modem rates.

WebEdit Pro hooks into your browser for testing through a browser pre-view button, but there's also a "Quick Preview" button that shows a less sophisticated view of your page. This can be valuable for testing things like <noframes> </noframes> tags, which are difficult to test properly in a frames-capable browser.

WebEdit Pro includes an FTP upload function, a hex number converter, and a *link checker*. You also get the opportunity to configure the toolbars, and set up the program's behavior in many ways—like whether to start a new line before or after certain tag types. WebEdit Pro is an excellent buy at $49.95. Try it free for 30 days from www.luckman.com.

areas, no matter how straightforward the images on the map seem to you. Text "fly-outs" people see when they pause the mouse over a picture and get the "ALT=blah blah blah" spiel that's tacked onto the <IMG> tag don't always work on image maps. And it won't do to simply have words appear nearby via a script when people pause their mouse over the picture, the way it does in the Postal Service image map in Figures 2–31 and 2–32, even though that's a nice way to give enlarged descriptions of the titles on the image map. Text-only menus are an absolutely necessary addition to the page, but even they don't excuse an image map that has no clear labels telling the visitor where he will go if he clicks here or there. If a poorly marked image map forces people to use the plain-text menu or stop and play games with the mouse to decipher the way, why have an image map at all? Incorporate graphical text into it to let your customers know you are more concerned with their convenience than with your artistic prowess. Always include plain text for people with plain-text browsers, speech syn-thesizers, Braille output devices, etc.

FIGURE 2-31 *As you pause the mouse over different options on this menu, the image in the box explaining the option changes.*

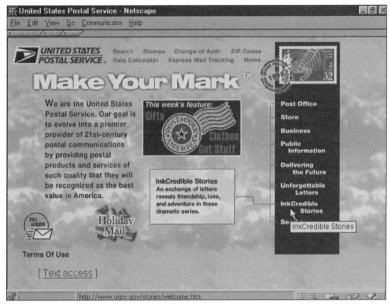

FIGURE 2-32 *As in Figure 2-31, when you pause the mouse over different options on this menu, the image in the box explaining the option changes.*

Downloadable Java Link Applet

The Java Boutique offers link.java, a downloadable applet that lets visitors select links from a drop-down menu. Check it out at http://javabou tique.internet.com/appindbut.html.

Necessary Ways to Say "We Care"

- Put your plain-text menu bar—usually two lines of short words that get to every major area's top page—in the same spot on every page at the site.
- Put a contact e-mail address on every page.
- Design the site so that every page is accessible within *two clicks* from the top page.
- Get beta testers. Make sure *users who don't know the site* can get to every page they need *within two clicks*.
- Update new page-to-page links globally with a tool such as Net Objects Fusion (trial download at www.netobjects.com) to ensure that you can get there from here.

Hint: Working on new pages? "Under Construction" signs are like beer bottles lying around the yard. Few things on the Web draw more disgust than the bogus urgent message "This site is constantly under construction, so come back often." Burn the construction sign and replace the message with a quiet, classy item that speaks volumes: put up today's date or the "week of" date each day or week as you modify the site. What? You don't modify the site every day or every week? In a few weeks or months that date would make you look bad? Then please, don't say anything about "constant construction" unless it's:

> This site is constantly under construction but, as so often happens in real life with bad help, the contractor has inexplicably disappeared and left signs and rubble all over the place.

Avoid Navigational Nightmares

Good site planning and design are just part of keeping your site navigable. Here are a couple of simple rules to follow to keep visitors on course and save you time.

Absolute vs Relative Links

Make an informed decision about using absolute or relative references to files (images, sounds, local pages, and other objects). Absolute links are URLs that specify a file name with a full directory path, so that it's a complete URL that would work just by typing it into a browser. Relative links are URLs that either specify just a file name (which is in the same directory as the referring page), or the file name and part of the path, relative to the directory the base URL is in, such as "…/Images/Cougars.gif."

Be cautious about using links that include any directory names, because all those links will break if you move the page, the images, or both to a new directory. Whenever it's manageable, put all pages and images in a single directory and specify only file names in URLs. If an unwieldy number of files requires that you split them up into directories and specify directory names, use good site management software, such as NetObjects Fusion, to update the links globally. (You can download a trial of NetObjects Fusion from www.netobjects.com.)

Meta Moving/Forwarding

Leave a forwarding address with the "refresh" command when you move to a spiffier, faster site. At the old address, create a page announcing the move and the new URL. You can push people to the new site automagically with the "refresh" attribute of the <META> tag, like so:

```
<HTML>
<HEAD>
<TITLE>Y-Haul Has Moved!
</TITLE>
<META http-equiv="refresh" content="5;
url=http://www.newdigs.com">
</HEAD>
<BODY>
<H1>
<CENTER>We've moved to www.newdigs.com.</CENTER>
<CENTER>Hang on a second and we'll give you a lift!</CENTER>
</H1>
</BODY>
</HTML>
```

The "5" in the <META…> line is the number of seconds to give the visitor to read your message before you schlep him off to the new land. You can use that page to remind him to bookmark the new site and ask him to notify Webmasters who are still pointing to the old site.

Finishing Touches: Make navigational cues topical, without being overly cute. For example, a side page at the Carousel site (www.carousel.org) has a carousel button and text reading "Around again to Carousel . . ."

Help Others Get With the Program

Once you have a great layout, get together with others throughout the company to see that everyone is using the same technology and that other departments will turn in material that:

- Fits the site
- Doesn't require formatting on your part

The directory for color files you created under the "Finalize Color Scheme and Make it Handy" section earlier in this chapter is the ideal place to store pristine embryonic templates of page types you create with your handy dandy color set. Those templates will save you time when expanding and updating your site, and they'll also help everyone who contributes to your site Do the Right Things. There are other things you can do to make life easier on yourself and Web contributors throughout the organization.

Templates

If people are going to contribute content to your site, offer them templates with your basic layout and color scheme and comment marks that tell them where to add their content. Invest a little bit of time teaching key contributors from various departments how to deliver completed pages that integrate perfectly with the rest of your site. What could save you more time?

While you're at it, see where their original documents are coming from, and look at ways to standardize everyone in the company on the same formats, from word processing document templates to graphics files and presentation formats. It will make conversion of legacy documents easier when the time comes, and make updates easier with search-and-replace operations across multiple files. Consistency now will make all the difference.

Hint: Use descriptive file names, rather than numbers, for all content, from HTML pages to images, sounds, and multimedia. Windows users should try to be descriptive within the boundaries of 8-character-plus-extension file names if any of your software still truncates names, including software for backup media, FTP, and editors. If you turn a file around in an editor and it goes back onto your site with a shortened name, links to that file won't work.

The "Look" Is Free—the "Feel" Costs Extra

One thing you've surely noted about well-dressed companies and professional sites is that they've sprung for a proprietary domain name (real or virtual). For example, you don't see Mercedes-Benz at:

`www.some-isp_named_jake.com\~mercedesbenz\index.html`.

You can simply guess, then type:

`www.mercedes.com`

and get to the site. You also get the car company if you type:

`www.mercedes-benz.com`

which was my second guess. Wouldn't it be nice if your customers could find you so easily?

Registering the right domain name(s) not only makes your site look more professional, it lets people find you without a hassle. As of this writing, it costs $70 every two years, payable to the InterNIC, which maintains the records. If you have an ISP instead of your own node on the Net, the ISP will also charge for its part in the setup. My provider, Eskimo North (eskimo.com), charged me a $50 setup fee, and charges $10 a month ($120 per year), thereafter. Since my unlimited account at Eskimo North costs only $120 per year (and even less if I buy two-year or five-year stints), I'm certainly not complaining.

Hint: If you don't have your own node on the Net, talk with your own ISP about setting up a domain name, rather than a third party. There are some places on the Net other than the InterNIC that let you check domain name availability, and also offer to register the name you want for a fee. If they're not your ISP, then you may wind up paying setup costs again. If you have neither a node nor an ISP yet, and you want to secure one or more domain names, you must provide the InterNIC with the numbers for two DNS servers—and that is where the third-party folks can come in handy. You're actually paying them for the privilege of using a couple of numbers on your InterNIC form, but it may be the only way to secure the names you need.

Warning: Don't try to be cute and register the names of big businesses if you don't have a legitimate claim to them, hoping to sell the names to their owners later. Domain names are first-come, first-served at the start, but people and companies with certain rights to the names can win them away from you. See the InterNIC's formal dispute policy at http://rs.inter nic.net/domain-info/internic-domain-6.html.

Business Value   Instead of having www.eskimo.com/~rrohan for a Web address, I now have www.bitcave.com, which sounds kind of cool to a geek like me, but there's more to it than that. Mail comes to me at anyname @bitcave.com. My family and friends send mail to rrohan@bitcave.com, doodihead@bitcave.com, and other names I won't go into here. That means your business can have one domain name that gets mail to:

- info@yourbiz.com
- sales@yourbiz.com
- special_offer@yourbiz.com
- contest@yourbiz.com
- flavor_of_the_week@yourbiz.com
- you_bleeping_jerks@yourbiz.com (you want to know, don't you?)
- you_great_guys@yourbiz.com (aw, shuuuucks . . .)
- sally@yourbiz.com
- ed@yourbiz.com
- yuor_name_but_not_your_domain_name_misspelled@yourbiz.com

As long as your ISP configures your account correctly, any name at your domain name will reach you—the ISP doesn't have to configure individual names. Put that together with a mail program that has filters, such as Eudora Pro 3.0, and the mail will automatically go into mailboxes for the right departments or individuals. That means the right people can see and take care of business right away.

Caution: Any time you want to share an account with multiple users, make sure to follow your ISP's rules about paying business or multiuser rates.

Put that name flexibility together with an autoresponse feature like the "reply with (stationery)" feature of Eudora Pro 3.0, and you can have mail come into autoinfo@yourbiz.com, meeting_notes@yourbiz.com, schedule@yourbiz.com, specials@yourbiz.com, etc., and let Eudora respond to it with the appropriate prepared letter! It's easy—all you do is click boxes in the dialog box under Tools/Filters on Eudora Pro's menu bar. The message Eudora sends to the inquirer is simply a letter you create without a recipient, and File/Save As/ a Stationery file in the Eudora/Stationery directory. You can have lots of these "stationery" files, which would be more aptly named "ready-letters" or "templates-missing-only-the-recipient's-name." Eudora fills in the name for you when a letter is received—and queues the letter to go out the next time you connect to the mail server to check mail or send another letter. You do nothing—you can even set it up so the inquiry letter is sent directly to the appropriate folder and the reply sent without your seeing it.

Hint: Test what users will get by sending an inquiry to yourself.

Save Money! Do Some of That without a Virtual Domain Anyone can use Eudora to filter mail by subject line, body text, the From: line, and more—they don't have to filter by user name. Whatever part of the e-mail is chosen, you can specify that it contain, not contain, start with, end with, and so on, whatever content you like. Eudora's filters can combine two conditions from two parts of the letter and respond with many actions such as transfer, respond with (prepared letter), reply, forward, and much more. Good filters are an incredibly powerful way to alleviate communications burdens on staff.

Eudora is available for Windows and the Mac, but there are other autoresponders for other platforms. Autoresponders are a great way of providing information to people who have only e-mail, and not Web access. You'd be surprised how many people have free e-mail services and nothing else, or just e-mail through a work account.

Important: Be sure to tell people that they're getting an automatic response, that it's for their convenience because it's quicker than a staff response, and that they can get a live person at some_other_address@yourbiz.com.

✪ ***Danger!*** To avoid having your mail box and an inquirer's mailbox get into an endless loop of mailing automatic responses to each other, be sure that your letter is set up with a REPLY TO: address *not* connected to an autoresponder. Many a machine has gone down under the weight of a mindless exchange between mail robots.

By the way, if you don't know the name Qualcomm, the makers of Eudora, you don't have to—you can get to their Website at www.eudora.com as well as www.qualcomm.com. It's unusual to name a site for a single product but, in this case, the extra domain name probably helps a lot of lost sheep find their way in. Give some serious thought to securing the domain names you might really want. And do it today. The top three names on my list were taken—including my own! It might be relatively easy to avoid being the only "Star Tech Enterprise" or "Strike Force Tactical Communications" in your city, but someone in the world has already taken startech.com and strikeforce.com—not to mention rohan.com. Check out domain name availability at the InterNIC's site (http://rs.internic.net/cgi-bin/whois) to see if your name picks are still available.

Finishing Touch—Webmaster's Contact

Make your job title reflect your business and your site's look and feel. Why call yourself a Webmaster when you are so much more? Where it's appropriate, you can make your enterprise seem more friendly, creative, or even more uptight with the right title in your contact line. In keeping with my write-minded profession, I was Little Web Writing Hood for a season. A more button-down soul might favor "Web Administrator." You'll find dozens of alternatives below.

You can say "Contact the Web Concierge at webmaster@swell hotel.com" and never have to worry about changing your e-mail address from webmaster@swellhotel.com. You can even tie the title directly into your e-mail address and address line. First, check to see that mail from the outside will reach your site at anyrecipient@company.com, then, if you aren't the sole user, get the sysadmin to hook the chosen alias to your mailbox. Be sure to test the setup from outside the company before you take it public; otherwise your public relations coup could turn into a public relations poup.

✪ *Danger:* Don't use a line like:

```
Contact webconcierge@swellhotel.com
```

when the underlying address is different. In other words, if the text that people view says:

```
webconcierge@swellhotel.com,
```

but they're actually clicking a mailto: address that says:

```
webmaster@swellhotel.com,
```

and webconcierge@swellhotel.com won't be routed to you, you'll have problems.

Some people will always copy the address they see and try to use that, rather than using your mailto:link with their browser. Why? Because their browser isn't hooked up to a mail program they like and they don't know how to configure it, or because they're gathering your addresses for their address book and will write you when they have more time. I do it myself because I may have something to say to more than one Webmaster when I'm writing an article. (That's why some folks who only use a form for their mail and hide their mailto: address can lose opportunities for press coverage, business, and more. All else being equal, I'll contact someone it's easy to contact—and that means being able to grab an actual e-mail address, not try to fit my carefully prepared request into their form.)

But you should be perfectly safe exchanging the boring:

E-mail comments regarding this Web site to <a href="mailto:webmaster @spacelytowers.com">webmaster@spacelytowers.com</a>

to the more interesting:

You may approach The Great Web Oz by knocking at <A REF="mailto:web master@spacelytowers.com"><I>webmaster@spacelytowers.com</I></A>.

If your professional culture allows it, try a title from Table 2–7. After all, the Web artiste is today's corporate cowboy. Take it from the Chief Guano Spreader at The Bit Cave™.

TABLE 2–7 *Alternatives for the "Webmaster" Line*

At the Web Helm	Technoid	Web Schlub
Bit Bender	The Fly In The Web	Web Slave
Bit Brain	Web Brat	Web Slinger
Bit Director	Web Concierge	Web Slob
Bit Marshall	Web Curmudgeon	Web Spider
Bit Tender	Web Diddley	Web Spinner
Byte Bender	Web Doll	Web Superman
Byte Minder	Web Engineer	Web Tender
Caught in the Web	Web Fairy	Web Thrall
Chief Geek	Web Foot	Web Troll
Chief Webbons Officer	Web Gal	Web Vader
Geekazoid	Web Guy	Web Weaver
HTML Slinger	Web Hand	Web Weevil
HTMLper	Web Head	Web Wonder
Java Master: Tea. Earl Grey. *Not.*	Web Jockey	Web Wonder Woman
Master of the Web	Web Mechanic	Web Wrench
Master of Web Minions	Web Meister	Webbles
On the Bit Bridge	Web Mole	Webbons Engineer
OverByte	Web Monitor	Webby-dooby-doo
Power Behind the Site	Web Monkey	Webel Without a Cause
Soul of the Web Machine	Web Monster	Webley
Spidey	Web Nut	Webrandt
Tech Droid	Web Poke	

CHAPTER 3

Objects Part 1: Images

Most creatures love show-and-tell: bees dance out a 3-D restaurant guide for their friends; wolves call "Good-night, John Boy" in the night; dogs tag fences, and human beings are rapidly evolving from projector-toting, laser-pointing critters into mondo-media Web designers. Our species seems just *this* close to digitizing star dust and flash paper for The Perfect Magic Show. We may not have the star tech to put a hard-light holo-port in every room, but we can do a lot with objects on the Web. The technology is already more elegant than what most of us have to say, let alone what most of us will put to good use. Think of all the things you can drop into a Web page—there's a small sampling in Table 3–1.

The sheer variety of options can put a forward-thinking Webmaster ahead of the competition. What *useful, relevant* thing could visitors to your site do that they can't do at your competitor's site?

Putting It All In

The machine driving the mondo-media Web is the ability to insert complex objects into HTML pages—once with <APPLET> </APPLET> tags and, with HTML 4.0, <OBJECT> </OBJECT>tags. (With HTML 4.0, the <APPLET> tags were deprecated.) The all-in-one <OBJECT> tags can contain any

TABLE 3-1   *Sample Objects You Can Drop into Web Pages*

3-D virtual worlds	MathCAD documents
Animations	Movie clips
Business-quality WYSIWYG forms	Photos
Cam-feeds	Remote access to computers and machines
Chat boards	Searchable address books
Chemical structures	Slide shows
Collaboration software	Spreadsheets
Databases centralizing input and output	Streaming sounds
Dynamic calendars	Terminal emulations
Interactive games	Windowed Windows applications
Kiosks	Zoomable vector drawings
Layered maps	. . . and much more.

kind of content, using the appropriate parameters. A great thing about the <OBJECT> tag is that you can specify a series of content types, and the browser that supports the <OBJECT> tags will parse the first content type that it can, from the first to the last. People will generally start with the most complex types of objects, for example, an executable application, and move down to more common types, such as an MPEG movie, then a static image, then plain text. The browser glomps on to the first type it can play and ignores the rest.

Here's an example of the <OBJECT> tag at work, offering a python applet, followed by an MPEG video, then a GIF image, and then plain text—the hope being that the browser will parse the higher-end object type:

```
<OBJECT title="The Likely Behavior of Volcano X"
classid="http://www.vulcan.spew/VolcanoX.py">
  <OBJECT data="VolcanoX.mpeg" type="application/mpeg">
    <OBJECT data="VocanoX.gif" type="image/gif">
      The likely behavior of Volcano X.
    </OBJECT>
  </OBJECT>
</OBJECT>
```

There's little new to deal with, other than the opportunity for layering object types from the top down.

If you would have used the <APPLET> tags with a Java sound player like this:

```
<APPLET code="AudioItem" width="15" height="15">
<param name="snd" value="volcano.au|erupt.au">
Java applet playing sound of erupting volcano
</APPLET>
```

you would now use the <OBJECT> tags like this:

```
<OBJECT codetype="application/java" classid="AudioItem"
width="15" height="15">
<param name="snd" value="volcano.au|erupt.au">
Java applet playing sound of erupting volcano
</OBJECT>
```

Even though it's easy to switch to the <OBJECT> tag, and tempting to use its drill-down object-type model, wait until everyone you want to reach has browsers that support the <OBJECT> tag, such as Netscape's and Microsoft's 4.0 browsers. In the mean time, you'll need a tag supported by almost all the browsers and browser versions out there. The objects themselves must be supported either by the majority of browsers or through add-ons such as Netscape Plug-ins or Microsoft ActiveX controls. Unfortunately, just delivering to both Netscape's and Microsoft's browsers can be a challenge, depending on the type of file you're trying to get across to visitors.

Covering Bases, Hedging Bets

Netscape and Microsoft may not tell you on their own pages whether their competitor's browser supports an add-on, so be sure to visit the plug-in vendor's site to see if you're shutting out visitors before you tie your site to a browser-centric technology. Note which platforms are supported, too—do you really want to put up something that only Windows 95 users can see? Don't you have customers—or want customers—on Windows 3.1, UNIX, OS/2, Macs, and Amigas? Check browser betas and watch magazine previews to see what file support will be integrated into the next versions of Netscape's and Microsoft's browsers. Today's browser plug-in may be tomorrow's built-in features. It pays to keep up with what the latest betas are reading as you finalize your commitment to a certain file type.

You shouldn't have to choose between Netscape and Microsoft to show a crucial species of file on the Web. Check out Chapter 1, the section called

"A Word about Standards and Webbons of Choice," and if you can't deliver the same format to both platforms, include a format for each platform. Most businesses and organizations benefit from reaching as many receptive heads as they can. If you rein in your content providers and let them know the standards they need to conform to, you shouldn't be in a position of designing two versions of a page. Look for the most universal format first. We'll cover conversions to near-universal formats for images, animations, sounds, and more, including places to download conversion tools. And since the widest audience isn't measured by eyeballs alone, we'll talk about text alternatives to multimedia visuals that the blind can hear and text-only visitors will love you for.

The next three chapters will cover various object types: Chapter 3 "Images," Chapter 4 "Sound," and Chapter 5 "Ready-Made Drop-Ins: Java Applets, JavaScript, Active X, and Plug-Ins."

Images

This first section covers image objects, beginning with an image overview, then moving to the most universal object format on the Web—the Graphics Interchange Format (GIF) image file, in its standard, transparent, interlaced, and animated forms. (We'll point you to both free and pay software to help create and work with it.) Next we'll work with varieties of JPEG—the only graphic format to gain the support that GIF has within virtually every graphical browser. We'll also talk briefly about other formats, including the Portable Network Graphics (PNG) format, which is now a W3C Recommendation meant to replace GIFs.

There's more to images than file types—like adding special effects, reducing byte count, capturing stills from video, getting photos developed as graphics files, doing better scans, getting screen shots, watermarking and signposting images to help defend your intellectual property, and buckets more. (If you want to know how to conceal entire images within other files, see Chapter 8, "Hiding In Plain Site: Keeping and Sharing Secrets on the Web.") We'll end the image chapter with Net sources for many thousands of free images—including thousands of free animated GIFs. Chapters 4 and 5 cover objects as sounds, video, objects for plug-ins, Java applets, scripts, ActiveX controls, and more. A reception with free goodies will follow.

The Right Graphic for the Job: Bitmap, Vector, or Metafile

Graphics files are stored in three basic ways: as bitmapped (or raster) formats, vector formats, and metafile formats.

Bitmaps

Bitmaps are often created by paint or image-editing programs. They store information about what color to display for each and every pixel making up the image. You can tell that color information is stored for individual pixels because, when you stretch a bitmapped image, you wind up with more pixels than information about what to display in them, and you get the "jaggies." Try it with a Windows BMP (BitMaP), PCX (PC Paintbrush), or GIF (Graphic Interchange Format) file, then see our tips for smoothing those jaggies.

Bitmaps are still perfectly good files—and they're easy to edit to the tiniest detail at the pixel level. Any decent image-editing program lets you jack up pixels to the size of sugar cubes—or half the screen—if you have bad eyes or a shaky mouse hand. If you appreciate the reassuring "griddiness" of cross-stitching, or if you've ever enjoyed playing with LiteBrite or painting by number, you'll love the directness of editing bitmaps.

GIF and JPG—the two nearly universally accepted Web image formats—are both bitmap formats, and newer versions are increasingly versatile. Between the two, you have the power to put up animations, transparent images, progressive builds, and files compressed to within an inch of their lives. The sheer universality of GIF and JPG makes them the right choice almost every time it's possible to use them.

Tips for Smoothing Bitmap Jaggies

- When enlarging, go back to the source and rescan at a higher DPI, rather than stretching a small image.
- Reducing normally doesn't create jaggies unless you're shrinking an image containing text. Get a program such as Wextech's Smooth Scaling (www.wextech.com) when reducing a screen shot with menus, or a scanned advertisement or poster with text.
- JPGs are bitmaps, but because their lossy compression makes them less sharp than GIFs, some JPGs may actually scale *up* more smoothly than GIFs. Remember that GIFs are 256 or fewer colors by nature—simply converting from GIF to JPG won't stretch out the number of colors. Try to find an original in JPG, rather than GIF, or start with any 24-bit

color image, then scale up before reducing colors and converting to GIF.

- Use feathering, blurring, "smoothening," and other effects found in image-editing programs.
- Use options for antialiased type in programs like Photoshop as you create text, or with the lasso tool when moving portions of pictures.
- Use antialiasing techniques, such as supersampling, which takes multiple samples to compensate for lack of information in shaded areas. See examples in the Syndesis Megahedron manual at www.threedee.com/mhedron/html/manual/alias.html.

Note: If you like pi (that's not the eatin' kind), you'll find what are probably fascinating lecture notes on antialiasing at Stanford. See www-graphics.stanford.edu/courses/cs248-95/samp/samp1.html.

Vector Images

Vector formats are commonly found in drawing programs, such as Corel-DRAW (CDR) and Lotus Picture (PIC). Vector files define objects such as ellipses and lines, and store the mathematical descriptions of those objects instead of information about specific pixels. Vector images expand much more smoothly than bitmapped images, since a circle is a circle and a square is a square, no matter how big it gets.

Vector images are practical even for complex drawings, *if* the program and hardware drawing them don't take forever to put all those objects on screen. Frankly, it can take too long on your own machine for some vector graphics to display, so waiting for them to be displayed over the Web would be like being stuck in a tar pit. If you're going to create a vector drawing, but really only need the static image on the Web, snap a bitmap of it with a screen capture program (see "screen captures" later in this chapter) and save it as a GIF or JPG—there's no point keeping it in vector format if people aren't supposed to interact with it.

Vector plug-ins exist for browsers, but Web visitors need a very good reason to download and configure them. "Because I made a vector drawing" isn't a compelling reason, but the need of visitors to zoom your drawing all over with multiple magnification levels might be. (See a listing of vector browser plug-ins in Chapter 8, Table 8–2.) Consider this alternative: If they only need to zoom a few exact blown-up views, you can stick with simple GIFs and JPGs. Just capture the normal view of your drawing, then capture the critical exploded views. Use the normal view as a basis for an image map, and link parts of that image map to the corresponding exploded views. (See "image maps" in Chapter 2.) For example, clicking on one of eight sections on a city map could bring up the corresponding neighborhood. There's no reason to stop there—you can link the neighborhoods to increasing street detail, and all you're doing is adding one simple link from whatever the last view was.

Last I checked, it was nearly impossible to convert, say, a photograph into a vector format. Programs that trace individual objects within such a complex image generally turn them into horrible monstrosities at worst, or mere outlines of their former selves at best. It would just take too many individual objects to be faithful to each segment of color in most photographs. But tech marches on, so it's probably just a matter of time.

Metafiles

Metafiles are a little bit vector and a little bit map—er, bitmap. Metafiles define shapes and fills using vectors, but they map pixels where there's complex shading. Common metafile formats are CGM (Computer Graphics Metafile) and WMF (Windows Meta File). Again, plug-ins are available, but reasons to display metafiles on the Web instead of turning them into GIFs or JPGs are few and far between.

Use GIF and JPG Bitmaps Whenever Possible

Special circumstances may require dynamic formats like Software Publishing Corporation's (www.spco.com/) ASAP slide show. Used with a plug-in, ASAP lets users advance through a slide show without changing Web pages. And your Web visitors may need to fly through virtual worlds with VRML. But you can meet most other needs with GIFs or JPGs. No matter where you develop your Web graphics—in a CAD program, from a video capture board, or even a ray-tracing or 3-D rendering program—if the result is a static image or a simple animation, you should convert it to a GIF or JPG, because virtually everyone can see those formats.

Between GIFs and JPGs, you have options for transparency, interlacing/progressive appearance, great compression, and animation. *Anyone* can create GIF animations with simple downloadable tools—animations that can take the place of difficult applets, scripts, and plug-in objects created for the sole purpose of animation. Animated GIFs don't call for any programming, and your visitors won't have to download plug-ins.

Refresher: The IMG Tag

GIFs and JPGs are easy to pop in with the standard HTML <IMG> tag, like so:

```
GIF
<IMG SRC="maindish.gif" ALT="Poached Possum on Wild Rice"
HEIGHT=200 WIDTH=320>
```

```
JPG
<IMG SRC="maindish.jpg" ALT="Poached Possum on Wild Rice"
HEIGHT=200 WIDTH=320>
```

Remember there is no closing, or "</IMG>," tag. Be sure to use ALT ="Text" to clue in people who have images turned off, Lynx users, and folks waiting for your image to display. With Netscape Navigator and Microsoft Internet Explorer, users who see the picture but aren't sure what it is or why they're looking at it can pause their mouse over the image and see your ALT text pop up in a yellow flag to explain.

The <IMG> HEIGHT and WIDTH attributes are important, too: Browsers use that size information to reserve empty borders for images. That makes it easier for the browser to lay out your page and start displaying text and other objects for visitors to view while the image fills in. You can get the height and width information from any decent image-editing program, usually from a menu that lets you view information about a file, such as View/Photo Properties in Ulead's PhotoImpact, View/Image Information in Jasc's Paint Shop Pro, or Image/Image Size in Adobe PhotoShop.

For additional <IMG> tag attributes, see Appendix B.

❂ *Tip:* Remember that the <IMG> tag inserts images *inline,* which means they load directly onto the page unless a visitor disables automatic image loading. If you want to install images on side pages and let users choose them either with thumbnail image links or with text links, use the standard HTML <A HREF> </A> tags to surround the thumbnail source, like this:

```
<A HREF="bigpicture.gif"> <IMG SRC="thumbnailpicture.gif"> </A>
```

or to surround the text you want hot, like this:

```
The word <A HREF="picture.gif"> here </A> will be hot and lead
to the picture.
```

❂ *Tip:* Beat broken image link symbols by using absolute and relative links appropriately. See Chapter 2 under the heading "Avoid Navigational Nightmares."

✪ *Tip:* Another way to beat broken image links is to make sure you've set the permissions on your images so others can see them. If your permissions are set incorrectly, you will be able to see your graphics, but nobody else will. Always have friends or co-workers on other systems check your page. Consult your server's manual or your operating system's MAN pages for details on using CHMOD or other commands for setting perms.

Choose between GIF and JPG for Each Individual Image

GIF and JPG files have unique properties that work better on different images. It's not a decision to make once and for all, but for each individual picture on your site. A little thought about what you want each picture to do will guide you to the best format choice. You'll find brief guidelines for matching the right format to the job in Table 3–2, followed by more details on working with GIFs and JPEGs.

TABLE 3-2 *GIF or JPEG?*

Desired Result	Use GIF or JPEG?
Animation	GIF (currently the only option).
Bigger possible color palette	JPEG can handle 24-bit images. GIF can handle only 8-bit or lower, but you can use images with optimized palettes so the GIFs look exactly the same as their 24-bit color original.
Most faithful color reproduction	GIF always reproduces colors faithfully. JPEG is a "lossy" compression.
Smaller file size	JPEG gives the smallest files for images with photorealistic color, photorealistic grayscale, many colors and shades, and gradations. GIF gives the smallest files for images with few colors, black and white images, and images with large blocks of identically colored pixels.
Sharper image	GIF (almost always).
Speed filling in an interlaced GIF or progressive JPEG	JPEG (almost always).
Transparency—page backgrounds show through background or other specified areas of image.	GIF. (Transparency isn't possible with JPEG at this time. JPEG is a "lossy" compression, substituting some colors for others, and transparent bitmaps depend on the ability to specify the exact colors to eliminate.)

GIFs

GIF stands for Graphics Interchange Format. Early on, CompuServe wanted an efficient format that all its users could view, and the GIF, developed with UNISYS' LZW compression, were the answer. Today's Webmasters and surfers also need an efficient, platform-independent file format, and the GIF still fits the bill rather well, especially in its 89a, rather than earlier 87, format. GIFs can be quite small compared to other bitmaps, such as Windows BMPs, decreasing download time dramatically. GIF uses a "lossless" compression method, storing information about blocks of cells that contain identical pixel colors. Since no information is lost about a pixel's original color, compressing GIFs never extracts a price in image quality.

GIFs and Color Palettes

Since GIF compression is based on saying "all the pixels in this patch of blue are the same," GIFs are best at compressing pictures with lots of identical color patches. You can save complex photo images to GIF format, but drawings with few colors, cartoons, and pictures with thick, single-color borders are better candidates. GIFs only use 256 (or fewer) colors, but GIFs are capable of storing optimized 256-color palettes that make the GIF image look identical to its original 24-bit color image. Consider how much information that saves by looking at the exponential increase in complexity with increased color depth:

Bit Depth	Math	Number of Colors
4-bit	2 (for binary on/off) to the 4th power	16 colors
8-bit	2 (for binary on/off) to the 8th power	256 colors
16-bit	2 (for binary on/off) to the 16th power	65,536 colors
24-bit	2 (for binary on/off) to the 24th power	16,777,216 colors

GIFs can go even further when they store information for only the colors used in an image. If the image has only five colors, you may choose to save only those five colors. Contrary to popular notions, none of those saved colors have to be black or white, and that can save two more spots on the palette.

You do need a program capable of optimizing palettes with the best colors and fewest colors to take advantage of these capabilities. Reducing the number of colors in a poor program will change the colors, since the program grabs whatever colors are on its default palette. For the best Web image-editing software I've seen, download a free trial of PhotoImpact by Ulead Systems (www.ulead.com/), or just its Web utilities plug-ins for Photoshop. Ulead's excellent program is easy for non-graphics pros (me included) to use, but has incredible options for optimizing Web images, as well as powerful image-editing features like special effects. PhotoImpact lets you save a GIF the normal way, but if you choose SmartSaver from the File menu instead of Save, you're in for a treat:

First, PhotoImpact's SmartSaver lets you start with a 24-bit image, even though GIFs don't store color depth information for more than 8-bit images. In some programs, that would mean having to reduce the colors to 256 or fewer before you even get an option to save the image as a GIF. PhotoImpact's SmartSaver not only eliminates that step, allowing you to go straight from a 24-bit image to a GIF of 256 or fewer colors, it cuts out all colors from the palette that your image doesn't need. See Figure 3–1, where PhotoImpact's SmartSaver automatically displays byte sizes for the original image and the same image compressed and using a palette of only the colors used in the image. The image size jumps from 57,600 bytes to 1635

FIGURE 3–1 *Ulead's PhotoImpact's GIF SmartSaver module (www.ulead.com) reduced the file size from 57,600 bytes to 1,635 bytes and reduced the palette to the seven colors in the image.*

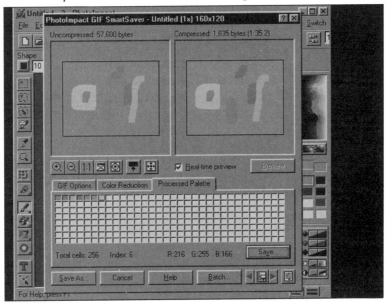

bytes—and I didn't have to think about a thing. At the bottom of the screen, on the Processed Palette tab, you see the mere seven colors this GIF file has to store—none of them black or white.

Note: I don't plug many for-pay products in this book, and I have never made a paid endorsement in 10 years of reviewing software professionally. In fact, I get *all* my software free—which has a way of leveling the field for the best products to stand out. A professional graphics artist might prefer Adobe Photoshop to Ulead PhotoImpact, but I have both programs and I use PhotoImpact because it's easier for me to do the things I do, even though Ulead's PhotoImpact's suggested retail price is $139, and Adobe Photoshop's is $895. Adobe Photoshop is the premier image-editing program, but it's way more program than I know what to do with. (Now you can also download a standalone of Ulead's SmartSaver for GIF, JPG, and PNG for under $40.)

Adobe Photoshop 4.01 (www.adobe.com/) has a File Export GIF89a feature with an "adaptive palette" option that limits the number of colors, though it takes a little more effort to use than Ulead PhotoImpact's SmartSaver, since you have to discover and set the number of colors yourself. Photoshop users can download a free trial of Ulead's plug-ins for Photoshop.

Transparent, Interlaced, and Animated GIFs

The GIF 89a specification—now supported in good graphics programs and browsers—allows for transparent, interlaced, and animated GIFs, which we're going to dive right into. But you can amaze people at certain kinds of parties with this factoid: Even the GIF 87a spec allowed for interlacing and for very basic animation. But many image programs that could save to the GIF 87a format weren't equipped to handle information about interlacing or multiple image storage. OK, that factoid may not make 'em splurt Alien Ale on their costumes, but it's the kind of thing that can get you noticed.

Transparent GIFs

You want a picture of a cheetah leaping gracefully across your page—without the big ugly rectangle that makes up the background of the image. How about tiger-eye-shaped navigation buttons without square backgrounds, or claw-marks that seem to rip directly through your Web page? You need to create a transparent GIF to make the image background—or any other pixels you don't want to see—disappear.

✪ *Tip:* Never simply paint the background of your picture to match your page color, and never fill in the background of your picture with bits of your page's background texture file. Some visitors don't see background textures—only a page color. Other visitors override incoming page colors and see only the color they've specified in their browser. In either case, when these people see your picture, the "matching" background will stick out like a red leather miniskirt at a funeral. Besides, you may decide to change your page color or page background texture in the future. (Trust me.) A transparent background will continue to serve.

As of this writing, there are no transparent JPEGs. The JPEG compression standard is a "lossy" compression, and colors may not be exactly the same as the originals once compressed into the format. For transparency to work, the colors have to remain the same, because you specify an exact color to make transparent. A couple of guys in Sweden were working on transparent JPEGs a while back, but the last thing I found about it at their Website was an invitation for people to help with the public domain project. It isn't impossible for someone to develop a transparent JPEG, but for the moment of this writing, you'll want a transparent GIF.

Transparent GIFs: How-To   If you're creating an image from scratch, some programs allow you to set the background to transparent before you even start to draw, but most of us non-artists are trying to take images we've found elsewhere—like that leaping cheetah—and remove the area "behind" him. (To remove something between the cheetah and the viewer, use a cloning tool to copy part of the cheetah's fur and put a patch over the object that's in the way, then use feathering and smudging tools to make it blend in.) Our job here is to cut out the wild surroundings so the cheetah can leap directly onto your Web page.

First, make a backup copy of your image. Never work on an original.

Second, make sure that everything you want to get rid of is one color— one color that appears nowhere else in the picture. If your image is already reduced to 256 or fewer colors, you might not see a color that you're sure isn't part of the image. With a palette that's already been reduced to only the colors in the picture, it's even less likely you'll find one, unless a program has made the wrong-headed assumption that it needs to put black and white in a palette of an image that doesn't use them. The way around this is simple: Convert the image to 24-bit color. You should see the option in your program right away but, if you don't, simply create a brand-new file, specifying a 24-bit canvas as you do. Copy and paste the entire image into the new 24-bit window and save the file. You're done with the old one, and you can close it.

Pick a new color—one that's obviously not a part of the cheetah picture—from the 24-bit color bucket, and place a little glob of it on the background of your new cheetah file. Now use the palette-optimizing feature of a program such as Ulead's PhotoImpact (in File/SmartSaver–GIF), or Ulead's SmartSaver PhotoShop plug-in or standalone SmartSaver, or Digital Frontiers' HVS ColorGIF 2.0 (www.digfrontiers.com) to export to a GIF file using the fewest possible colors (as discussed earlier in the GIFs and Color Palettes section). You now have a unique color that you can spread all over portions of the cheetah picture that you want to eliminate. Jack up the zoom and pick up the new color with your eye-dropper tool, and carefully color all the undesired pixels with the foreign hue.

Now you've fingered sections of the image for termination. Both PhotoShop 4.01 and PhotoImpact 4.0 will let you make that color transparent by clicking on it in a mock-up of the image from within their export GIF dialog boxes. In fact, if you have a simple picture with just a few colors, it may be easier to skip the re-coloring steps and just mouse-pick one color after another to get rid of.

Jasc's Paint Shop Pro 4.0, which you can download for a free trial at www.jasc.com/, lets you specify a color to get rid of by palette number in it's Save As GIF dialog box. To find the palette number, you single-click the representation of the current foreground or background color under the color picker on the right side of the screen. That action opens a table of colors in the palette. At first glance, the color squares in the table appear unnumbered. In the drop-down list box above the table, choose Palette Order for the sort order. Click on the undesired color, and its palette number appears in the lower left corner of the color table window. Note that this isn't the RGB or BinHex number, but a number between 0 and 255 that corresponds to the order of colors in a particular graphic's palette. It is this palette number you'll plug into the transparency number box in Paint Shop Pro's Save As GIF options.

Hint: Don't be confused by what some programs refer to as "transparency." Some drawing and paint programs are talking about making colors seem to show through each other, as if, say, a thin piece of soft blue tissue paper were lying partially over a bright red Christmas ornament. You'd get the illusion that the Christmas ornament shows partially through the "transparent" tissue, but the graphic would simply be a 100% solid block of picture on your Web page. To be sure you're dealing with GIF89a transparency, look for "GIF" in the Help file, or check out the options where you save files to GIF format.

Hint: If your program offers to let you save a GIF with a transparent "background," that doesn't mean the logical background—the tree branch behind your lizard, or the skyline behind the Statue of Liberty. We're talking pixels here, and pixels don't know from branches or skyline. Most paint programs have two blocks of color displayed to represent the current foreground and background colors. Often you change the foreground color by dipping your brush into a color picker with the left mouse button, and change the background color by dipping into a color with the right mouse button. It's this official background color that covers your canvas when you create a new file. If your paint program lets you make backgrounds transparent, use that knowledge to your advantage when you create new graphics for the Web. Start with an odd background color, then just punch it out when you save the image to a transparent GIF.

✪ *Cheat:* Fefe's Transparency Apparatus at www.inf.fu-berlin.de/tec/soft ware/public/public_html/otrans/english.html lets you convert a normal GIF to a transparent GIF right over the Web. Upload your GIF to your on-line directory and type its URL into the form at the Fefe site. Follow the directions at the site, and you'll have your transparent GIF file in just a few clicks. Save the changed GIF with the normal right-click "Save As" action. You won't notice the difference—the transparency—until you put the graphic on a Web page with the <IMG> tag and view the page in your browser.

✪ *Tip: All* transparent GIFs must be put on a Web page with the <IMG> command in order to see the benefit of the transparency.

Table 3–3, in the following section, shows programs and utilities for various platforms—many shareware or free trial—for making transparent and interlaced GIFs.

Interlaced GIFs

Unless visitors arrive at your site via T1, they'll probably have at least a short wait to see all of your images clearly. But this is *your* outer limits—you control the vertical, you control the horizontal, and you decide whether images appear slowly, with crystal clarity, as in Figure 3–2, or all at once, gradually building up from a blur to a sharper image, as in Figure 3–3. The images that appear slowly but clearly are non-interlaced. To give a GIF that crescendo of interlacing, just use a program that supports it—many are free for the downloading—and check the "Interlaced" box as you save or export the image in GIF89a format. Ulead's PhotoImpact works that way when you choose File/SmartSaver, and you'll find similar options when you save or export in Jasc's Paint Shop Pro, Adobe Photoshop, and many other image-editing programs, as well as single-purpose utilities.

FIGURE 3-2 *Non-interlaced images appear slowly but clearly. The inset shows the finished image.*

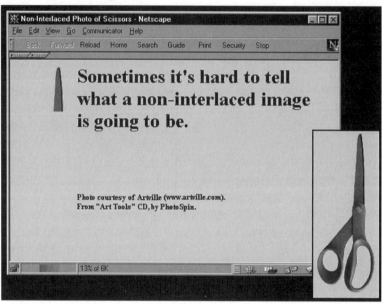

FIGURE 3-3 *Interlaced images appear quickly, all at once, but out of focus, gradually sharpening. The inset shows the finished image.*

To Interlace or Not?   Like many things on the Web, interlacing is a matter of judgment and taste. Is there an element of surprise that would be diminished by a gradual appearance of the image over the entire graphic area at once? Would the graphic gain or lose impact with the standard line-by-line appearance? Are you likely to lose visitors if they don't see anything but empty frame for a while? You can minimize the urgency of these issues by simply keeping the number of files so low and the size of files so small that all pictures appear quickly no matter how you choose to reveal them.

Does interlacing make a file's byte count larger or smaller? A sample drawing in WMF format shoved through the GIF SmartSaver in Ulead's PhotoImpact immediately showed a "before" size of 76,608 bytes and an "after" projection of 2,187 bytes with interlacing. Unchecking the box for interlacing brought the estimated output size down to 2170—a savings of a mere 17 bytes. That's 17 *bytes,* not kilobytes. The teensy byte penalty for interlacing can be more than offset by the Web visitor's perception that something is happening on the screen.

Of course, if you don't like the feel of interlaced pictures sharpening over time, or think they detract from a particular image, that's your call. A Website dedicated to convincing a church council that the Internet can be a dignified forum for viewing religious paintings might be a poor choice for the pixelated look of some interlaced GIFs. A Website meant to convince a parent group to allocate money for a computer lab might benefit from the "high tech" look of pixels and the added movement on the screen brought about by successive "passes" of an interlaced GIF.

Should you decide to interlace, check the options in your graphics package when you save GIFs, or see Table 3–3 for a utility you can download. Whether your GIFs build up over alternate groups of lines or with pixel-like squares depends on the style of the interlacing utility you save it with. Download several and see which results you like best.

If you like the idea of interlaced GIFs, check out "Progressive JPEGs" later in this chapter. Progressive JPEGs give images buildup effects like those of interlaced GIFs, but can do so much faster and in a smaller file space for most images.

Animated GIFs

You understand the principle of animation: draw Felix the Cat reaching into his bag of tricks one frame at a time, and then flip the frames, as with a deck of cards, put the frames on film, as with a cartoon movie, or save them to a GIF 89a file for an animated GIF. The same principle applies to

TABLE 3-3   *Transparent and Interlaced GIF Programs and Utilities*

Program	Platform	Comments*	URL
Fefe's Transparency Apparatus	Web—on-line through form	Transparency	www.inf.fu-berlin.de/tec/ software/public/public_html/ otrans/english.html
GIFConverter	Mac	Interlacing	www.kamit.com/ gifconverter.html
GifTrans	DOS	Transparency	http://sunsite.unc.edu/pub/ packages/infosystems/WWW/ tools/giftrans
giftrans.c	UNIX	Transparency use with XV 3.10 (ftp://ftp.cis. upenn.edu/pub/xv/ xv-3.10a.tar.gz) to get color index numbers	http://sunsite.unc.edu/pub/ packages/infosystems/WWW/ tools/giftrans
IMGWORKS	SGI	Transparency and interlacing	In your system software
Paint Shop Pro	Windows	Transparency and interlacing	www.jasc.com or ftp.jasc.com
Photoshop GIF89a plug-in for Sun and SPARC	Sun and SPARC	Transparency and interlacing	www.adobe.com/ supportservice/custsupport/ LIBRARY/psunix.htm
Photoshop trials and GIF89a plug-in for earlier versions	Windows	Transparency and interlacing	www.adobe.com/ supportservice/custsupport/ LIBRARY/pswin.htm
Photoshop trials and GIF89a plug-in for earlier versions	Mac	Transparency and interlacing	www.adobe.com/ supportservice/custsupport/ LIBRARY/psmac.htm
Transparency	Mac	Transparency	http://sunsite.unc.edu/pub/ packages/infosystems/WWW/ tools/mactrans
WinGIF	Windows	Interlacing	www.partner.digital.com/ www-swdev/pages/Home/ TECH/software/WNT-roadmap/ wingif.htm

*__Note:__ Entries indicating transparency and/or interlacing tell what we believe is there, but don't imply what's missing. We have not tested all programs, and new features are constantly added to programs.

photographic-quality movies, and you can turn video clips from any movies into animated GIFs as easily as drawings. However, since GIFs are better at compressing images with lots of identically colored pixels, the result may be byte-bulky. The real limitation to animated GIFs at the moment is the inability to store sound in them, but you can set an audio file to play automatically when someone reaches the page your GIF is stored on, which we'll get to a little later under sound objects.

You'll need a program to save your multiple frames to GIF 89a format. GIF animation programs are plentiful, and often free, inexpensive, or available for a free trial. Your graphics software or Web creation software might already have an animation module, but we've got a list of some you can download in Table 3–4.

✪ *Danger!* Animations are *way* overdone. Most often there is no reason for an animation to be on a page. Why annoy people with a longer download just so your logo can spin or, worse, so the logos of all the vendors who made your favorite browser and Web server can spin? My goodness—do you really want to build the site to honor them? Is there no higher purpose to your efforts? Remember the e-zine *Suck,* where the word "Suck" on a white page was artistically swirled and sucked back into the page? That was purpose. That was art. Put *purpose* first, and you'll know when—if ever—to animate. Here are some helpful hints:

- Only one animation on a page.
- The animation should be good enough, and relevant enough, to be the major (read "only") piece of art on the page.
- The animation should be integral to the page, not something nailed onto it as an afterthought. (See and believe Chapter 2, "Page Elements, Layout, and Navigation.")
- If the animation causes your disk to make ongoing noises like a running toilet, kill it.

Note that most GIF animation programs animate only preexisting images—therefore, you'll need a separate paint, draw, or image-editing program to create source frames saved as separate, standard image files. Different animation programs accept different formats, with GIFs one of the most common. Windows AVI (video) files are becoming increasingly popular imports in animation programs such as Ulead's GIF Animator, which converts the video clips into animated GIFs, even when the AVI is a full-blown photographic-quality movie clip.

Planning Your Scene   Think about the effect you want your animation to have. Will visitors watch an object move within the frame, as though you

TABLE 3-4   *GIF Animation Programs*

Name	Platform	Cost	URL
Alchemy Mindworks GIF Construction Set	Windows 16- and 32-bit versions.	Free trial, $20 registration	www.mindworkshop.com/ alchemy/alchemy.html
GIF Builder	Mac	Free	www.download.com/Mac/ Result/Download/ 0,21,0-21523,00.html
GIFConverter	Mac	Free 15 day trial, $30 registration	www.kamit.com/ gifconverter.html
Giffy	Windows	Free trial $19.95 buys	www.web-ready.com/
GIFmation	Mac		www.boxtopsoft.com/
GIFMerge	SunOS4, SGI, HP-UX, ELF-Linux, OS/2, Atari-ST, DOS/NT	Free	www.iis.ee.ethz.ch/ ~kiwi/GIFMerge/
MD+F Animated GIF Writer (Modular Dreams)	OS/2 as plug-ins for SPG ColorWorks V2	$37.99 MSRP	www.modulardreams.com/ mdfcwpi.html
MPEG2GIF	Windows 95	$25	http://nergal.boxtop soft.com
Ulead GIF Animator	Windows 95	Free 15-day trial version or $29.95 for retail copy. Also comes as part of Ulead's PhotoImpact retail version, which includes image editing, special effects, and special tools for creating Web buttons, backgrounds, etc. for a street price under $100.	www.ulead.com/ products/framens.htm
VRL's Imaging Machine	Creates animated GIFs right over the Web through a form	Free	www.vrl.com/Imaging/ animate.html

had a still camera watching a ball bounce or an airplane fly by? Would you rather the "camera" seemed to pan or zoom the object? Would it be more dramatic for an object to come toward the viewer? When at its closest point, will the object theoretically whoosh past the viewer's left ear, or will it go right through her head and disappear? Will there be an element of cuteness, like the cat that pulls the screen around himself just before using the litter box, or perhaps a surprise, or something that instills a sense of wonder?

Just because you can throw an animation together with lightning speed doesn't mean you should. Rough out a story board before you dip your paintbrush into the pixels. Make sure to consider all these things:

- Story line or action—keep file size in mind.
- Medium or "look"—dark, intricate cartoon; light, balloonish cartoon; real video, etc.
- Graphics style—how must it fit with the image you want the site to project?
- Colors—especially how colors will go with the Web site colors.

Natural Animation   When appropriate to your design, consider an organic pulse, rather than a frenetic blink or a predictable and, therefore, boring spin. Robert Lunday, an ISP and Webmaster (www.hemp.net), and one of the kind folks who previewed this book, says:

> I personally like animation that has a more "natural" movement to it, like a flag or a branch in the breeze, or perhaps a flowing stream. It seems the brain can filter these images a lot better. . . . It may even place the viewer in a subconscious state of peace as you have provided a welcoming environment rather than one that assaults them.

There's a lot to be said for a site that is, above all, inviting.

Animating over the Web   You can get around the need for an animation program on your local machine by creating animations right over the Web at VRL's Imaging Machine (www.vrl.com/Imaging/animate.html). Just put up to 25 files into TIFF, GIF, PNM, HDF, PS, or MIFF format, number them consecutively, put them in your public_html directory on-line, and type their base URL into a form, specifying the delay time, and number of times to repeat the loop. (The default values are a good place to start.) Press the "Do it!" button and you'll get a form with a field for each file name with the base location already filled in for you. Type in the actual file names, and your new animation appears in motion. Just download the GIF and pop it into your Web page.

Animation Programs—Learning the Basics in the Best   Most animation programs use files you've prepared elsewhere, so you'll need the program, the files, and the type of nonstick double-decker meatloaf pan that lets the grease drain to the lower pan as you bake. That way, you can shape the loaf flat for even browning. (The last part is only necessary if you want to bake a meatloaf while you animate GIFs.)

I use Ulead's GIF Animator for Windows 95 in the following example, because it's the most luxurious GIF animation program I've used, and you can get a free trial or buy the full stand-alone version for $29.95. It was great in version 1.0, but 1.5 is like a whole-number upgrade, with an animation wizard, support for converting AVI files instantly, and lots more. I highly recommend buying the retail version of Ulead's PhotoImpact which you can find for under $100 street, and contains both GIF Animator and my favorite paint/image-editing program, with special tools for creating 3-D Web buttons, Web background textures, special effects, and the brilliant GIF SmartSaver and JPEG SmartSaver for making everything the smallest and best it can be.

The basic purpose of a GIF animation program is to put individual image files from other programs into a single GIF89a—preferably making use of the ability to control frame display duration, decide how palettes should be optimized, and handle transparency and other issues neatly. Different programs make different use of the possibilities. Ulead's GIF Animator 1.5 takes care of all that, plus extras like adding animation to a single image instantly with transition effects such as Venetian blinds and wipes. Another menu option takes a single image and turns it into a rotating 3-D cube, and another lets you animate individual colors or a select group of colors within an image. The program also offers instant animated banner text.

Ulead's GIF Animator accommodates a lot of work styles. You can start with an animation wizard, a blank animation, an existing animation, or a sample animation. Press a button to add an image file as a frame, and just keep adding them, mixing and matching formats if you wish. A split screen offers either a list or thumbnails of frames on the left, and the currently selected frame on the right. Preview effects instantly with the click of a button. Another button adds whole AVI files, which import already converted to individual animation frames. Comment lines like your copyright notice show in the list at left as though they were a frame, even though they're invisible to those viewing your GIF on the Web. Cut superfluous frames with the familiar scissors icon, the Edit Cut command, or the Delete key—tools work the way a Windows user expects them to.

"Offsetting" means positioning frames within the GIF's overall space in relation to one another. Offsetting is an important tool, because it can save you lots and lots of work and bandwidth. It saves you work because you don't have to make all the frames the same size. You can align a small blinking eye frame over a big entire face frame. Rather than counting pixels and adding coordinates to the file by hand, you can drag the eye frame to the correct position with the mouse, or scroll to (or type in) pre-measured coordinates in Ulead GIF Animator. Don't despair if your program is less fancy. The X-offset is simply the number of pixels you want the frame positioned from the left edge of the GIF's working space, and the Y-offset is how many pixels from the top. It is nice, though, to drag the frames with the mouse and not have to think about it. You'll save file space by positioning the small closed eye over the face with the open eye rather than using a second whole face with one eye closed.

Controlling other factors is refreshingly easy in Ulead's GIF Animator, too. Just click on a frame in the list of frames running down the left of the screen, and click and unclick buttons and boxes for transparency, interlacing, and duration of the frame on the screen ("delay"). The delay feature saves you lots of file space, too, because you can make a single image persist rather than inserting a lot of frames with the same picture when the action is supposed to slow or settle. A drop-down box offers four options for disposing of the last image viewed—a handy set of choices that makes it easy and practical to leave that whole face up as the eye opens and closes, or to chase off a large image that you don't want showing up behind the coming small one.

❂ *Tip:* If your animation doesn't loop, make sure the final image is one that makes sense to leave on the screen, even if it's a solid-colored frame or a closed curtain.

You can merge frames, crop, rotate, and more. When you think you've done everything you can to make a great animated GIF and make it as small as possible, Ulead's GIF Animator makes it smaller. Choose Optimization Presets to let the program have its way without bothering you with the nitty-gritty details, or let the Optimization Wizard guide you through choices like whether or not to create a "super-palette"—a dynamic global palette that grows from frame to frame only as necessary. You get prompts to set the bit depth, decide whether to allow dithering, remove redundant pixels between image layers, and remove comment blocks. You can always save your image to a backup name, then go with the suggestions Optimization Wizard makes—or even try scrunchier values than it suggests. You'll see the projected size of the output file before making the final decision, so you can try various settings and see if they're worth the size savings.

If you don't have a file size optimizer in your program, check out the over-the-Web shrinker GIF Wizard at http://webreference.com/services/gw/. Sign up for the GIF Wizard Email Newsletter at gwnews@raspberry hill.com for the latest, or send e-mail to gwnews@raspberryhill.com.

The foregoing stroll through Ulead's GIF Animator covered most of the things you'll deal with when creating animated GIFs, though less luxurious programs may require more grunt work, or even cobbling a couple of your platform's programs together to get the same result.

Converting Other Video and Animations to Animated GIFs   Why convert? Animated GIFs allow almost everyone to see your videos inline—within the Web page—seamlessly. Visitors don't have to download any plug-ins or viewers, and if their browser is too inept to run an animated GIF, it's likely to show the first frame of the GIF file, so it's possible for people to see that first or last frame and be completely unaware that they've missed anything. But almost everyone browsing the Web today can see your GIF animations. (Do try to leave a nice first image up, just in case folks aren't getting the animation.)

Animated GIFs take <IMG>, one of the most basic HTML tags, and make it do a sophisticated job without Java, without JavaScript, without putting anything in your service provider's CGI-bin, and without having to know a single command or line of code. With a program like Ulead's GIF Animator, you can turn a string of images or an existing video clip into an animated GIF with a few brainless clicks, then lick the back of an <IMG> tag and mount it on a Web page faster than you could put mounting corners in a real photo album.

Animated GIFs also let you control many elements easily, such as duration of individual frames, disposition of a finished frame, and the number of times to repeat the animations, as we saw during the run-through earlier in this chapter. It's easy to add comments such as copyright information and how people can send you lots and lots of money if they want to show your artwork on their page. And since the GIF 89a spec supports plain-text banners, you don't have to resort to learning code for those, or depend on your visitors allowing Java or JavaScript.

Once you've converted a couple of video files to GIF and realize how easy they are to share with the world, you might be inspired to buy an inexpensive video capture board and grab a bunch of moving clips from your product demos, your home movies, or even your favorite action/adventure flick. That's the kind of special touch that can aid customers in a buying decision, touch family members, or get a laugh from your buds. Warning: It would be illegal to capture and display video from a video you don't own, so make sure that favorite action/adventure flick is one you shot yourself, OK?

Table 3–5 shows some downloadable utilities for converting from AVI, QuickTime, and MPEG movies to animated GIFs.

✪ *Danger!* Never edit an animated GIF in a program that doesn't create animated GIFs. Non-animation GIF editors may save your entire multi-frame animation as a single image.

Wrong Starting Format for Movies? If you have animations in other formats, or can't find the right conversion tool for your platform, take the necessary intermediate steps to get to AVI, QuickTime, or MPEG, then use these tools to convert to animated GIFs. This can involve going through a couple of conversions in different programs, or simply opening the movie in its native editor and taking a screen shot of each frame with a screen-capture utility. (You can find a screen-capture program in Table 3–6.) With all the bridging software among various platforms and file types—not to mention the ability to exchange files over the Internet—situations where files are truly dead-end are rare.

✪ *Danger!* If you begin an animation file by using the "Open" button in some programs, such as Microsoft GIF Animator and Ulead GIF Animator, then choose the Save button instead of the Save As button, you will overwrite your first GIF file. Microsoft's downloadable GIF Animator has no standard menu, and won't let you use the Insert Frame button until you have at least one image on board, so begin by pasting an image, rather than using the Open button—or at least remember to use the Save As button, which looks like several floppies, instead of the normal Save, when

TABLE 3–5 *Conversion Utilities from Movies to Animated GIFs*

Starting File Type	Platform	Use This Program	Vendor	URL
AVI to animated GIF	Win 95	GIF Animator 1.5	Ulead	www.ulead.com/
AVI to animated GIF	Win 95	MPEG2GIF 2.0	BoxTop Software	www.boxtopsoft.com/
QuickTime to animated GIF	Mac	GIFBuilder 0.5	Yves Piguet	www.download.com/ Mac/Result/Download/ 0,21,0-21523,00.html
QuickTime to animated GIF	Mac	GIFmation 2.1	BoxTop Software	www.boxtopsoft.com/
MPEG to animated GIF	Win 95	MPEG2GIF 2.0	BoxTop Software	www.boxtopsoft.com/

TABLE 3–6   *Screen Capture Utilities*

Screen-Capture Utility	Platform	URL
Collage Complete	Windows	www.innermedia.com/
Easy Capture	UNIX	www.autograph.dk/htdocs/cap/cap.htm
Screen Catcher	Mac (also reads and writes progressive JPEGs)	www.stclairsw.com/scatcher_bg.html
SnagIt	Windows (also captures scrolling screens)	www.techsmith.com/
HyperSnap	Windows 95 (also captures scrolling screens)	www.hyperionics.com/

you first save the animation. Ulead's GIF Animator will let you start your animation with the Insert Frame button, and has a menu with a Save As option—but you have to remember not to use the Open button for your first frame if you're likely to hit the Save button or File Save option for the first save. If you do overwrite the first frame in either program, take a screen capture to recreate it. (See Table 3–6 for screen-capture utilities.)

Animated GIFs in Complex 3-D   Ah, here we are. A place to trash what we know about saving bandwidth. Not! Think about it—why should a 3-D image contain any more pixels than a 2-D image? After all, depth in a flat medium is all illusion. Forget what you know about the processor time and memory it takes to *render* a 3-D object. You'll render it in the privacy of your own software, then just take snapshots of successive frames with a screen capture program. (See Table 3–6 for screen-capture programs.) That spinning 3-D skull carved from stone or that top hat that turns itself inside out to become a rabbit is no "deeper" than a 2-D puppy running across the screen after a butterfly. We're not doing VR—we're still just putting one frame after another.

To render the original objects, you'll need real skills or the help of a pro. There are plenty of 3-D modeling packages, ray-tracing programs, and even software that renders only 3-D text. To get the Persistence Of Vision (POV) ray-tracing program POV-Ray for DOS, Windows 3.1/Win32s/ 95/NT, Mac, i86 Linux, SunOS, and Amiga, visit www.povray.org. Source code is available for more ports.

Animated GIF Text Banners (Marquees)   GIF 89a plain-text banners are an easy way to create marquees—simply type text into a box in Ulead's GIF Animator and the program animates it for you instantly. It's best to use a static background image or no background image for your marquee, since the scrolling text is actually built with a series of frames, just as a pictorial animation is. During playback of the file, each frame of the text banner must play in succession, and the frames from a picture animation won't be playing at the same time—they'll play before or after. This will either make the picture animation stop or disappear, depending on what you tell the program to do with the previous images once they've played.

If you really need to have both a picture animation and scrolling text animation playing as one, you can copy the text frames to a drawing program or image editor and edit in the successive picture frames, or use a frame merge feature in your animation program for each pair of frames. You'll not only have a picture and marquee animated simultaneously— you'll have one file and one file size to deal with, instead of two.

Free Animated GIFs—Ready to Dance!   Take a big pail and go picking! Lots of professional design companies try to attract business by offering a set of free animated GIFs. Then there are plenty of folks who just like to create and share. Never has so much that's so good been so free for the taking. Check out some examples in Figure 3–4, then go raid the URL list in Table 3–7.

FIGURE 3–4   *Download animated GIFs like these, from WebProMotion, Inc. (www.webpromotion.com/stock.html).*

TABLE 3-7 *Free Animated GIFs*

Name	Free Animated GIFs	URL
AGL ("The Animated GIFs Library")	Different authors post their wares—you try to find what you need engine. Hint: Type "*" into the search through the animated GIF search engine field (without quotes) to see everything quickly.	www.arosnet.se/agl/ indexhome.html
Andy's Art Attack (Andy Evans)	Animations, Bullets, Points, Arrows, Buttons, Backgrounds, Counter Digits, Bars & Lines, Letters. Give a credit line and/or link to author's page.	www.andyart.com/ fimages.htm
Bill Gavin	Splendid water cooler, puffy disk, snowman-snowglobe, flashing arrow, and more.	www.tiac.net/users/ gstudio/an1.html
Caboodles Animated GIFs	Gaping fish, winking ASCII smiley, animated "Frames Free" symbol, Halloween divider bars, and Christmas cheer. Personalize your animated mailbox on-line.	www.caboodles.com/ animated/
Denton's Animated Images	Denton offers over 50 cool little spaceships and pieces of techno stuff. Metaphorical imagery of Windows/Mac wars and general protection faults (GPFs), and joke visitor counter. Fast loaders.	www.copzilla.com/ dimensions.html
Gif Animation Thrift Shop	Too-cool CAD-quality lava lamp, plus blow gun, spilled Ezra, light saber, and other unique movers and shakers.	www.tiac.net/users/ stacey/gifshop.html
Kulacrosse's Clip Art Stable	Variety of animated horses and riders, and more.	www.kulacrosse.com/ clipartstable/index.html
Mars Hotel	The Mars Hotel offers glorious pseudo-photographic object animations, divided for use on various backgrounds. Silver toaster popping toast, pink ceramic pig snurfling its nose and tail, metronome keeping time, a racing Starship Enterprise, and multiplying tribbles. Put the animations on your site, but provide a link somewhere on your site in thanks.	www.themars hotel.com/originls/ animaa.htm
Page Works (Kitty Roach)	Too cute for words. Dozens of animated drawings and photos include dragon doing handstand, little mermaid swimming, kitty blinking, snow globe snowing, turtles hiding in flowers, etc. Some are quite large and slow, which won't be as big a problem on an intranet. Some have optional smaller versions. You might want to shove them through an optimizer yourself. Must include a credit if using animations.	www.snowcrest.net/ kitty/hpages/ index.html
PhotoDisc	PhotoDisc's 10 free GIF animations are wonderful moving photos of chattering teeth, a construction sign with blinking light, a chalkboard with the chalk writing out "Welcome," a ringing phone, a hand choking a rubber chicken, a rotating fan, and more.	www.photodisc.com/ animate/

Name	Free Animated GIFs	URL
Pixelator Web Graphics	Pixelator drew its 13 free animated GIFs in a style reminiscent of Virgin Games. The chess king, jackknife, and even the flashing light bulb have a wooden or medieval feel. Swaying palm, weird car chase. Must provide a link to the site in appreciation. Also non-animation freebies.	www.pixelator.com/ pixanim-list.html
ProMotion	ProMotion offers 36 wonderful photographic GIF animations, including a spinning Porsche or T-Bird, waving hand, blinking eye, spinning basketball, DNA doing what scientists imagine DNA to do, and lots of navigational animations to point to FAQs, search engines, help, etc. Great visual picker lets you see small iconic representations of all 36 animations on a single page to save time as you choose.	www.webpromo tion.com/stock.html
Roy's World	Roy Jones put up 12 interesting animated GIF images, including a really good planet Earth spinning backwards, and a rotating guitar.	http://roysworld.com/ animation.html
SSA Custom Design (Stepping Stones Animation)	SSA Custom Design offers about 100 free drawn animations in GIF format. Most are drawn, some are dithered, and some look quite solid, but almost all are wonderful and imaginative. The wide variety includes blinking Christmas lights, spinning skulls, a swinging monkey, and pulsating and swirling Web-page navigation words, such as "Next."	http://ssanimation.com
The GIF Animation Site (Chuck Poynter)	Animated drawings of a prowling cat, dancing people, jumping Santa, business people, seasonal images, bombers, Pegasus, mailbox, and more. Anyone may use the GIFs, but commercial Web pages must furnish acknowledgment of the artist's ownership somewhere on the Web page. **Warning:** The audio might make you spill your coffee.	www.cswnet.com/ ~ozarksof/
Victorian Animated GIFs	Victorian dancing girls, lady in corset, wreath, and more—some made relevant to Web, such as carriage pulling "What's New" sign behind it, or a feathered pen writing "Email."	www.victoriana.com/ animate/animated.html
Web GraFX-FX	5,000 animations. Click "GIF89 Animation" sign, pick a category, such as "Cat" from the drop-down list, and hit "GO." Choose a name like "Sylvester," and hit "GO" again. Nice animations, but a lot of steps to see the basic images one at a time. Many images labeled "unknown artist" look suspiciously like familiar cartoon characters, so use discretion.	http://webgrafx-fx.com.
WWWeb.Ready!	WWWeb.Ready! makes cartoon-like animations for sale in packages of 250, and offers these 15 pro-quality samples in one free download (.ZIP for Windows or .HQX for Mac). Hammer slams nail, mailbox runs with letter, etc.	www.web-ready.com/

JPEG, JPG, and JPE

You probably know that JPEG stands for "Joint Photographic Experts Group"—a group whose prime directive is to produce standards for efficiently shrinking photo-like images. But did you know that "JPEG," "JPG," and "JPE" are not actually file formats?

What most people think of as JPEG is the public-domain format JFIF (JPEG File Interchange Format) created by Eric Hamilton of C-Cube Microsystems. The JFIF format, commonly known as JPEG, JPG, or JPE, uses part of a set of compression algorithms devised by JPEG (the group). According to Richard Clark of Elysium Ltd., JPEG's Webmaster and editor of Part 3 of the JPEG's standard, only the group of people—not even the set of compression algorithms—can properly be called "JPEG."

Why didn't the Joint Photographic Experts Group specify a format? As Clark puts it, "JPEG as a group did not want to set hard and fast assumptions about what users of its algorithms would want to do with it. It just happened that, as a result of pressure from users who wanted a file format rather than a basic set of tools, Eric Hamilton, who was at the time Convenor of JPEG and a C-Cube employee, hacked together a 'quick and dirty' file spec—JFIF—and, as they say, the rest is history." Other file formats, including a TIFF variant, also use JPEG extensions. Naturally we're going to call the files JPGs.

Put JPEG History to Work   You could mingle at parties, correcting people who misuse the term "JPEG," but there are better ways to use your knowledge of JPEG formats. Since the JFIF format isn't the only format using the file extension ".JPG," you'll occasionally run across ".JPG" files that choke your graphics program or won't display properly in your browser or HTML editor. The file may be non-JFIF—try it in another image-editing program. You may have to rename it with other file extensions in programs that don't detect the file format from the data directly. I fell in love with Ulead's Image Pals, the predecessor to PhotoImpact, because it opened formats that other programs rejected—even if they had the wrong file extension. (Ulead PhotoImpact carries on that tradition.) Before there were graphical newsreaders for Windows, Image Pals would even display moth-eaten multipart files I downloaded from Usenet without all the parts! The lesson is to try a "bad" file in as many programs as you can get your hands on and, once you get the file open, save or export it to the proper format you need for the Web. If you'd rather snap on the rubber gloves and stick your hand up the actual code and feel around, you'll find instructions for identifying different files that pass themselves off under the JPG label at www.cis.ohio-state.edu/hypertext/faq/usenet/jpeg-faq/part1/faq-doc-15.html.

JPG Wins as Big Loser

"Lossy" compression discards data that the human eye isn't likely to miss, and JPGs actually change the color of pixels slightly. To make the most of JPG's nature, your image-editing or conversion software should also let you decide where to strike a balance between making the file small and retaining image quality. Look for the means to achieving the right balance—perhaps under an "Advanced" or "Options" button in the Save, Save As, or Export dialog box of your image-editing program. Since every image is different, the perfect balance will be different for individual images. Balancing quality and compression is not an exact science—you have to decide when a file's byte size is small enough without degrading the image. The only way to do that is to eyeball the image at different compression ratios.

❂ *Cheat:* The JPEG SmartSaver in Ulead's PhotoImpact has a real-time preview that lets you see both the original and proposed image. As you move the quality slider bar back and forth, you see the effect on the proposed image and original side-by-side, as well as the byte size for each, as shown in Figure 3–5. You can even zoom the pair of images larger or smaller with magnification tools, and do so for as many settings as you want before you save. This is an extreme time-saver that makes it easy to conserve bandwidth and quality. In the new PhotoImpact 4.0, you can

FIGURE 3–5 *The real-time previewer in Ulead's JPEG SmartSaver tool shows the balance between reduced byte size and quality.*

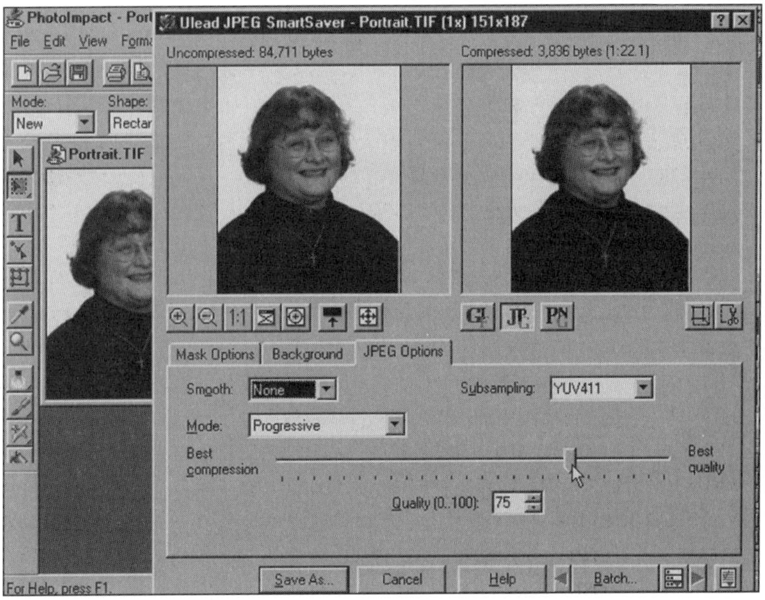

even switch among "SmartSaving" GIF, JPG, and PNG files in the same dialog box, comparing file sizes for the best format option, as well as the best bandwidth/quality trade-off. If you have a more convenient way to fine-tune your JPG speed/quality balance, you can probably roast marshmallows with the pointy end of your tail.

Converting to JPG to Save Space

Remember that files can be much smaller as JPGs than as GIFs if they're made up of continuous (photo-like) tones instead of abrupt color changes and broad areas of identical pixels like those you'd find in simple drawings. GIF is better at squeezing images with lots of identical pixels, and PhotoImpact also has a GIF SmartSaver that can actually reduce the number of colors in the GIF's palette to the exact number of colors in the image, without even taking up bytes with black or white entries in the palette if you don't use them in the image. GIFs are also better when you need to keep distinct fine lines, as with small text within an image. Remember that converting to JPG will destroy transparent areas and animation, too.

Warning: Never convert your *GIFs* directly to JPGs in order to save space. GIFs already have 256 or fewer colors, so there's little material for the JPG to work its magic with. Instead, resample—go back to the original scan, or scan again. If you don't have access to the original, convert back to 24-bit color, then convert to JPG.

Tips

1. Cut off single-color borders before converting to JPG.
2. Perform image-editing and touch-ups before converting to JPG. (JPGs deteriorate quickly with successive saves.)
3. Crop and resize before converting.
4. Convert to JPG only once.

Progressive JPGs

Progressive JPGs, like interlaced GIFs, make an image appear on the Web page quickly and out of focus, then sharpen. The fade-in can make Web visitors feel they're getting something while they wait. In a good image-editing program, you'll find a "progressive" option to check or pick from a drop-down list as you save your file.

Progressive JPEGs can look less pixelated than interlaced GIFs, have smaller file sizes, and appear faster. To really explore the best format for a given image—especially if the file isn't obviously meant to be a GIF or JPG according to the criteria we've talked about—you may want to take your best and smallest version of the image and try it as both an interlaced GIF and a progressive JPG. It costs just a few seconds to try it both ways. Table 3–8 points to some tools for making your JPGs fade in to hold visitors' attention.

PNG Files

By the time this book is in your hands, you may be seeing PNG (Portable Network Graphics) files where GIF and JPG usually tread. PNG is pronounced "ping." (For the record, JPG is pronounced "jay-peg," and GIF is pronounced with a hard "g," since it stands for "Graphics Interchange Format.")

TABLE 3-8 *Progressive JPG Utilities*

Name	Platform	URL
akJFIF datatype	Amiga	www.amigaworld.com/support/akjfif/
GIFConverter 2.4	Mac	www.kamit.com/gifconverter.html
Lview Pro	Win 3.1(with 32s extension) / 95/NT	ftp://gatekeeper.dec.com/pub/micro/ msdos/win3/desktop/
Paint Shop Pro	Win 95/NT	www.jasc.com
PhotoImpact 4.0	Win 95/NT	www.ulead.com
Photoshop 5.0	Mac	www.adobe.com
Photoshop 5.0	Win 95/NT	www.adobe.com
PMView 0.92	OS/2	www.wilmington.net/bmtmicro/pmview/ pmview.html
ProJPEG	Mac Photoshop plug-in	ftp://ftp.boxtopsoft.com/pub/
XV	X Windows	ftp://ftp.cis.upenn.edu/pub/ xv/xv-3.10a.tar.gz
zgv 3.0	Linux	http://sunsite.unc.edu/pub/Linux/apps/ graphics/viewers/svga

PNG support is already built in to the current versions of PhotoImpact, Paint Shop Pro, Photoshop, and lots of other graphics editors, but that's a bit of a waste as of this writing, since neither Netscape 4.01a nor Microsoft Internet Explorer 3.0 would read them during my tests. (Calling up an external application, treating a PNG as a download, or requiring a plug-in just doesn't cut it.) Microsoft's Internet Explorer 4 beta is said to have partial support, but if you want everyone to see your graphics, wait for Netscape support as well as full Microsoft support, along with support from a number of the "little" browsers.

PNG is recommended by the W3C (World Wide Web Consortium), but that may be a bit premature. PNG was brought to the forefront during a time of crisis, when it looked as if the GIF format were going to be yanked from popular usage. At the time it seemed that publishers of programs implementing GIF would have to pay royalties because the CompuServe GIF used the LZW compression method, which Unisys had patented without notifying CompuServe. That crisis passed, but the attention drawn to PNG lingers on, since there are some nice things about the format.

Why consider PNG once it has more browser support? PNG uses a lossless compression that shares a common ancestor with LZW, but isn't patented, and compresses files a little smaller than GIF. PNG also supports 24- and 48-bit True Color, more complex interlacing and transparency, and gamma correction (to control brightness across different platforms). There's more—read up on it and keep up with browser support at the PNG home pages maintained by Greg Roelofs (www.cdrom.com/pub/png).

Good Things, Small Packages

As Webmaster, you're painfully aware that people won't sit watching the Web skies, praying that your graphics will appear before they have the technology to just transport themselves into your showroom. This is the *Real-World* Wide Web, and whether you control a high-powered commerce site for a Fortune 500 company or a page about your cat, you either master it professionally or you don't. Some of the biggest corporations in the world flaunt their cluelessness by presuming that their content is worth a ridiculous wait. It never is. This is the "big fish" mentality that makes the companies themselves lose to fast, hungry piranhas.

Check it—if you knew that every time you called a business they would keep you on hold for 15 minutes, how often would you call? Only when you had to—and you'd have all that time to think nasty things about that company. If Web visitors spend one second for each K of data at 28.8, what will they be thinking of your company while a 70K ego file appears? That's the kind of math question you can answer with four-letter words. Transfer speeds can be faster—or slower. During busy times, your graphic may be showing up on people's monitors at 200 bytes or fewer per second.

○ *Tip:* Offer a plain-text paragraph or two near the top of the first screen for people to read while even small images appear. Be sure to use the HEIGHT and WIDTH attributes with all <IMG> tags so the text will know where to go and appear quickly.

The Golden Rule(r)

No screenful of data should take longer than 25 seconds to load. Assume 1K per second at 28.8, and that allows you 25K of data. If you interlace the GIF or make the JPEG progressive, double the allotted time to 50 seconds or 50K.

Remember, that's for the entire viewing area of the monitor, so you can have several small files, one large one, or some other mix, but make sure the aggregate byte count stays within the 25/50 guideline. There is no good reason to violate the rule. It goes for static graphics, animated GIFs, pictures of your mother, and live cam-feeds from the site of aliens landing. You *can* make it fit under The Golden Ruler. The tools and skills to make files smaller are available to everyone. Remember, too, that the 25/50K Golden Ruler is the maximum. The most. The outer limit. Do better than that. I'd love to walk by an IS department and hear Webmasters bragging about how they fit a 4" by 4" photo of an elephant into a 3K file without losing a single peanut.

Exception to The Golden Ruler: If you label text or iconic links to larger pictures with their file sizes, and people choose them, that's fine. But they'll visit more of those links—or actually wait for the first one to load—if you make it with as few bytes as possible.

Decreasing Byte Count

You found information about reducing palettes for GIFs and increasing the compression rate of JPEGs under the GIF and JPEG sections earlier, and we mentioned cropping and resizing, which we'll spend some quality time with now before we move on to illusions that help cut the wait.

Cropping and Downsizing   Before cropping or downsizing:

- Make a copy of the image.
- Make sure you're viewing the image at 100% size (also called 1:1 Zoom or Actual View). Some people are surprised to find that reducing a file

by a factor of four or five leaves them with a "bigger" picture. That happens when the picture they began with was actually displayed several times smaller than actual size.

• Make sure you're in 640 X 480 mode (or the mode you've committed to for your site if you have a captive audience at a higher resolution). If you're eyeballing proportions, this will make it simpler.

Cropping   Cropping an image gets rid of everything outside the rectangular area you specify. Cropping doesn't just paint over the area, it cuts it off, leaving a file that takes less space on screen as well as less space on disk. It's as if you used a paper cutter to trim a photo on up to four sides at once.

To crop an image, hit your image editor's Select tool (shaped like a square marquee) and drag a rectangle around the part of the image you want to keep. You don't have to start at any particular point in the image, so you can trim off more, less, or none from the right, left, top, or bottom than other areas. Then use the Crop command from the proper menu to eliminate everything outside your selection. In PhotoImpact, the menu command is Edit/Crop. In Paint Shop Pro and Photoshop, it's Image/Crop.

Don't waste your time selecting nonrectangular areas for cropping. Image files are rectangular, and even if an image editor lets you choose the Crop command for a nonrectangular selection, you'll just get an irregular shape on a plain rectangular background. Use the Crop command for trimming down a file—use transparency procedures for making irregular areas within the remaining image disappear.

The good news is that you can put irregular cropping to some good use. Since PhotoImpact and Paint Shop Pro will let you use the Crop tool to cut irregular areas of paint off the remaining canvas, you can use the Crop tool to quickly make those areas one color, then choose that color to make transparent. You can also achieve this in Photoshop by making your irregular selection, then, from the menu, choosing Select/Inverse, then Edit/Cut. (The Inverse command on the Selection menu switches the focus from what you selected to what you didn't select, so instead of cutting out what you selected, you are cutting around it.)

If you use this method in any program to turn unwanted areas into a single color so you can make that color transparent, make sure the background color selected is not one used in the image, or turning that color transparent will put peep holes all over your picture. See the section on transparent GIFs for more information.

❂ *Tip:* If you experiment with the Select tool and change its setting from rectangular to square or elliptical (usually from a drop-down list called "Shape" on the menu bar), remember to set it back to rectangular. You can drive yourself crazy trying to drag a wide or tall rectangle with a square tool. (Yes, I'm blonde, but I don't see how that's relevant.)

Downsizing   To make a whole image smaller, you probably won't have to re-scan at a lower resolution. Easy menu commands are available when originals to scan aren't. In PhotoImpact, choose Format/Dimensions. The dialog box shows several option areas. Under "Apply to," make sure "Entire image" is selected. Under "New image," check "User defined," and "Keep aspect ratio" should be checked. The "Unit" should be Percent. Change the value for *either* Width or Height. The remaining dimension will change automatically. The beginning percent was 100, so if you choose 25, the new image will be one-quarter the size of the one you started with.

In Paint Shop Pro, you can choose "Image/Re-size," and make sure "Maintain aspect ratio" is checked, even though you can type the number of pixels you want in both the height and width areas of the dialog box. The Image/Re-size command is best with simple images with 16 or fewer colors—the kind of image that makes a good candidate for the GIF format when you're all through messing with it.

Another alternative in Paint Shop Pro is resampling. Use the Image/Resampling command, which only appears on the menu when the color depth is more than 256 colors. You can increase the color depth with the Colors/Increase Color Depth command. Don't worry—there are lots of commands in lots of programs you can't get to unless you increase color depth first. You can always reduce the colors again later. From there, choose Image/Resampling and work it the same way you'd work Image/Resize above. Resampling is better for more complex (photo-like) images—good candidates for the JPG format once you're through editing. (Remember that you shouldn't edit a JPG—edit the original format and then save to JPG.)

In Photoshop, choose "Image/Image Re-size." (Don't use Image/Re-size Canvas, which will crop (cut off the edges of) your image, not make the whole picture smaller.) In the dialog box, make sure "Constrain Properties" and "Resample Image" are checked. Under "Pixel Dimensions," choose Percent instead of Pixels in the drop-down lists, and type in the percent size you want. Ignore the printer settings. The drop-down list options Nearest Neighbor, Bilinear, and Bicubic (shown in Figure 3–6) are interpolation options, which tell Photoshop what method to use when adding or deleting pixels. Choose Bicubic, which is smoothest and best. Bilinear is medium quality, and Nearest Neighbor is poorest. With the size of images you'll be working with, you won't notice the speed difference that might tempt someone to use a lower-quality interpolation method.

FIGURE 3-6 *Choosing the bicubic (best quality) interpolation option when re-sizing in Photoshop by selecting it from a drop-down list.*

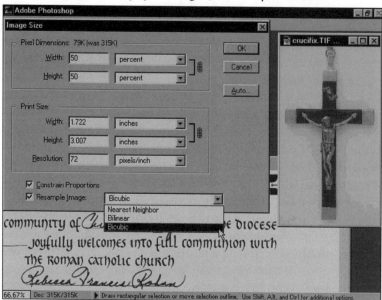

Clean and sharpen the reduced image. Your picture should look pretty good, but if things are really screwed up, try again with different settings, or crop a little more so you don't have to shrink the file so much.

Text that's part of an image doesn't usually shrink gracefully—you may have to go in and clean it up pixel by pixel. You can also reduce more smoothly with a product like Wextech's Smooth Scaling, as mentioned under "TIPS for Smoothing Bitmap Jaggies" earlier in the chapter. Another alternative is to wipe out the existing text, then use a text tool to recreate it in the smaller file. Use antialiasing options if they're available, as they are in Adobe Photoshop, Jasc Paint Shop Pro, and Ulead PhotoImpact.

When you reduce the size of a screen image, it doesn't sharpen like a paper reduced in a copier. You'll probably need to sharpen the image. In PhotoImpact, choose Effect/Blur & Sharpen/Unsharp Mask, and pick one of the preview frames offered. In Paint Shop Pro, choose Image/Normal Filters/Unsharpen, and experiment with settings. (Paint Shop Pro can be a little scant in the Help department.) In Photoshop, choose Filter/ Sharpen/Unsharp Mask, and slide the pointer and drop it at various points on the bar to preview various settings before applying. As usual, Photoshop has excellent detailed instructions. Photoshop really comes out on top with the heavy editing stuff where, if you're like me, you run into new words like "interpolation," or find out why something called "unsharp mask" makes your image sharper. (Unsharp masking is an old film compositing technique that increases the contrast among adjacent pixels—and Photoshop's Help has a lot more to say about it that will help you fine-tune the settings.)

Split It Up

Page byte totals will drop dramatically if you divide your content and let people go straight to the images they want, as implied above under "Exception to The Golden Ruler."

If you have large images—maybe original artwork or photos of an alien cockpit—or a lot of medium-sized images—perhaps a gallery of product models or background textures—or even a lot of relatively small (10K) images, let people know what they are and how big they are, and offer either text or iconic links to them.

Put large images on pages by themselves, and split up medium and small images into reasonable groupings that fit on from one to three screenfuls. Good, descriptive text links will obviously show up faster than graphical links, but if thumbnail images of the real thing will be more helpful, there are several ways to get them. One is to follow the directions earlier in this chapter for cropping and downsizing images, but cropping and downsizing in the extreme. We're talking about thumbnails of 32×32 pixels, 48×48 pixels, or 64×64 pixels at the absolute outer limit. (Don't forget to add size descriptions to both text and thumbnail links so people can make informed choices. Visitors will like you better while they're waiting if they've given conscious consent to downloading a given file size.)

⊗ *Cheat:* If the thumbnail quality isn't terribly important, you might save some time getting image browsing programs, such as Ulead's PhotoImpact Album, to generate all your thumbnails at once. Album programs can take a whole directory of files and reduce them to thumbnails for display within their own browsing programs. Take screen shots of those album pages, then cut and paste thumbnails to individual files in an image-editing program. Set the thumbnail files into simple tables to keep them neatly organized and spaced as they lead to your full-size images, properly mounted and centered on HTML pages. (You never want to just point to a graphic's file name and let it slam into the upper left corner of someone's browser when they select it.)

If you want more control over thumbnail quality, skip the album programs and follow the downsizing instructions earlier in this chapter.

However, albums can be a very nice shortcut with many image types and sizes. Ulead's free trial of its album (also included with PhotoImpact) is at www.ulead.com/webutilities/album/al_main.htm.

✪ *Tip:* Never take one big picture of thumbnails and use them in an image map. It wastes space and, unless you provide good text alternatives for each area of the image map, it makes it difficult to impossible for people with text-based browsers and speech synthesizers to find their way to what they need.

✪ *Tip:* Never abuse the height and width attributes of the <IMG> tag to shrink an image by forcing it into a smaller area than the actual picture. Not only do you risk distorting the image, it's a waste of bandwidth. If you want to make an image appear smaller, make the actual image smaller.

✪ *Tip:* Do use the height and width attributes of the <IMG> tag to help browsers map out pages before your image downloads. This allows users to see the page setting up and view the content that appears in its allotted space first.

Space-Saving Illusions

A magician doesn't use a scarf the size of Miss Liberty to make her disappear, and artists don't have to paint tigers orange all over, then add black stripes over the orange. Illusion can save time, effort, and lots of bandwidth. Web background colors and textures provide an excellent opportunity to make big, impressive graphics out of practically nothing.

Background Basics   The <BODY> </BODY> tags let you paint the whole page one color and/or toss up a small wallpaper image that repeats to fill the entire screen. While plain white backgrounds are best for most Websites, colored backgrounds and wallpaper can be excellent opportunities to save bandwidth on a page with a strong theme. A classic example is a thin horizontal strip: On the extreme left of the strip is a bit of spiral notebook wire. The remainder, stretching to the right, is a line of ruled notebook paper (just a thin light blue line drawn on a white background). Repeated down the Web page, the effect is a spiral-bound notebook, open to a page of ruled notebook paper.

Coupon Net (http://coupon.com/coupon.html) used the spiral theme with plain white paper, which is best if you're going to put text on the page using HTML. The notebook motif works with very small graphics files for the section of spiral and sample of paper—typically, 18 to 35 pixels high by 2000 pixels across. You can guess the reason for the width—if the graphic didn't reach the far right of someone's monitor at its highest resolution, a parallel spiral would appear in the page.

Rule: Make page backgrounds wide enough for the largest screens, so patterns don't repeat unexpectedly, but design so that everything else fits on a single 640 × 480 screen. <BODY BACKGROUND> graphics are special in that someone using the lower resolution *won't* have to scroll to see the wide background.

Another Webmaster used a plain white background color on the rectangular screen as a virtual envelope, adding a small postmark graphic and stamp graphic, and plain text where the addresses would be. But one of the most heavily awarded examples of making a small background file do a lot is a family Website—Faherty Web at www.ultranet.com/~fahertys. Check out Figure 3–7, which shows the whole screen as the front of the Faherty's virtual house. Figure 3–8 shows the tiny vertical strip (www.ultranet.com/~fahertys/iback.gif) that makes up both the awning and the porch. Note how busy the animated cat can be while using just 18 frames and 11.8K.

The Faherty door makes good use of large areas of identical color that GIF's LZW compression can squeeze right through a keyhole. And the sound files for the intercom, doorbell, wind chime, door, mat, and cat don't play until you click on their images. For a site that's been around for a few years now, Faherty Web showed bandwidth savvy early on.

Think about your screen, your background, and your background color as byte-saving canvases with a first coat of graphics for your Website's theme.

Table Tricks (No Tablecloth Required)   Use HTML tables to replace rectangular graphics, like picture frames. Create a large set of drawers using just table commands and small doorknob graphics. You can even "draw" the recessed drawer pulls with hyphens or dashes—creating graphics with no image files at all. When you decide on a theme for your page, think of ways to use table cells to replace other graphics. For example, create a table with no borders and color certain cells to make a stairway, making the remaining table cells match the background color. If you want a logo to have a large, plain background, put it in a single-cell colored table, center the table, and center the logo in the table. You can remove the border or pop it out in 3-D, but the only thing that will cost you in bytes is the graphic in the center.

Recycling Bytes   Save bandwidth by repeating one graphical bullet down whole lists of items. It's probably not worth the bandwidth to use bullets of different colors or shapes instead of a single file. Even if your HTML calls for GOLFBALL.GIF 10 times, visitors only have to download it once.

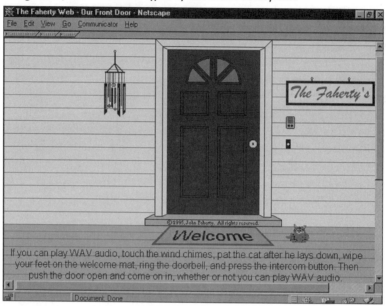

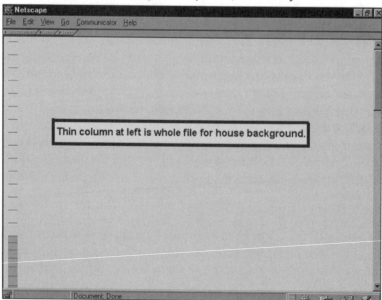

Speed Test   When you move your page on-line to test it for speed, remember to go into your browser's options, clear both the RAM cache and hard-disk cache, and reboot before each test. Ask your friends with other ISPs to test your site for speed, too, and to dump both their caches and reboot between tests, as well.

Grabbing Graphics

If you can see it, you can probably nail it up on your Web site quickly and easily. Just make sure you hammer up stuff that's yours, that's public domain, or that's used with permission of the copyright holder. Use good judgment if something looks like it doesn't belong in the public domain. Honor requests to give credit to the artist.

Free Clip Art

One message you'll see at a lot of freebie art sites is: "Please do not link to these images. Download them to your own site!"

Obviously, it would put a lot of drag on the art site's server if everyone linked to them and, in turn, had all their visitors pulling down the art from their server instead of yours. It could be bad for your visitors, too, if they're trying to get an image from an overloaded donor site. To visitors, it's *your* site that will seem slow. And if the owner of the originating server removes, moves, renames, or corrupts the file, your page will show a "broken image" icon.

To get your own copy of an image, follow directions at the site. The most common way to scarf up graphic goodies is to right-click once on an image (with Netscape Navigator or Microsoft Internet Explorer), and choose the Save option from the menu that pops up beneath your mouse pointer. Some sites offer zipped, tarred, or gzipped collections so you can get everything at once and sort it out at home like a sack of Halloween candy dumped on the carpet. Table 3–9 offers lots of clip art sites to paw through, and you can get a preview of what's out there in Figure 3–9.

Screen Capture

Lots of programs—including free and trial utilities—will take what you've got on your screen and save it to a file. In fact, Windows 95 users can simply hit the Print Scrn key and use the Edit/Paste command in any reasonable graphics program to copy a screen. Whatever your platform, check your graphics suite for a utility with a name containing "capture," "grab," "thief," "screen," or "snap." If you want more power, try a program

TABLE 3-9   *Free Clip Art*

Name	Free Graphics—Drawn	URL
Arbeau (1589)	Black and white drawings of the swords-people and others of the time.	www.pbm.com/~lindahl/arbeau_images.html
Barbary MUSH Victorian Faces	Few, but interesting, faces.	www.best.com/~gazissax/barbary/faces.html
Bear Clip Art	Bear clip art (teddies, grizzies, paws, signs, cartoons) and photos.	http://esther.la.asu.edu/personnel/ramsey/bear_ca.html
Bicycle	Cartoons, drawings, clip art, logos and photos	http://blueridge.infomkt.ibm.com/bikes/gifs/Pix.html
Big Dave's Cow Page	Who'da thunk there were this many moos?	www.gl.umbc.edu/%7Edschmi1/cows/clipart.html
Celtic Clip Art	Borders and such in black and white	http://celtic.stanford.edu:80/pub/misc/celtic_art/
Cemetery Clip Art	Angels and death, graves, coffins, hearses and funerals, and worse.	www.best.com/~gazissax/silence/clipart.html
Christian Webmaster Graphics Gallery	Jesus, crosses, angels, Christmas, and miscellaneous images. (Protestant.)	www.njwebworks.com/churchweb/gallery/
Christmas Clip Art	Nice collection of classic Santas, reindeer, and sleighs. Borders, too.	www.christmasgifts.com/freeart.htm
Christmas Pages	Christmas icons and larger images. Includes cute mouse sleeping in ornament box. Also MIDI Christmas music.	www.geocities.com/HotSprings/2210/noel.html
Clip Art Collection	Collection of 28 categories, from "Alphabet" and "Animals" to "Weather" and "Words."	www.clipartconnection.com
DanceArt.Com	Dancers, shoes, hats, canes, barres, logos, and more. Lots of ballet.	www.danceart.com/clipart1.html
Dinosaur Illustrations	A window onto good dinosaur art all over the Web. You have to check for rules or ask each owner for permission to use it.	http://web.syr.edu/~dbgoldma/pictures.html
Diving	Mostly black and white drawings.	www.ukdiving.co.uk/index.html
Flags	National, United States, Canadian, and Australian flags.	www.globalserve.net/~photodsk/flags/flags.html
Flowers	Bright and colorful drawings—lots of purple, plus blue, white, and red.	www.geocities.com/Silicon Valley/Heights/6355/flowers.htm
Froggy Page	Frog icons, clip art, and photos, including colorful poison arrow frogs and bug-eyed tree frog.	http://frog.simplenet.com/froggy/

Name	Free Graphics—Drawn	URL
George's WedPage	Large wedding-related pieces by a variety of acknowledged artists. Angels, cupids, cherubs, balloons, party Items, bells, Bibles, brides, grooms, candles, churches, crosses, doves, flowers, hearts, wedding rings, wedding cakes. Various types and sizes. Sorted by topic.	http://barrow.uwaterloo.ca/ ~ghballin/wedpage.html
Not Just Another Golf Page	Golf clip art by the keeper of the site, plus golf art he's gathered from other sites or scanned. Includes golf icons and bullets.	www.sover.net/~sbound/ golf4.html
House Ravenscroft Scriptorium (Celtic Art)	Many patterns suitable for borders. Requires a credit line to the artist.	www.geocities.com/SoHo/Lofts/ 3374/index.html
Kulacrosse's Clip Art Stable	Mounted cowboys, Pegasus, rocking horse, knight, cartoon horses in clothes, trotting horses, horse logos, guest book icon with horseshoe-mark signatures, race horses, Western horses, and many more. Includes animation section.	www.kulacrosse.com/ clipartstable/index.html
Library— Surf Madison	Clip art libraries in about 42 categories— many in PCX format.	www.surfmadison.com/ library.htm
Lori's Collection of Craft Clip Art	Images of arts and crafts, and the tools that create them.	www.geocities.com/~sewdoll/ CraftClips.htm
Insects	Drawings of creatures so fantastic, it's hard to believe they're real. They are. From University of Illinois.	www.life.uiuc.edu/Entomology/ insectgifs.html
Jewish Clip Art	Adonai, menorah, dreidel, tablets, star, and more, in black and white GIF format.	www.stud.ntnu.no/studorg/ laget/clipart/jewish/
Juggling Picture Gallery	Drawings, promo pics, photos, cartoons, clip art, and ASCII art.	www.juggling.org/pics/
Neferchichi's Egypt Clip Art & Backgrounds	Gods & Goddesses, Tut Artifacts, Carvings & Statues, Amulets & Jewelry, Mummy Stuff, Flora & Fauna, Paintings & Imagery, Pyramids & Sphinxes, and Backgrounds. Really awesome.	http://members.aol.com/ crakkrjack/egypt.html
Railroad	Cars, diesels, heralds, people, signs, steam, structures, traction & electric.	www.rrhistorical.com/art/
Religious and Holiday (Highland Graphics)	Religious and holiday clip art, Christian and Jewish.	www.itsnet.com/~highland/ index.html

(continued)

TABLE 3-9 *continued*

Name	Free Graphics—Drawn	URL
Religious Icon and Image Archive	Protestant clip art, especially United Methodist, plus Christmas.	www.aphids.com/susan/relimage/
Religious Orthodox Iconography	Color images of Orthodox Christian icons, plus incredible inside of a Romanian church. Get permission to use via e-mail.	www.mit.edu:8001/activities/ocf/icons.html
Safety Clipart	Industrial hygiene, labs, noise, medical, personal protection, safety management, and more. Large black and white images.	http://haz1.siri.org/graphics/
School clip art	One of the few sites that allows you to link to images from their server if you don't want to download them for some reason.	www.bev.net/education/schools/admin/pics.html
Science—Softshell Online Clipart	Scientific glassware, computers, science symbols, "no food or drink" symbol, etc.	www.softshell.com/Resource/FreeArt/Freegifs.html
Scouting	HAM radio, nature, badges, knots, and other scout subjects.	ftp://ftp1.scouter.com/usscouts/ftpindex.html
Shawn's Web Art	Shawn's modern cartoon hands, heads, bodies, and Yuletide and Halloween stuff. Don't miss the "warning symbol" cartoons, such as "Audio Enhanced," "Vegetarian," "Carnivore," "Cat Appropriate," "Java-Free Zone," etc. Nonprofit use only.	www.inforamp.net/~dredge/
Strange Benedictions	Interesting black and white gargoyles and monstrosities.	www.geocities.com/Paris/8319/
Studievereniging GEWIS Clipart Library	Studievereniging GEWIS Clipart Library isn't created by the people who host the site, so copyright is iffy. Medical, mythological, and more, mostly simple black and white drawings.	www.gewis.win.tue.nl/general/clipart/index.html
Varian's AngelDream	Black and white and grayscale angel clip art, plus links to more angel art sites.	http://users.aol.com/dreamweavn/angeldreams/clipart.html
Zo's Online Barn & Equestrian Clipart	Horses and horse-related objects.	http://ourworld.compuserve.com/homepages/zoerider/

FIGURE 3-9 *Some of the clip art available for download. This from DanceArt.Com at www.danceart.com/clipart1.htm*

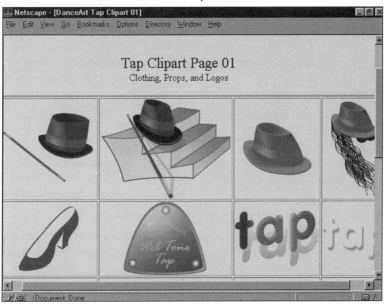

like SnagIt 4.0 for Windows 95, which lets you capture screens that scroll beyond the viewing area, capture animations of user actions, reduce colors, scale images, capture text as text, capture DOS screens, and save to GIF, JPEG, TIF, PCX, BMP, and compressed BMP. Download SnagIt from www.techsmith.com and register for $39.95 if you like it.

Artistic License(ing)

A couple of words about using art others have created—but bear in mind that I'm not a lawyer and don't play one on Web TV.

"Royalty-Free" Doesn't Mean Freeware or Shareware   "Royalty-free" usually means that you pay for a disk and can use the art over and over without paying each time. It doesn't mean it's free—and it may be a good idea to take steps to guard it by putting up a copyright notice on behalf of the publisher, who owns it. (Your money probably bought you a license to use it—not ownership.)

You May Not Have Web Rights   Even if you've paid for the right to use a CD full of art, you haven't necessarily paid for the right to put the art on the Web. Some art publishers are willing to grant you a license to put their art on the Web for a higher licensing fee and/or a copyright notice. Check the license before you buy.

Video Capture

Get a video capture board and you can grab content from your video camera, video tape, or TV. Whether your card can collect still images or video footage depends on the card you buy. If you have a still image capture card, realize that the images you capture are likely to be fuzzed, since NTSC signals weren't meant to be still images. When TV is broadcast digitally, perhaps the situation will improve. If you plan to do videoconferencing, consider getting a video camera made for computers that mounts on top of your monitor.

If you buy a motion video capture board, the quality of output for nice-looking source video will depend on your hardware's horsepower, especially processor speed and RAM, though you'll want a nice big hard drive for footage of any length. The perception of smooth action in film depends on the number of frames per second (fps), and an underpowered computer will drop frames, resulting in choppy output.

Look for a capture board that sends output to industry-standard file formats such as Windows AVI, Apple QuickTime, or MPEG. Make sure your board comes with video editing software to get you started. MGI VideoWave (www.mgisoft.com) lets you produce AVI, QuickTime, or MPEG videos.

Once you get some nice footage and edit it to give the best quality in the fewest frames (to save bandwidth), you might want to look into streaming video software that lets Web visitors start viewing the movie when just a little is downloaded, the way RealAudio does with sound. Prices are dropping and license agreements improving. Be sure to choose software that charges once only—for the software—instead of charging by the number of visitors to your site.

Look at Progressive Networks' RealVideo at www.realaudio.com and Vivo Software's VivoActive Producer at www.vivo.com, to get an idea of what's available. RealVideo is made by Progressive Networks, the makers of RealAudio, and its RealPublisher makes streaming audio and video from existing WAV, AU, AVI, and QuickTime files and costs $49.95. VivoActive Producer also takes standard input and creates streaming output for $199.

Digital Still Camera

Still digital cameras are getting better and cheaper—they're a great way to gather images in the field and upload them to a Website that everyone can see at the home office, or vice versa. Look for a camera that:

- Can operate away from your computer on battery power
- Doesn't lose information if the battery dies
- Stores lots of photos before requiring a download to the computer
- Is color, not just grayscale
- Has a flash

Scanners

The great thing about scanning for the Web is that you won't need the high-DPI models required for dense print publishing. Chances are you'll never need more than 150 DPI. So get that "low end" 600- or 1200-DPI machine. I got my 24-bit color flatbed Mustek TwainScan II SP for $249 at the local price club. (I decided at that price point not to add shipping costs, and to do a simple return if it didn't work. It's fine.)

Make sure you get a legal-length or longer flatbed—never a sheet-fed scanner. (What if you want to scan something from a magazine or book?) And don't even think about those silly photo-size scanners. What a waste! Of course you'll want a TWAIN-compliant scanner. I heard a few years ago that "TWAIN" literally stands for something to the effect of "This Word Ain't Initials for Nothing" or "The Worthless Acronym (something something)," but the TWAIN Working Group claims in their FAQ at www.twain.org that TWAIN is not an acronym—that "TWAIN is TWAIN." Perhaps they're using "twain" (literally "two" or "pair") as in "the twain shall meet"—getting the stuff out here into there. But I can't help but wonder if there's an inside joke.

Whatever is behind the word, TWAIN is a cross-platform standard that lets various programs use your scanner and other acquisition devices directly—usually with a command such as File/Acquire, as seen in Figure 3–10. That way you don't have to open one program to scan and then use another to deal with the image. (The File/Acquire command may be disabled on menus until you have a TWAIN source, like a scanner, configured on your system.) The TWAIN standard also helps ensure that an art program you buy today will support new types of TWAIN-compliant devices as they're invented.

But even the "cross-platform" TWAIN standard splinters into TWAIN, TWAIN32, and TWAIN_32. Make sure your prospective scanner supports the proper model for Windows 3.1 or 95/NT, etc., by looking for specific operating system support on the scanner box.

Don't buy a scanner until you see:

- Support for your operating system and version listed on the box
- Evidence of an interface card (hardware, circuit board) for your

FIGURE 3-10   *Pulling in a TWAIN source—in this case a scan— through the File/Acquire command in Ulead PhotoImpact. The Mustek scanner's TWAIN software comes up to help.*

computer (make sure you have room in your computer for that inter-face card, too.)

- Driver disk for your operating system (open the box—if it's a return it might be missing)

Finally, try to get a scanner that comes with image-editing and OCR (optical character recognition) software so you'll know you're set. (OCR software lets you store text pages as text, which you can manipulate and set up as normal text with HTML, instead of as a big picture of the words.)

Ask questions if you're not satisfied—especially "Can I bring it back without paying a restocking fee?"

Film Development on Disk or E-mail

If you've got film and no scanner, get your film developed someplace like Seattle Film Works, which sends your photos on diskette, along with prints and negatives, for very little over normal development and printing costs. Call them at 800-445-3348. They'll also scan your old pictures for a very reasonable price.

If you do use Seattle FilmWorks or a similar service, convert the files to GIFs or JPGs when you get them. There's one woman on the Web who leaves them in the original format and tells people they have to go download Seattle FilmWorks' software to view her images! (Ouch—I had to bang my head on a table when I saw that.)

Graphical ASCII Text Banners

That's not an oxymoron—you can use graphics-like text banners where plain text characters make up larger characters in various styles or "fonts." The banner words will show up for graphical visitors, as well as for people who view your site with LYNX or other plain-text browsers. Remember that such banners will sound like nonsense to the blind, because the text that makes the banners up is just whatever characters happen to make good visual building blocks.

It's easy to turn words into ASCII banners with the Figlet program. See Figure 3–11 for various styles of banner text made with Figlet. Try a Figlet server on the Web from Table 3–10. Just type in your word, choose a Figlet "font," and press the Submit button for the results. Or download the Figlet program for your platform from the sites listed in Table 3–11.

FIGURE 3-11 *It's easy to create ASCII banners in various "fonts" with the downloadable or Web-based Figlet programs.*

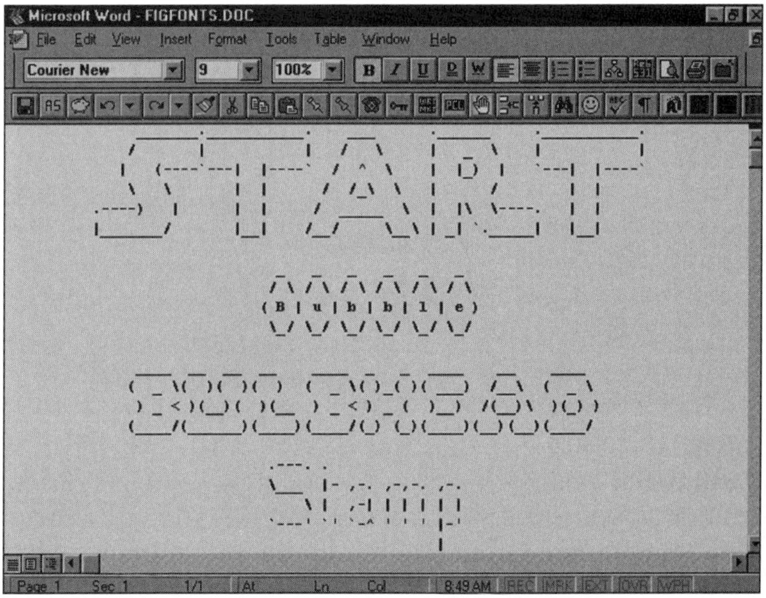

TABLE 3-10   *Web-Based Figlet Servers*

Web-Based Figlet Servers	URL
Fancy ASCII with Figlet	http://ntd.intro.nus.sg/~rudi/figlet.html
Figlet Factory	www.pixelsight.com/cgi-bin/web_figlet
Figlet Service	www.inf.utfsm.cl/cgi-bin/figlet
Lonster's Figlet Server	www.schnoggo.com/figlet.html
Web Figlet	www.sconnect.net/figlet/index.cgi

TABLE 3-11   *Downloadable Figlet Programs*

Figlet Program	URL
Figlet Program FTP Site	ftp://ftp.internexus.net/pub/figlet/
Acorn	ftp://ftp.internexus.net/pub/figlet/program/acorn/
Amiga	ftp://ftp.internexus.net/pub/figlet/program/amiga/
Apple II	ftp://ftp.internexus.net/pub/figlet/program/apple-ii/
Atari ST	ftp://ftp.internexus.net/pub/figlet/program/atari-st/
DOS	ftp://ftp.internexus.net/pub/figlet/program/ms-dos/
Mac	ftp://ftp.internexus.net/pub/figlet/program/mac/
NeXTstep	ftp://ftp.internexus.net/pub/figlet/program/nextstep/
OS/2	ftp://ftp.internexus.net/pub/figlet/program/os2/
UNIX	ftp://ftp.internexus.net/pub/figlet/program/unix/
Windows	ftp://ftp.internexus.net/pub/figlet/program/windows/

There's a wonderful Figlet page with more details at http://st -www.cs.uiuc.edu/users/chai/figlet.html.

Join the Figlet listserv to learn of updates and discuss all things Figlet by writing LISTSERV@postoffice.cso.uiuc.edu with "subscribe figlet-l your full name" (without the quotes) in the *body* of the letter. You'll get a confirmation letter with instructions to make sure you really want to subscribe and some jerk didn't sign you up on that and every other list in the universe.

ASCII Text-Based Pictures   You'll find everything from castles to alien bartenders created from ASCII text on the Web. I believe ASCII art is every bit as important artistically as the American quilt, and has a lot in common with needlepoint in terms of the constraints of the medium. These sites offer a great intro to what's becoming a lost art with the rise of the graphical Web. See an example of ASCII art by Joan Stark as seen in Netscape in Figure 3–12, and the same art as seen in Lynx (a text-only browser) in Figure 3–13.

ASCII Graphics	Description	URL
Spunk's Gallery (Joan Stark)	Electronics, household items, tools, musical, animals, holidays, people, food, sports, and more. Huge, categorized collection of images.	www.geocities.com/SoHo/7373
SuperNova Productions, Inc.	Dragons, castles, robots, mice, and skulls.	www.supnova.com/ascii.html

Special Effects

Every moment you spend with a graphic, up until the time you save it as a GIF or JPEG, you have an excellent opportunity to do something spectacular without eliminating half your audience, pumping in extra bytes, or adding technical variables that increase the likelihood of foul-ups. Some of the best tools for creating great content—effective content—whether subtle, sophisticated, or outrageous, are sitting idle in your image-editing program, under a menu titled "Filters," "Special effects," or something similar. These simple tools can add quality and power to a site, whether you're simply sharpening a graphic, adding a drop shadow, or using techno effects like "Plastic Wrap" (in Photoshop) or "Turnpage" (in PhotoImpact).

Caution: Always make a duplicate image to operate on—never put your original under the palette knife.

Reminder: Most image-editing programs won't let you apply special-effects filters to images with palettes with fewer than 16 million colors, but it's easy to convert to 24-bit color. In our three popular example programs, the commands are:

Example Program	Menu Choice
Paint Shop Pro 4.0	Colors/Increase Color Depth/16 Million Colors
PhotoImpact 4.0	Format/Data Type/True Color
Photoshop 4.0	Image/Mode/RGB Color

FIGURE 3-12 *One of many pieces of ASCII art by Joan Stark (www.geocities.com/SoHo/7373/) as seen in Netscape.*

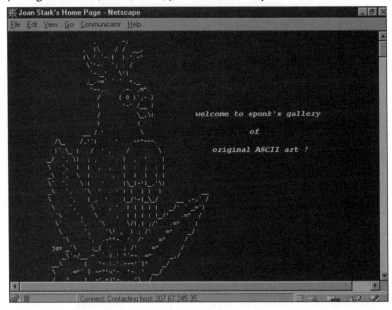

FIGURE 3-13 *The same ASCII art by Joan Stark (www.geocities.com/SoHo/7373/) looks just as good in the text-only browser Lynx.*

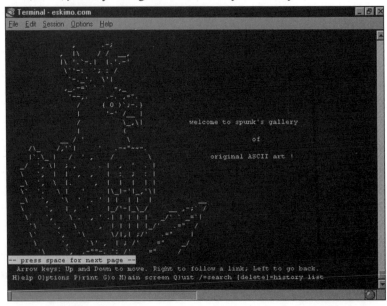

One of the most professional-looking effects on the Web is "Turnpage," found in PhotoImpact. Turnpage makes it look as if an edge of your photo is curling up, revealing a page underneath. All you have to do is choose Effect/Magic/Turnpage, and you get a dialog box with a Before and After preview of your photo. Figure 3–14 shows the effect with the default settings. Just drag the movable line in the Before photo to change the amount of photo that's curled in the After photo. Figure 3–15 shows how pressing different buttons changes the type of curl from rounder to more triangular, which of the four corners is curled, the angle of curl, lighting direction, background color, and more. You don't have to understand a single graphics concept—just push buttons and flip dials. All of it will show up on the trial "After" photo on the right.

Buried Treasure: You may already have Kai's Power Tools, which is often bundled with art applications and art content disks. Your copy of Kai's Power Tools may include "Page Curl" (similar to Turnpage), among other effects.

PhotoImpact offers the same ease of use in its dialog box for the Kaleidoscope effect, which can create some astonishing results. I didn't expect to create the very different images from a single photo of my daughter seen in Figure 3–16. The images were each created in seconds by moving a shape tool around the original and choosing different kaleidoscopic patterns from the icons shown in Figure 3–17. You'll be rewarded a lot for just fiddling around a little. While you may see more applications for the Turnpage effect than for the Kaleidoscope effect, Kaleidoscope could be wonderful with product shots like a shiny tri-colored soda can or a painted nutcracker's head.

If any image editor has spellbinding special effects, it's Adobe Photoshop 4.0. Photoshop's daring collection is arranged by category under its Filter menu. Photoshop, like PhotoImpact, has dialog boxes that let you experiment with various settings and, like PhotoImpact, the defaults often produce fabulous results. You can see some examples of Photoshop effects that were produced with no fuss and no muss in Figures 3–18 through 3–22. Torn Edges and Plastic Wrap are some of my favorites. Compounding effects can make them even better, such as "Chalk & Charcoal" on top of "Torn Edges." "Torn Edges" makes a figure appear to be made from torn paper, and "Chalk & Charcoal" gives the appearance of very rough, textured paper. The resulting mix looks like a creation made of torn black paper on textured light paper, as seen in Figure 3–23.

Jasc Paint Shop Pro 4.0 has preview dialogs for some of its effects, and it's an inexpensive place to start—especially considering the free trial download.

FIGURE 3-14   *The "Turnpage" effect from PhotoImpact, using the default settings.*

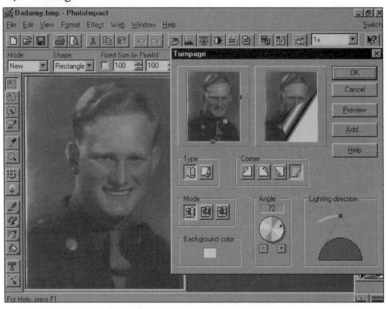

FIGURE 3-15   *Play around with dials and bars to change the "Turnpage" curl in the real-time previewer.*

FIGURE 3-16 *Both the "Cat Face" and "Botticelli on Saki" were taken from a single photo of my daughter Marcia with PhotoImpact's "Kaleidoscope" effect.*

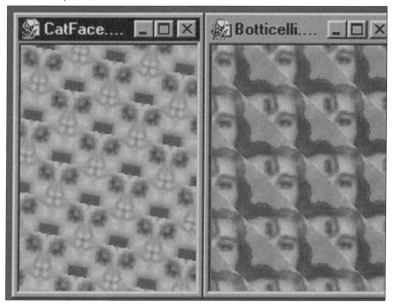

FIGURE 3-17 *You can create lots of different images like these in seconds by applying and adjusting the kaleidoscopic patterns shown on the PhotoImpact icons.*

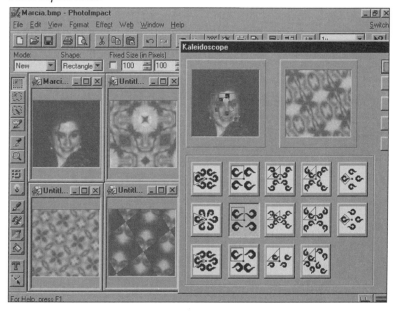

FIGURE 3-18 *Check out these examples of Photoshop effects, beginning with the base image: a glorious Cattleya walkeriana orchid grown and photographed by Nicholas Plummer (http://www-personal.umich.edu/~nplummer/).*

FIGURE 3-19 *Nicholas Plummer's orchid under wraps—Photoshop's "Plastic Wrap" effect.*

FIGURE 3-20 *Nick's orchid with Photoshop's "Cutout" effect*

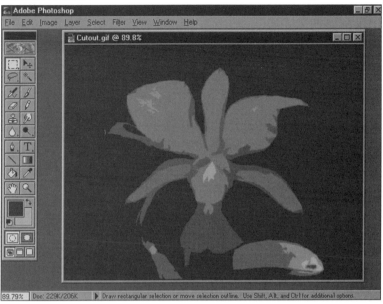

FIGURE 3-21 *Nick's orchid with Photoshop's "Glowing Edges" effect*

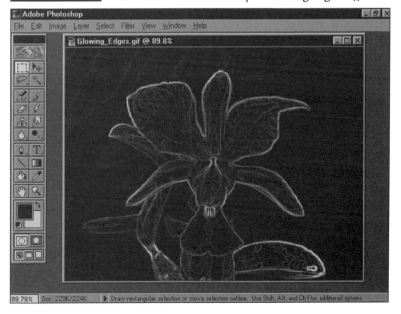

FIGURE 3-22 *The Cattleya walkeriana with Photoshop's "Wind Blast" effect*

FIGURE 3-23 *Compound effects for fabulous new options—here's a photo of my daughter Marcia with Photoshop's "Chalk & Charcoal" over its "Torn Edges."*

See a sampling of some of the more exciting special effects from our three model programs in Figures 3–24 through 3–28. Tables 3–12 through 3–14 tell which special effects you get in each of our three popular image editors.

Drop Shadows

You can ignite more interest in your page by adding drop shadows to your pictures—check out the subtle but dramatic shadow in Figure 3–29. Shadows are one of those oft-overlooked tricks that can help separate the professional site from the amateur. They can add area to your image, too, so take that into account when you're planning the size of your image and deciding how big a shadow to cast.

Some professional CDs of photo objects come with separate cast shadows and drop shadows for each object. Those CDs usually come with specific instructions for attaching the shadows to the images. But if you have an object or whole photo without a shadow, and you're feeling a bit like Peter Pan looking for a way to put his shadow on, forget Wendy's needle and thread and just Tinker with your image-editing program.

FIGURE 3-24 *Nicholas Plummer's orchid again, this time with Ulead PhotoImpact's "Charcoal" effect*

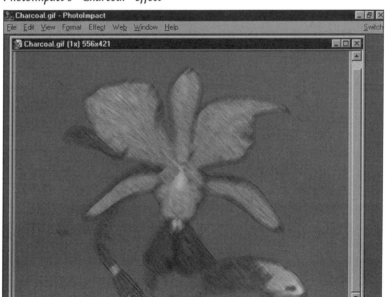

FIGURE 3-25 *Orchid with Ulead PhotoImpact's "Colored Pen" effect*

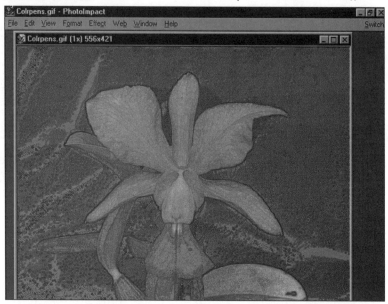

FIGURE 3-26 *Orchid with Ulead PhotoImpact's "Ripple" effect*

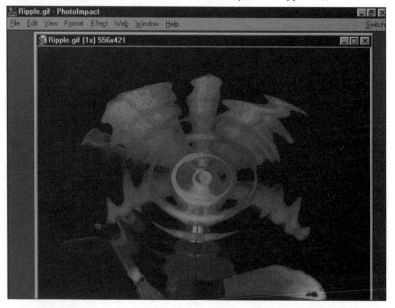

FIGURE 3-27   *Orchid with Photoshop's "Ocean Ripple" effect*

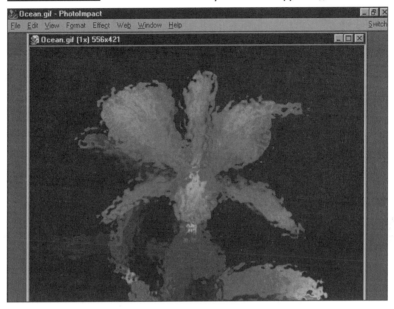

FIGURE 3-28   *Orchid with Jasc Paint Shop Pro's "Circle" effect*

TABLE 3-12   *Adobe Photoshop 4.0 Special Effects*

Accented Edges	Dust & Scratches	Motion Blur	Smart Blur
Add Noise	Emboss	Neon Glow	Smudge Stick
Angled Strokes	Extrude	Note Paper	Solarize
Bas Relief	Facet	NTSC Colors	Spatter
Blur	Film Grain	Ocean Ripple	Spherize
Blur More	Find Edges	Offset	Sponge
Chalk & Charcoal	Fragment	Paint Daubs	Sprayed Strokes
Charcoal	Fresco	Palette Knife	Stained Glass
Chrome	Gaussian Blur	Patchwork	Stamp
Clouds	Glass	Photocopy	Sumi-e
Color Halftone	Glowing Edges	Pinch	Texture Fill
Colored Pencil	Grain	Plaster	Texturizer
Conte Crayon	Graphic Pen	Plastic Wrap	Tiles
Craquelure	Halftone Pen	Pointillize	Torn Edges
Crosshatch	High Pass	Polar Coordinates	Trace Contour
Crystallize	Ink Outline	Poster Edges	Twirl
Cutout	Lens Flare	Radial Blur	Underpainting
Dark Strokes	Lighting Effects	Reticulation	Unsharp Mask
Despeckle	Maximum	Ripple	Video De-Interlace
Difference Clouds	Median	Rough Pastels	Water Paper
Diffuse	Mezzotint	Sharpen	Watercolor
Diffuse Glow	Minimum	Sharpen Edges	Wave
Displace	Mosaic	Sharpen More	Wind
Dry Brush	Mosaic Tiles	Shear	ZigZag

TABLE 3-13 *Ulead PhotoImpact 4.0 Special Effects*

Add Noise	Creative Warp	Motion Blur	Stagger
Adjust for NTSC	Despeckle	Oil Paint	Thin
Adjust for PAL	Emboss	Painting	Tile
Artist Texture	Emphasize Edges	Particle	Transform
Average	Facet	Pinch	Turnpage
Blast	Fat	Punch	Type
Blur	Find Edges	Puzzle	Unsharp Mask
Charcoal	Gaussian Blur	Remove Moiré	Warm
Colored Pen	Kaleidoscope	Remove Red Eye	Warping
Cool	Light	Ripple	Watercolor
Custom Effect	Magic Gradient	Sharpen	Whirlpool
Custom Filter	Mosaic	Sphere	Wind

TABLE 3-14 *Jasc Paint Shop Pro 4.0 Special Effects*

Add Drop Shadow	Cylinder	Hot Wax Coating	Sharpen More
Add Noise	Despeckle	Median	Skew
Blur	Dilate	Mosaic	Soften
Blur More	Edge Enhance	Motion Blur	Soften More
Buttonize	Edge Enhance More	Pentagon	Trace Contour
Chisel	Emboss	Perspective Horizontal	Unsharpen
Circle Horizontal	Erode	Perspective Vertical	Wind
Circle Vertical	Find Edges	Pinch	
Create Seamless Pattern	Find Horizontal Edges	Punch	
Cutout	Find Vertical Edges	Sharpen	

FIGURE 3-29 *Drop-dead easy drop shadows in PhotoImpact*

Paint Shop Pro 4.0 adds drop shadows through the Image/Special Effects menu, and it's good for quick and dirty shadows along two edges of a selection, whether straight or drawn with the excellent freehand tool. Make your selection, and choose Image/Special Effects/Add Drop Shadow. The dialog lets you choose the shadow's size and position, as well as its opacity and blur. Opacity lets you control how much you see through the shadow to the picture's background. Blur lets you fray the shadow a bit so it's not a harsh, straight line that looks like it was applied with a highway painter's truck.

PhotoImpact lets you add simple drop shadows to whole images when you choose Format/Frame & Shadow, then make further selections from a dialog. But PhotoImpact also lets you create truly beautiful shadows around selections very easily. When I say beautiful, I mean shadows that look like real shadows—and you don't need to know a palette knife from a palette spoon. Select the area you want shaded with a selection marquee and click the right mouse button as you hover over the selected area. A pop-up menu appears under your mouse. Choose "Convert to Object." Right-click again and choose "Add Shadow." Accept that and you'll have a foggy-looking, realistic shadow. As beautiful a shadow as the defaults create, you're free to change the details, and even preview them before making your final decision.

✪ *Tip:* If the dog eats your defaults, make the controls read 10 pixels each for the X and Y Offset values, 50% for Transparency, and 10 for Edge Blending.

Ulead's PhotoImpact gives good instructions for creating diffused halos and other shadow-related effects. Go to the Help Index and type in "Shadows" and hit Return, then double-click "Shadows:Overview" for detailed information.

In our final example program, Photoshop 4.0, put the area to be shadowed on its own layer by simply cutting and pasting it once. Next, double-click the Airbrush tool so the Airbrush Options tool window shows. The drop-down list in that Airbrush Options window probably shows "Normal"—change it to "Behind." Hold the shift key and began airbrushing your shadow, which will fill in behind your object.

Spectacular Cast Shadows

Increase the drama of your "cutout" objects or "photo objects" with cast shadows. A straight-edged or blobby-fog drop shadow is perfect for an object with a frame, border, or undistinguished shape, but a cutout like an isolated apple, drill, china cup, or seahorse will look much more dramatic with a cast shadow, which mimics the shape of the object like a real shadow would, with just the right distortion. Some, but not all, photo object CDs come with pre-created drop and cast shadows for each photo, but once you start scanning your own photos of objects, you'll need to create your own. This is one of the places Adobe Photoshop really earns its money, making it relatively quick and easy to create an intricate cast shadow by copying and distorting an image and positioning that distorted image beneath and behind the original object. Photoshop 4.0 comes with a tutorial CD that teaches the cast shadow technique step-by-step in both movie and text formats. You cannot fail.

Easy Drop–Cast Shadows
for Text in Paint Shop Pro

Paint Shop Pro 4.0 lets you add instant shadows to text—shadows that have some of the traits of cast shadows and some of the traits of drop shadows. Hit the Text tool and create your text, but leave it selected, then choose Image/Special Effects/Add Drop Shadow from the menu. Your letters get individual shadows, shaped like each letter, but not distorted. You can change their position under and behind the original text by dragging a box over a shadow in the dialog.

  ✪ *Tip:* For creating text with shadows in Paint Shop Pro 4.0, choose a color, such as blue, and use a dark, strong version for the foreground and a medium version for the background color.

  ✪ *Tip:* Leave the Blur option set to zero when adding shadows to text.

  ✪ *Tip:* Don't pass up the Antialiasing option within Paint Shop Pro 4.0's text dialog—it will make your text appear smoother.

Special "Framing" Looks

You've probably seen photos in special frames that make the image seem to be set into the Web page like a feathered cloud. (See the example in Figure 3–30.) You can buy special packages that work with certain image editors to create special frames, but we'll do without those for the moment and create a feathered oval frame with just our example image-editing programs, a toothpick, and a bowl of popcorn. We'll go into detail with Photoshop 4.0, then run briefly through PhotoImpact and Paint Shop Pro. You

FIGURE 3-30 *Easy feathery frames in Photoshop*

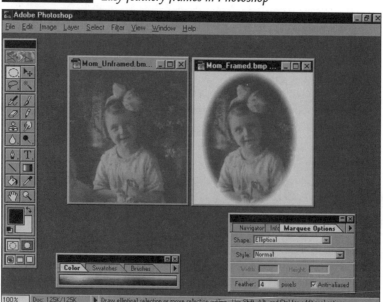

should be able to get similar results by finding corresponding commands in other image editors.

In Photoshop, make your background color white. Double-click the Marquee (selection) tool to open the options window for it. In that Marquee Options window, make the Shape Elliptical, the Style Normal, and the Feather value 4. Drag an ellipse (or Shift+drag a circle) around the area you want to frame. You can move the circle or ellipse by releasing the mouse button, positioning the mouse over the center of the circle or ellipse, and click-dragging the marquee where you want it.

From the menu, choose Select/Inverse. The second set of marching ants means you've inverted the selection from what was inside the marching ants before to what lies between the original marching ants and the outside of the picture. It's as if you lived inside your house before, but now you live everywhere outside your house, and what's inside your house is the outdoors.

From Photoshop's menu, choose Edit/Clear. You'll see your feathery framed image. Restore the Marquee settings to Shape Rectangular, Style, Normal, and Feather value 0. Finally, trim off excess white by selecting the smallest necessary rectangular area and choosing Image/Crop from the menu bar. Eat the popcorn as you compare your results with the Before and After images in Figure 3–30. Clean the kernels from your teeth with the toothpick.

In PhotoImpact, change the Selection tool to a circle or ellipse using the drop-down Shape box just above the work area. Drag your selection. Choose Edit/Select/Invert from the menu. Choose Edit/Select/Soften from the menu and make the value 4. Choose Edit/Clear. Choose Edit/Select/None.

Paint Shop Pro 4.0 seemed most straightforward of all. Selection Type and Feather value are directly above the work area. Set them to Ellipse or Circle and 8, and drag an ellipse or circle. Choose Selections/Invert from the menu. Choose Edit/Clear from the menu. Choose Selections/None from the menu. That's it.

Note: You may want to adjust the feather value up or down in whatever program you're using.

And whatever program you're using, you should be able to figure out the commands to use, even if they're not in the Help file, just by looking for similar commands to those used here. Believe me, it's hardest for me to dig this stuff out and learn it in the first program, but once I understand the principle, as you do now, I know what I'm looking for and where to look. So will you.

✪ *Tip:* When you want to invert your selection in any program, don't accidentally invert the colors to negative, or turn the photo upside down or flop it over by choosing a command that has to do with image formatting instead of area selection. (But you are working on a duplicate image, right?)

Other Framing Effects

You can create incredible frames—stunning frames, artistic frames—either by learning more about your image-editing program or by purchasing CDs full of pre-created frames. Not your two favorite alternatives? Download free samples of frames from Auto F/X at www.autofx.com. In fact, you can download a few free samples from their PhotoGraphic Edges, Typo-Graphic Edges, Ultimate Texture Collection, and PhotoGraphic Patterns. The samples are for Windows 95/NT or the PowerMac, and work with Canvas 5.0, Fractal Painter 4.0.3, Paint Shop Pro 4.1, Corel PhotoPaint 6.0, 7.0, PhotoDeluxe 1.0, Photoshop 3.0, 4.0. Pagemaker 6.0, 6.5, and Freehand 7.0.

Hint: If you're using Photoshop and the Auto F/X demo doesn't ask you where Photoshop is, drag the Auto F/X directory tree into your Photoshop Plug-in directory, then start Photoshop. The plug-in will appear on the Filter menu, under Auto F/X.

There's so much more you can do with wonderful grainy borders and other special effects with the tools in your image editor. Get into your manual or, better yet, the on-screen tutorials that came with your image-editing program. You'll be amazed at what you can create as soon as you get the feel of a few tools. Take it from someone who can't draw a smiling sun—the digital tools do most of the work. Spending a little time with the tutorials for your image programs can make those tools do more for you—exponentially more.

Page-Top 3-D Text

What would James Bond's 007 logo be if it were just three flat numbers? You don't have to be an artist to create great page-top headers in turned-out 3-D letters. Your company name can merely be up in lights, or it can be banged out of metal pipes or molded from plastic tubing with light coming from an invisible source just off-stage. Your name can be a neon sign with a pink flamingo attached. It can be drawn in toothpaste squeezed from a tube or screeched across the page with skid-marks from tires—just use your imagination, fit the visual metaphor to your business, and let the 3-D software do most of the work.

The bad news is that most 3-D programs are difficult to learn and use. The good news is that you're only working with the text tool, which limits the number of variables you have to deal with. Some variables you might encounter are:

- Font (typeface, size, and format, such as bold or italic)
- Material (metal, stone, clouds, radial color, etc.)
- Shape of material (tube, extrusion, etc.)
- Degree of extrusion
- View (top, bottom, front, etc.)

The closer a program is to a full 3-D object rendering package, the more you may have to learn about moving a dolly, moving a light source, and other modeling concepts to turn out a good 3-D text effect. If you plan to create ray-traced spheres and other virtual objects, it's as good a time as any to learn, and a full-featured package like Fractal Design's Ray Dream 3-D Studio 5 will take care of your text, your spinning spheres of light, and your indoor and outdoor scenes.

If you're interested in making only text 3-D and don't have any desire to learn traditional modeling, try Ulead's Cool 3-D, a WYSIWYG program exclusively for creating exotic, textured 3-D text. Type your text and choose a typeface. Choose the look you want, from gold metal to wood to cool blue droplets on stone. Rotate the object with your mouse. Get great results without having to understand or learn any rendering concepts, and without dealing with cryptic buttons or commands. The $39.95 program from Ulead (www.ulead.com) has a free trial that's fully functional, except for a semitransparent watermark.

There's also 3drender.zip, a Windows program you can download from ftp://gatekeeper.dec.com/pub/micro/msdos/win3/demo/, or check out lots of ray-tracing programs at www.cm.cf.ac.uk:80/Ray.Tracing/. Even if there's no program with striped gel toothpaste as an initial option, you'll be OK if it has toothpaste-shaped (round tube) letters, and the ability to make custom materials, like white opaque matte and aqua glossy semitransparent gel toothpaste. Make sure your program lets you create custom materials, if not custom shapes, or import them from other sources—and that it lets you use your own fonts.

Another feature that will save you time and keep you from tearing your hair out is a decent preview as you work. If a program has to "render" your text, your preview isn't going to be exactly like the rendered product, but look for a program that gives you a pretty good idea. And Webmasters who crave motion will want a 3-D program that supports animation. Both Ray Dream 3-D Studio 5 and Ulead Cool 3-D support animation. Who knows—

5 years from now you might wind up making intros for shows like "Tales from the Crypt" and have a Silicon Graphics Workstation at home by your bed for doodling. Just remember that we don't all have T1s, and stay in touch with the section of this chapter on keeping file size down.

Morphing

Morphing is definitely a niche technology, but it could have applications for your Web page beyond mimicking late-night television's sight gags—you know the ones where they project the progeny of the prestigious. (Pththt—I sound like Daffy Duck.) For example, you could use the steps between the beginning and ending objects to create an animated GIF, MPEG, or QuickTime Movie where an ugly duckling comes into contact with your product and morphs into a beautiful swan.

One of the first Web sites I chose for review was a site about Kabuki, which featured the Kabuki artist morphing from his normal look into a beautiful woman character. You can check out the review-worthy Website "Kabuki for Everyone" at www.fix.co.jp/kabuki/kabuki.html, and see this textbook-perfect use of morphing at www.fix.co.jp/kabuki/movie/man jiro_morph.mov for inspiration. Once you're inspired, check out the morphing tools seen in Table 3–15.

Figure Modeling

If you need a posed human figure in your artwork, you may want to spring for Fractal Design's Poser. Creating realistic human poses on the screen doesn't get much easier. Poser lets you position adult male, adult female, adolescent, skeleton, and stylized wooden mannequin models, either by manipulating body parts with the mouse or by applying libraries of positions

TABLE 3-15 *Morphing Programs*

Morphing Program/File	URL
bmorph30.zip	ftp://x2ftp.oulu.fi/pub/msdos/programming/utils/
wmorph10.zip	ftp://x2ftp.oulu.fi/pub/msdos/programming/utils/
Algobit Plastic Morph	www.algobit.com/
Black Belt Systems WinImages	www.blackbelt.com/blackbelt/bx_top.html

and lighting effects. If you move one body part and other parts would have to move in a real person, the Poser models move the same way.

Once your model is poised to make your point, render it into a fully fleshed-out human or mannequin. You can apply clothing textures to the models that are shaped as if they're wearing clothes, but the nude bodies look finished as they are except for the bald heads and coloring. Figure 3–31 shows the male dressed in detail for business as he appears after simply selecting his type and hitting the rendering command.

If you aren't an artist, stick with the wooden mannequins. They are completely finished on rendering with the simplest choices—no worries about adding hair or clothing. The mannequin shown in Figure 3–32 is an interesting vehicle for making a point with an "EveryPerson" character.

Poser makes it extremely easy to move and turn the whole figure in apparent 3-D space with the mouse, without fiddling with degrees of yaw or other axes-related numbers. Very cool—and you can create AVI movies from within Poser. (Consider converting them to QuickTime, MPEG, or Animated GIF format before you put them on the Web.)

Virtual Reality

If you weren't already thinking about VR, all this figure-turning in Poser and 3-D scene creation in Ray Dream Studio has probably made you think about it. The idea of VR is to let the viewer decide where to go in an online environment, as they would if they were running down halls in a game of Doom, or "flying" around an object to see it from various angles.

More support for Virtual Reality Modeling Language (VRML) is turning up in browsers, and the specs are racing forward, even though the bandwidth just isn't there to make cruising big, complex virtual worlds practical for the majority of your visitors. However, new technologies are pushing their faces through the walls of 3-D houses. In particular, applications that support multiple avatar environments (environments where your 3-D character interacts with other people's avatars) are beginning to cut down unnecessary data relative to a given participant, such as the movements of avatars outside the given player's immediate surroundings.

Unfortunately, the real (as opposed to virtual) reality is that even VRML 2 can look very poor and simple compared to other forms of multimedia, because it still takes too much bandwidth to express many angles of many gizmos of any complexity. Even though you can fly around photo-quality environments with technologies like Apple's QuickTime Virtual Reality (QTVR), it took a 2Mb download to fly around the outside of the

FIGURE 3-31   *One of poser's male figures is dressed in detail for business as he appears after simply selecting his type and hitting the rendering command.*

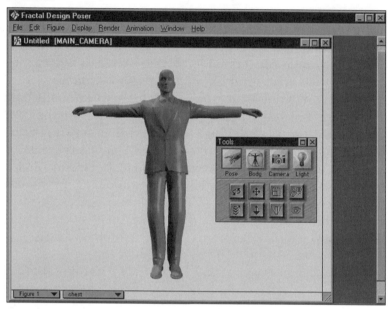

FIGURE 3-32   *Poser's mannequin figure is an interesting "EveryPerson" character that is finished on rendering—no worries about adding hair or clothing.*

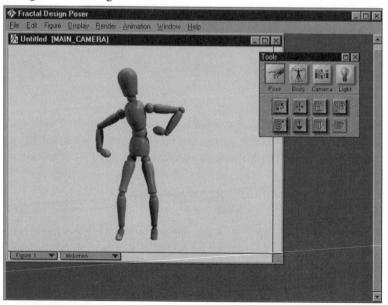

yellow Ferrari at the Ferrari North America site (www.ferrari.com/Automo bili/index.asp).

I don't expect the situation to change until the technology changes radically or everybody has big bandwidth. Two years ago I interviewed a highly placed official at a huge technology company, who said that within 12 to 18 months (from back then), people would expect Websites to have a 3-D virtual space. The person said any holdup would be due to a lack of the right skill set—people with both artistic and programming talent. As you can guess, the artistic tools for creating VR without much programming knowledge are evolving: that's a given in the software industry. The bandwidth just isn't there, and recent interviews with ISPs for Web Week's ISP World didn't make me expect a big change soon. Remember that your T1 doesn't mean a thing to the visitor with a 28.8 modem. But it's not how big the bandwidth is—it's making the most of it with skill and illusion.

Special Symbols

If you're using math, chemical, and other special symbols in your normal work day, you probably have programs to display them. Simply capture the screen, crop it, and make the background transparent. If you don't have programs that produce your kind of symbols, try the downloadables in Table 3–16, or search the Web for similar software.

TABLE 3-16 *Specialty Image Programs for Special Web Pages*

Program	Platform	Description	Cost	URL
ChemWeb	Windows or Mac	ChemWeb makes chemical structure drawings and saves them to GIF format for use on HTML documents.	Free	www.softshell.com/FREE/ ChemWeb/cw-pages.html
Mathbrowser	Windows 3.1/ WFW 3.11/ 95/NT 3.5	Download this special browser that reads Mathcad documents and snap pictures of the math symbols you see on the Web.	Free	www.mathsoft.com/browser/ index.html
Trial Mathcad Plus 6.0	Windows or Mac	15-day fully functional trial of Mathcad itself— set up your equations and snap their pictures. See other scientific programs at the site.	Free	www.adeptscience.co.uk/as/ products/mathsim/mathcad/ files/download.phtml

If you have big graphics programs, look in your documentation for hundreds of included fonts, including symbol fonts, that you may not have installed. You can find fonts made of symbols for everything from musical notes to math symbols to office layout icons to animals. Remember to capture the images and use them as graphics—don't try to display them as fonts, even if your Web-authoring software supports pushing your fonts onto people, because a lot of us don't have the same fonts, don't have a browser that accepts embedded fonts, or refuse to let people send their fonts.

Those same big graphics programs may come with graphic image collections under titles like "icons" or "symbols" that have just the symbols you need in individual graphics files. Check the program's book or on-screen image browser.

Art, Copyright, and Licensing Issues

I can't speak to what constitutes courtroom proof of on-line art ownership, either now or as technology and the law change after this book is in your hands. It's also possible for someone to put their "proof" of ownership on someone else's work. Therefore—and because I'm not an attorney—the following tips are intended to help honest people identify their ownership for other honest people who sincerely intend to respect their artistic property by contacting them for permission to use it. This isn't meant as protection from people who disregard your ownership—and it isn't legal advice.

Comment Lines in Animated GIFs

Animated GIF programs, especially registered versions, often have special hidden text frames that let you tell the world it's your artwork, or say anything else you want to. Some unregistered programs use this space to tell the world about their product and to proclaim that you're using an unregistered version. People only see the comments when they open the animated GIF in a GIF animation program that supports comments. This may help if your animated GIF winds up on someone's freebie page and an innocent party downloads and opens it for editing. Since not everyone will open your GIF in such an editor, you'd best also leave other clues around your site for all to see.

Watermarks

"Watermarks" mean at least four things to computer folk—Microsoft's proprietary non-scrolling background textures, the light-printing background logos used behind text in word processing documents for artistic effect, stains from a variety of geeky spills on cloth or wooden surfaces, and a means of identifying the owner of on-line artwork through a third party such as Digimarc. The fourth is the one we're concerned with here, and you may have already checked out www.digimarc.com when you heard about it, or followed a link from Adobe Photoshop 4.0, which has Digimarc on its Filter menu.

Digimarc acts as a go-between between artists and the world. For a $99 annual subscription, Digimarc assigns a code number to you, which you embed in your art. People encounter the code and get your information from Digimarc by e-mail or fax. At this writing, there is a free trial available to people with Photoshop 4.0, Micrografx Graphics Suite 2.0, or Micrografx Webtricity 1.0. Check current policies and look for currently supported art programs at www.digimarc.com.

Steganography

A free, easy way to add your personal mark to your graphics is to use the steganography tools discussed in depth in Chapter 8, "Hiding in Plain Site." Steganography is intended to add information to files without detection and will show up when run through a specific decoder. This is sort of like hiding a signature between layers of paint, rather than signing the picture where people can see it. If people manipulate your image, your information may be lost. Again, put plain-sight notice up that your art is copyrighted. Hidden proof isn't a deterrent. Hidden erasable proof would only help you in the most unlikely Perry Mason case ever not written.

For More Information

Find out lots about copyright at www.benedict.com. Keep up with advances in watermarking and other art identification technologies at the Watermarking, Cryptography, and Steganography site at www-nt.e-tech nik.uni-erlangen.de/~hartung/watermarkinglinks.html.

Copyright Notice

Remember that ownership is ownership, but the Web is the Web, and it's easy for people to just take things. You stand a big chance of being ripped off when you put something on the Web, but big scary copyright notices at the bottom of the page may encourage would-be sticky-fingers to click and save elsewhere. Another tack is to put the copyright symbol beside your image, with a hot link to your copyright notice or a credit and copyright notice for a third-party author. You can also link the image itself to a copyright page. If you make a link of the image and don't want a frame to show around it, set the border to zero. Finally, put copyright information in your source code with comments by everything you want to protect individually, as well as the whole page.

Don't know what to say? Drop by David Letterman's Top Ten page at www.cbs.com/latenight/lateshow, read the Top Ten, get a laugh, then go to www.cbs.com/about/legal. You'll see links for the two ways to read it: "as a lawyer" and "as everybody else." Click "as everybody else," and tremble in fear as you read CBS's giant copyright threat page, which they characterize as "translated for all you netheads" (sic). Indeed, the first word is "WOW!" and the page contains other clear and present phrases such as "don't even think about. . . ." This would be an excellent copyright notice to steal. (Just kidding, CBS! Down, boys! Nice lawyers!) But do look around corporate Websites for an idea. Then consult a professional attorney, physician, and stockbroker. I have to say that every 50,000 words, by law. Murphy's Law.

CHAPTER 4

Objects Part 2: Sound

Remember when you were a kid and got dragged to some store that was boring or dusty—like a thrift shop or an electrical surplus store? It seemed to take a life-time for your mom to look up through her bifocals at every book that looked collectible, or to wait with her while your dad went off through tables of cables and boxes of parts. When you finally arrived at the cash register, you were lifted onto the counter beside a little red machine with a turnie-knob and columns of wrapped mini-sticks of gum and even miniature Hershey bars. They gave you a penny and let you turn and view the wares and pick out a treat. It was magic. It changed the whole experience.

Of course you don't want your site to be boring or dusty anywhere—the whole site should be engaging—but a little sound is nice if it has a real purpose and fits well with other content. People know when sound is augmenting their experience or enhancing their understanding, and when it's like a mechanical chimp banging on cymbals. Example: Sound works when it gives a sense of something you can't get from transcripts, or when it helps softly insinuate an ambiance. It doesn't work when it makes some poor guy splash coffee all over his keyboard.

The right delivery method is crucial. If someone wants to hear one of the trained birds you sell, and she clicks the bird's audio button, do you really want a sound window to open and just sit there, blank, while the file transfers to her? A little Java applet you can download and drop into your page can prevent that scenario, as you'll see in this chapter. Would you even consider letting that blank sound window appear when a visitor *hasn't* requested a sound file? That surprise window is an open invitation to kill the sound and leave your site in a huff before the first word or note plays.

✪ *Tip:* Avoid tying a sound to simply loading your main or index page. Every time someone visits a side page and returns, they'll hear the same sound. After a while, no trip will seem worth the repetition. If you want to tie a sound to loading a page, make it a side page they'll only visit once. In general, these are the best things to do with audio:

a. Put an audio file behind a link and let visitors choose it voluntarily. This is great for useful audio items that people will actually want to hear. Examples: keynote addresses by important people, discussions and forums that are more interesting to hear than read, a cut from your album, or a holiday greeting from your family. (**Hint:** Include text transcripts for sound grinches and the sound-deprived.) The link to audio can be hypertext or a small graphic with descriptive text beside it. Either way, the link should describe the file well and give the size and format of the file. People should know what they're getting into, and if they can deal with it once they have it. The most professional way is to have one small, nonlinking graphic atop text links to a choice of at least two audio formats; AU and WAV. (SND is a good third choice.) Check out downloadable editor/conversion programs in Table 4–1.

TABLE 4-1   *Downloadable Audio Converters and Editors*

CoolEdit	Windows 3.1/95/NT	WAV, SAM, AIFF, AIF, VOX, AU, SMP, VOC, TrueSpeech	www.syntrillium.com
GoldWave	Windows 3.1/95/NT	WAV, VOC, AU, SND, RAW, MAT, AIF, AFC, IFF, VOX, DWD, SMP, SDS	www.goldwave.com
SoundHack	Mac	Sound Designer II, IFF, IRCAM, DSP Designer, SND, AU	www.hitsquad.com/smm/programs/SoundHack
Sox	DOS	IRCAM, AU, HCOM, SOU, Sndtool, Sounder, SND, RIFF, WAV, SMP, CD-R, AIFF, 8SVX	www.spies.com/Sox
Sox	UNIX	IRCAM, AU, HCOM, SOU, Sndtool, Sounder, SND, RIFF, WAV, SMP, CD-R, AIFF, 8SVX	www.spies.com/Sox

b. If you want to play a sound automatically, avoid problems with the way different browsers handle different formats by using a drop-in Java applet like the ones you find free at the Java Boutique at http://java boutique.internet.com. There are instructions at the site for installing the applets (no programming required), or see the general instructions in the Java applet section in Chapter 5. Basically, all you have to do is create certain directories and place the files in them, and cut and paste a few lines of HTML to your Web page.

I don't usually push Java, but it works with audio files in both Netscape Navigator and Microsoft Internet Explorer (and little else does, when it comes to sound). There are some smooth-running Java sound applets that load fast—and some don't really even show. Try them out at the site and note differences in whether controls show or not, and what triggers the sounds. These applets can be nice for playing little sounds that might amuse your visitors if they don't have to watch a window spring open. It's like what the advice columnist says about putting on makeup in public—everyone appreciates a well-groomed appearance, but they don't necessarily want to see how you got that way. The Web is most definitely "in public." It's showtime.

When you make decisions about showing controls, keep the social context in mind. When applet controls pop up unexpectedly, some folks either feel invaded or expect something better than what they'll actually hear. If a visitor chose the content, it's a different story. For example, if a visitor clicks to hear an interview, she probably won't mind seeing controls appear that will help her cue and review certain points. She won't be as thrilled when an application window pops up and makes a big production out of loading something as inane as "Welcome to our Web page," or a cartoon "Doh!"

Java Boutique's downloadable applet AudioItem plays AU files quickly each time the visitor loads the page, and also leaves a small button up so visitors can hear it again without reloading the page. The applet ClipControl puts up Play, Loop, and Stop controls that visitors can see right away while an AU file loads. The applet Cornholio puts up a single button and plays an AU file each time a visitor presses the button. The applet Vivace plays a file quickly and invisibly each time a visitor loads the page. ***Note:*** Click on the Java applets' source code links and read their text for permissions as they relate to commercial and noncommercial use.

✪ ***Danger!*** Getting fast results on big files? If you aren't streaming the audio, the speed may be because the audio file is (a) on your system or (b) cached on your system. Don't forget to flush your hard-disk cache and your RAM cache between each test, and call the file off your Website from a browser on a completely different system.

Table 4–2 offers a few sites with tons of audio tools for a variety of platforms.

<EMBED>, <BGSOUND>, <APPLET>, or <OBJECT> Tag?

The <EMBED> tag works on graphics and sound files in Netscape 4.0, but Microsoft Internet Explorer 4 completely ignored embedded graphics files in my tests and drew a gray area and partial controls for a sound file. The bar at the bottom of the gray area moved, but no sound played. If you expect any Internet Explorer visitors, forget the <EMBED> tag. If you have an all-Netscape audience, you can use the <EMBED> tag like this:

```
<EMBED src="Nobodydz.au" autostart="true" volume="250"
loop="true"
height="60" width="145" align="middle">
```

The <BGSOUND> tag works in Microsoft Internet Explorer 4.0, but not in Netscape Navigator 4.0. If you have a captive Explorer audience, feel free. Just remember that a background sound can get old fast if it's on a page people return to often.

Here's an example of the <BGSOUND> tag in use:

```
<BGSOUND src="sound_file_name.wav" loop=infinite>
```

In contrast, the Java applets mentioned in this section work in both Netscape and Internet Explorer. See "Adding Java Applets to Your Page" in Chapter 5 for instructions. The Java Boutique also includes complete instructions for adding its applets to your site, plus all the necessary files and

TABLE 4-2 *Multiple Audio Tool Sites*

Audio Tool Site	Platform(s)	URL
MPEG Tools	Windows 3.1/95/NT, DOS, Mac, OS/2, Linux, UNIX	www.mpeg1.de/mpega.html
Shareware Music Machine	Windows 3.1/95, DOS, Mac, OS/2, Linux, Atari	www.hitsquad.com/smm
Tools for Mac	Mac	www.nexor.com/public/mac/ archive/data/sound/soundutil
WinFiles.com	Windows 95	http://www.winfiles.com/ apps/98/sound.html

even the patch of HTML that will go between your <APPLET> </APPLET> tags.

The <OBJECT> </OBJECT> tags will supersede <APPLET> </APPLET> tags when "everyone" is using HTML 4.0-compliant browsers. The <EMBED> and <BGSOUND> tags are nonstandard and aren't even listed on the World Wide Web Consortium (W3C) Website's list of HTML 4.0 tags.

Sources for Sound

Sound is everywhere, and you need to keep copyright laws in mind as you use these methods and tools for collecting it:

Get lossless digital sound files from audio CDs with the downloadable DiDo CD Audio Grabber for Windows. DiDo saves audio in WAV format. The tiny 58K download contains the program, help file, and source code. Get the works at www.voicecrystal.com/software/dido4.zip.

Use a simple RCA cable to pipe sound directly from your audio equipment or other output source into the input jack on your sound card. (You'll probably need to turn your computer around to get to the exposed area of your soundcard, which may already have external speakers or a microphone hooked into jacks on the back.) Your sound card manual will show which jack takes auxiliary sound if the jacks aren't labeled.

Telephone recordings sound best when taken with equipment specifically designed to pick up phone conversations. You must obey local and federal laws about disclosing the fact that you're recording, if telephone recording is allowed at all where you live. The quality of your phone line is incredibly important. A slight hum in the line can completely overpower a conversation when taped. Radio Shack has traditionally had very inexpensive simple rubber suction pickups that attach to the outside of the handset, with a plug at the other end that goes into your recorder. More complex equipment with a modular phone connector is also relatively inexpensive. Once the conversation is recorded, you can use normal RCA cable to hose it from the recorder into a sound file.

Hint: In order to get the most data to work with, go from the source to an intermediary analog tape recorder before going to disk.

There are lots of places to download sound files, and we mention a few in Table 4–3 for testing purposes—they may not be meant for reproduction. You can buy good canned sounds effects on commercial software CDs. Check the license agreement for use on a Web page before spending your money.

TABLE 4-3 *Sound Sources*

Name	Description	URL
alt.binaries.sounds	Newsgroup hierarchy of dozens of groups for posting and downloading binary sound files in subjects from cartoons to MIDI.	news:alt.binaries.sounds
AISP MIDI Might	1504 MIDI files, 1140 MOD files, and 114 WAV files. Note that MIDI can sound *awful* with any player if your audience doesn't have 16-bit sound cards.	www.tech-net.net/
EarthStation II	Sounds from TV, movies, radio, and history.	http://earthstation1.simple net.com/homepage.html
Hollywood Online MovieTunes	RealAudio Tracks from movie CDs—maybe not the track you want, since they're trying to sell the CDs.	www.movietunes.com/

Sound Quality and File Size

No matter how much bandwidth you can or can't afford in the end, start with a quality source. Contrary to what you might think from files posted on popular sites, that means an RCA cable between source and sound card—not a mic next to the speaker on the TV. And don't try to do your sampling during a one-time performance, because you don't get a second chance to make a first impression. Make a videotape of television programs and sample the sound from the tape later, at your leisure, through the VCR sound jacks. Send radio directly to cassette tape—preferably internally to the sound system—and sample it later, too.

To play or record CD quality, your sound card and driver have to support 16-bit stereo at 44.100 kHz. If your card doesn't support that, then you'll have less paring down to do, because you don't have room for files that size on the Web unless you're streaming your sound, which we'll discuss later in this section. So, if you're not streaming—or working with an intranet—you'll want to start with the best quality source or recording you can get, then go for the best trade-off among the following variables.

Channels

Mono is one channel, stereo is two, etc. If you're not trying to wrap a race car around somebody's brain, mono is probably your best bet for the Web, since stereo will about double your file size. You can record in mono, but you can also cut out a channel later.

✪ *Tip:* If you don't see obvious means of cutting down to one channel in your speech editor, copy and paste the stereo sound to a new (mono) file and save it, or look for a File/Export command that gives an option for mono.

Sampling Rate

Like the frames per second (fps) rate in video, the audio sampling rate measures how many samples of the sound are recorded per second per channel. Sampling rates in the GoldWave sound editor run from 5500 to 48,000 Hz. Popular sampling rates are 8000 Hz, 11.025 kHz, 22.050 kHz, and 44.100 kHz (the CD sampling rate), and you should shoot for those common numbers. When you experiment with different sampling rates, experiment with the bit depth (below) as well. You're looking for a balance between size and quality, and that's best accomplished by manipulating both sampling rate and bit depth—in opposite directions.

Bit Depth

Like the bit depth of graphic image files, the bit depth of sound files tells how much data is stored about each sample—usually 8 bits or 16 bits. At 16-bit depth, there is more nuance to the sound. Use 8-bit any time you can get away with it, and 16-bit when nuances are important. If you drop or raise the bit depth, experiment with sampling rate as well. It's all about trade-offs; if you raise one, try lowering the other.

Lossiness

Lossiness and losslessness apply to different types of compression used by various file formats. As a general rule, lossiness is much more apparent in sound than in graphics.

Clip Length

Obviously, the shorter the sound clip, the smaller the file size. A sound editing program will let you select and cut out unneeded sections of a recording. Be sure to shave off periods of silence before and after a sound.

File Formats

The file type you choose is important for several reasons, including cross-platform capability (though most files are convertible with utilities written for most platforms), installed base of audio players (if the player isn't proffered by Java), potential for sound quality, and compression capabilities. Table 4–4 focuses on the all-important issue of pervasiveness on the Web and accessibility to the largest possible audience. Even perceived accessibility can be crucial: If a visitor's browser has built-in support for Barking Spider files, but he's never heard of Barking Spider files, he may bypass links to your great sound files, or say "No" to "Opening" the file when a dialog box appears.

Streaming Audio—
Now with No Media Server Required

Most of us already appreciate the importance of streaming audio such as Progressive Networks' RealAudio (www.realaudio.com), since it lets us start hearing a long sound file after downloading only a small text file and a tiny fraction of the audio file itself. But some of us were disappointed when we ran off to find out how to add streaming audio to our Web pages, only to learn that the server side is how the bills get paid. At the time, putting up streaming audio was not for the faint of wallet. Now, though, it's a whole different ballgame for the little guys. Progressive Networks itself has a serverless (and therefore free) solution that's great for small sites without a lot of demand. (Competitors are out there, too, driving rates down for larger sites.)

To put streaming RealAudio on your page, you'll need to first do one thing to the Web server—simply define two MIME types, or get your ISP to configure them—and you can use the HTTP method to stream audio from your Web page. Defining MIME types isn't a lot of trouble or risk—my security-conscious ISP, who has turned down riskier requests in the past, configured his Web server for these MIME types without batting an eyelash. Remember, this is done to the Web server—you don't need a media server at all. The method is kind of low-rent—and not for huge enterprises—but it works just fine. Hats off to Progressive Networks for making RealAudio an option for smaller Web pages as well as the big kids.

The MIME types to configure on the Web server (if they're not preconfigured before you ask) are:

Extension	MIME Type
RA or RAM	audio/x-pn-realaudio
RPM	audio/x-pn-realaudio-plugin

TABLE 4-4	*Sound File Formats*
AIFF, AIF	Audio Interchange File Format (AIFF or AIF) is an Apple format also used by SGI that is virtually unheard-of on the Web today, though there are tools to convert AIFF to a more universal currency.
AIFC	AIFC is a compressed Mac format also used by SGI, but seldom found on the Web. Lossy compression.
AU	AU is an extremely important format with roots in the μ-law (American) and A-law (European) telephony standards. What makes AU special for Webmasters at this moment in time is its roots in Sun machines, where it propagated itself in the world of UNIX that spawned the Web itself. Many of the people writing browsers and authoring Java applets that handle sounds seamlessly were raised on UNIX— and they know and choose AU. If you go to download sound files from the Newsgroups, you'll find lots of AU files, and they're very popular on the Web. AU files are quite small, but may sound "hissy." A "safe" cross-platform bet.
IFF	IFF is an Amiga format and, considering the Amiga market share, is an "iffy" choice. Optional compression.
MIDI	Musical Instrument Design Interface (MIDI) files don't record sounds from the world when you create them. Instead, they tell the computer how to play sounds from a repertoire of synthesized sounds meant to mimic musical instruments. Obviously there can be no vocals on MIDI as we know it today. On 8-bit sound cards, MIDI can sound like a chorus of metal cats.
MP2 (MPEG)	In addition to a video format, the work of MPEG (Moving Pictures Expert Group) has resulted in audio formats such as MP2. The compression is a little lossy, but puts a good squeeze on files. Not yet widespread, except maybe with some anime sound collectors.
MP3	The new MPEG Audio Layer 3 format—get a player from www.mpeg.org/~tristan/MPEG/mp3.html and check it out.
MOD or NST	An Amiga format that has spread to other platforms, MOD files are actually instructions for playing a bank of samples or "instruments." The instruments can be any sound you can record, not just synthesized musical instruments like MIDI plays.
RA (and RAM)	RealAudio is a streaming format. Your HTML directs the visitor to a text (RAM) file containing the URL of the actual RA sound file. As soon as the first little bit of the audio (RA) file downloads, the file starts playing as the rest of the audio file streams into the visitor's player. Not always the best sound quality, but an excellent choice for delivering long files that visitors can hear right away. See the section on RealAudio to find out how you can add streaming RealAudio to your Web page free—and now without a media server!
SND	The Macintosh sound format adopted by NeXT is getting less prevalent compared to the proliferating Windows WAV files, RealAudio, and the Webbiest format of all (AU), but you're still likely to run into it, and it makes Mac people happy.
VOC	SoundBlaster's format, not widely deployed on the Web.
WAV	WAVE (WAV) is the Windows sound format developed by IBM and Microsoft, and is taking over Web sound territory proportionately with the WinTel platform.

You might mention to your ISP that clients will be drawn to a site that lets them stream audio from their pages.

When to Stream

Streamed files at today's modem speeds may not sound as full-bodied as WAV files, but they make it practical to deliver long sound files over the Web with next to no waiting. Consider streaming speeches, interviews, commentaries, and discussion groups, but don't rule out music. RealAudio would also be a great choice for streaming speech to visually impaired people when the content would be unsatisfactory on a speech synthesizer. Run-of-the-mill synthesizers don't do well with lists of proper names, some symbolic notation, poems, stories, or dramatic readings—anything that needs a human brain and voice instead of phonetic spewing.

How to Stream RealAudio from Your Page

First get the latest RealAudio Plug-in and player package free from Progressive Networks at www.realaudio.com, as well as the free encoder for making and converting files to RA from other formats.

1. Download the free RA encoder and convert or create an RA sound file. We'll call it catsmeow.ra.

2. Create a plain text RAM file that contains only the complete path to your file, like so:

   ```
   http://www.myprovider.com/~mylogindir/catsmeow.ra
   ```

   Name that plain text file kittylink.ram.

3. In your Web page, create an HTML link to the RAM file, not the RA file, like so:

   ```
   <A HREF="kittylink.ram"> Feline Melody </A>
   ```

4. Upload the RA, RAM, and HTML files to your Web directory, and make sure the permissions are set correctly.

You can try an evaluation copy of another media-server-less streaming product at Vivo Software (www.vivo.com). Both the RealAudio and Vivo products stream both video and audio files.

Other options: Download the free EasyStart RealAudio server, a fully functional 60-stream EasyStart Server, or a 30-day trial of the professional version, at www.realaudio.com.

Editing Sound (Effects)

Your sound editing program probably offers a range of opportunities to enhance your sound file, whether you got it with your sound card, with your operating system, from the Net, or in shrink-wrapped cardboard. Table 4–5 shows the effects available in the downloadable GoldWave 3.24 for Windows (www.goldwave.com). GoldWave's options are a good example of what to look for in a sound editor if you can't use this Windows program. (For multitrack editing, mixing, and sequencing of WAV, VOC, AIF, and AU, look into the beta of Multiquence at the GoldWave site.)

TABLE 4–5 *Sound Effects in Downloadable GoldWave 3.24*

Doppler	Dynamically alters pitch the way a train's whistle changes pitch as it approaches.
Dynamics	Limits, compresses, or expands a range of amplitudes.
Echo	Hello? Hello? Set the volume and delay of an echo.
Exchange Channels	Swap left and right channels (stereo).
Filters	Goldwave's filters remove a range of frequencies to remove quiet parts of selections, boost and reduce frequencies, and much more. Users can even create custom filters.
Flange	Creates unusual sound effects.
Interpolate	Smooths out samples between start and finish markers to remove a pop or click.
Invert	Invert one channel of a stereo sound to create a surround-sound effect.
Mechanize	Robotic sound.
Offset	Changes the dc offset.
Pan	Pan left and right channels.
Playback rate	Make entire sound play faster or slower and higher or lower.
Resample	Recalculates data so new sample plays at original pitch and rate.
Reverse	Reverses sound so you can play it backwards. Ooooooh.
Silence	Mutes the selection.
Speed	Changes the speed by resampling.
Transpose	Changes the pitch by resampling.
Volume	Fade in, fade out, and more.

Cool Product: CoolEdit Pro

The 64-track "Pro" version of the popular CoolEdit lets you tweak files as large as 2 gigabytes, in about 25 formats. You'll know how to get going as soon as you open the program, and the interface has button flyouts to let you know what each tool does. Use Noise Reduction, Hiss Reduction, and Click and Pop Eliminator to make your sound files sound more professional.

You get the special effects you'd expect in a program of CoolEdit Pro's caliber, but I was shocked to find "Brainwave Synchronizer," based on a principle a college teacher of mine was having success with more than 10 years ago under the name "hemisync." The idea is that beta, delta, and theta brainwaves can be stimulated by simulating the correct frequency over headphones. Since the brain won't pick that up by listening to that frequency, the two hemispheres are "synched" by creating a difference of that frequency—just a few hertz—between two stereo headphones. CoolEdit Pro lets you lay down those brainwave-influencing tracks. (See Figure 4–1.) Be sure to tell Web listeners that to get the benefit, they need to listen with their stereo headphones.

A feature-packed, cool product. Windows 95/NT. $399. Demo download available from Syntrillium Software Corporation at www.syntrillium.com.

FIGURE 4-1 *CoolEdit Pro lets you lay down tracks to influence brainwaves.*

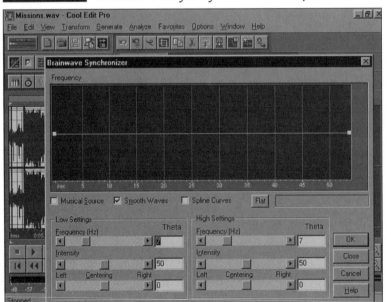

Sound Alternatives

Macs have built-in soundware, but remember that not everyone on the Web with a PC or other system has a sound card or sound chips. A visitor may be deaf, or may have turned off sound because a spouse or baby is sleeping or they don't want to disturb co-workers. Offer these folks links to the richest possible text alternatives and/or descriptions of anything offered to hearers.

CHAPTER 5

Objects Part 3: Ready-Made Drop-Ins: Java Applets, JavaScript, Active X, and Plug-Ins

You don't have to know how to program "Hello World" or anything else in Java to pluck and use applets offered by generous authors on the Web. To see for yourself, grab a gunny sack and visit The Java Boutique at http://javaboutique.internet.com.

The Java Boutique has been around for years and offers some cool applets, including a spoof visitor counter with constantly turning numbers, puzzles, games, animated buttons, an image flipper with sound effects, text animators and scrollers, image animators, audio players, clocks, an image ticker tape that parades small photos across the page, various explosions, an advertising banner, fade and melt effects, a stock checker, the old box-jumps-away-from-the-cursor trick, neon signs, charts, page password, image mappers, pop-up descriptions for an image map, a plotter, a simple spreadsheet, sound players, and more. There's even the "Kiss Me" app, which turns a visitor's cursor into smoochy lips and makes a kissing sound when the cursor touches your photo. (There's a suggestion at the site to change the kissing sound to a gunshot and the image to a bullet hole. That's one of the nice things about Java—you can substitute file names for photos, sounds, and so forth by replacing them where you spot them in the plain text source file.)

Adding Java Applets to Your Page

The Java Boutique provides instructions for adding the applets it offers, and puts everything you need for each applet on one convenient page. Here's the basic idea:

1. Download all the elements the site says to. This usually includes .java and .class files, and any accompanying media files (.gif images, .au sounds, etc.). The Java Boutique makes this easy with hot-links to the files.

2. Copy the few lines of HTML you're asked to and paste them into your test Web page. Make any necessary changes to the <APPLET> and <PARAM> tags to reflect your preferences. Credit the author of the applet and the Java Boutique. Save the test HTML file.

   Hint: Don't forget that your file needs the standard skeleton HTML tags, as shown in Appendix A.

3. Create the directories you're asked to in your public_html directory. In UNIX you will use the MKDIR command. You will probably add directories called "classes" and "Images" under public_html. The directory structure should look something like this:

```
public_html
public_html/classes
public_html/Images
```

   Hint: Copy the directory names exactly—including letter case—so they'll match the directories called from the Java file. If you have to go in and edit file, directory, or path names, simply make them match the names you've set up.

   Follow any other instructions at the site.

4. Upload the files if you're working off-line. Move the test .htm file and .java file into your public_html directory. Move the .class file into the public_html/classes directory. Move any images (perhaps a .gif file) into the public_html/Images directory.

   Hint: If you downloaded your files to a system that shortened the file names, be sure to restore the longer file names when you have them on the server.

5. Make sure permissions are set correctly.

6. Copy and paste the HTML into your Web page. This is the example HTML for the acNeilson Java applet, which puts a constantly spinning joke counter on your page:

```
<applet codeBase=classes code="acNeilson.class" width=75
height=20>
```

```
<param name=NUMBER_FRAMES value=10>
<param name=NUMBER_WIDTH value=15>
<param name=NUMBER_HEIGHT value=20>
<param name=HOW_MANY value=5>
<param name=DELAY value=1000>
<param name=VALUE value=12345>
</applet>
```

Remember that the <APPLET> </APPLET> tags were "deprecated" in HTML 4.0 in favor of the <OBJECT> </OBJECT> tags. (See the section "Putting It All In" in Chapter 1.) For now, the <APPLET> tags are the correct choice, but when the majority of Web visitors is using HTML 4.0-compliant browsers, you'll want to switch to the <OBJECT> tags.

7. Test your handiwork. If you have problems, check the site where you got the applet for troubleshooting tips or a FAQ or, as a last resort, write the author of the program.

Table 5–1 shows sites that offer downloadable Java Applets.

JavaScript gets cut and pasted right into your Web page and there are lots of downloadable scripts, as seen in Table 5–2.

Download other kinds of scripts—such as CGI, Perl, and htmlscript— from the sources shown in Table 5–3.

TABLE 5-1 *Downloadable Java Applets*

Applets from JavaSoft	Some Classics, including "Tumbling Duke," the little Java droplet guy.	http://java.sun.com/ applets/js-applets.html
Gamelan	Awesome collection of thousands of applets and related materials, organized into these categories: Arts and Entertainment (267), Business and Finance (218), Commercial Java (473), Educational (835), Games (1238), How-to and Help (71), Java-Enhanced Sites (791), JavaBeans (50), Miscellaneous (119), Multimedia (467), Network and Communications (440), Programming in Java (1329), Publications (172), Related Technologies (1421), Special Effects (856), Tools and Utilities, (693).	www.gamelan.com
JARS	The Java Applet Rating Site has thousands of resources: Business (86), Multimedia (348), Web Sites (72), Financial (66), Science (186), Utilities (256), Games (392), Programming (132), Other (38), and WWW (354).	www.jars.com/listing-Java.html
The Java Boutique	Great sample site—see description of applets at the beginning of the Java section in this chapter.	http://javaboutique. internet.com

TABLE 5-2	*Downloadable JavaScript*	
Cut-N-Paste JavaScript	Categories include: Travel and Tourist, Merchants, Retail, Malls, Technical, Engineering, Financial, Games, Toys and Effects, Clocks, Calendars and Locks, Christmas and Hanukkah Seasonal, Sponsors and Sponsor Rotation, Buttons, Image Changing, Animation, Cut-N-Paste JavaScript Newsletters, Miscellaneous Stuff, Web Page Design, Security.	www.infohiway.com/ javascript/indexf.htm
Java Goodies	Script Types: Calendars, Clocks, Calculators, Scrolling Text, Buttons, Links, Email, Color Scripts, Text, Images, Alert Boxes and Prompts, Cookies, Passwords, Counters, Games, Miscellaneous Scripts.	www.htmlgoodies.com/ javagoodies
JavaScript Developer	Educational (30), Example (46), Finance (36), Games (137), General (71), Graphics (69), How-to and Help (39), Search Engines (52), Utilities (190), Web Sites (203).	http://javascript. developer.com/

TABLE 5-3	*Other Scripts: CGI, Perl, and htmlscript*	
AGL	Master list of scripts pages.	www.arosnet.se/agl/ free/scripts.html
Matt's Script Archive	Over 900 CGI-related resources in 170 categories. Perl CGI, C++ CGI, and htmlscript Template Applications.	http://worldwidemart. com/scripts/

Table 5–4 offers Active X. But remember that the audience for Active X is currently very limited. Active X is a Microsoft, not a Netscape, technology and, as of this writing, Microsoft is only planning the broad platform support that Netscape has practiced for a very long time. (A Microsoft press release puts the UNIX version of IE 4 in the first quarter of 1998.) Even

TABLE 5-4	*Downloadable Active X*	
Active X Developer	Downloadables and other resources: ActiveX Collections (12), General (71), Graphics (49), Multimedia (33), Network and Communications (44), Publications (24), Special Effects (21), Tools (92), User Interface (54).	http://activex. developer.com

when Microsoft builds browsers for more platforms, those users can say "no" more easily than Windows users (if Windows 98 integrates Internet Explorer onto the desktop). And with the headline allegations involving Microsoft and the Justice Department, Internet Explorer may look slightly less like a boulder rolling down a narrow alley after every PC buyer.

Netscape Plug-Ins
(and Active X and Java Counterparts)

We've talked about standards throughout this book, and why it's not a great idea to depend on visitors to go download a plug-in just to see your content. For your convenience, we'll briefly run down the Netscape plug-ins in Table 5–5—just in case you have those special circumstances (like a captive audience) that may make a plug-in the right choice. Be sure to follow a link from the plug-in blurb at the Netscape page (www.netscape.com/comprod/products/navigator/version_2.0/plugins/index.html?—question mark included) to the manufacturer's site to get the most current information on:

- What the product required at your end (for creating content, or a server) costs you.
- Whether visitors have to pay for the plug-in.
- Whether there is an Active X counterpart or other means of broadening the base to both Netscape Plug-in and Microsoft Active X visitors. Some of these vendor sites list Java versions of their players—a cross-platform solution.

Note that the following brief descriptions are not reviews, but extremely condensed versions of information on-line, which will help identify products that may be right for you. Only products with sites I could reach are included, and new plug-ins are added often.

TABLE 5-5	Netscape Plug-Ins			
Plug-In	**Platform**	**Description**	**Vendor**	**Vendor's URL**
ABC QuickSilver	Windows 95/NT	View and interact with object graphics.	Micrografx	www.micrografx. com/
AboutPeople	Mac 68K, Power Mac, Windows 95	Browse and search address books on the Web.	Now Software	www.nowsoft.com/
AboutTime	Mac 68K, Power Mac, Windows 95	Get to appointment calendars on the Web.	Now Software	www.nowsoft.com/
Acordex ViewTIFF	Mac 68K, Power Mac	Display TIFF image files.	Acordex Imaging Systems	www2.shore.net/ ~cordant/ welcome.html
Acrobat Reader	Mac 68K, Power Mac, Windows 3.x/ 95/NT, OS/2, IRIX, Sun OS, HP-UX, OSF1, AIX, Linux	Navigate and print pop- ular Portable Document Format (PDF) files, which show files as they ap- peared in their originating applications. Very power- ful for training and other purposes—especially on an intranet.	Adobe	www.adobe.com/ prodindex/acrobat/ readstep.html
AnimaFlex	Mac 68K, Power Mac, Windows 3.X/ 95/NT	Photorealistic animation.	RubberFlex Software	www.rubber flex.com
Apple Electrifier	Mac, Power Mac	Vector typography, graphics, and animation.	Lari Software	www.electrifier.com
ASAP WebShow	Windows 3.x/95	View and advance slide shows quickly.	Software Publishing Corporation	www.spco.com/
Astound Web Player	Windows 3.x/95	Plays dynamic multi- media documents created with Astound or Studio M.	Gold Disk	www.golddisk.com
Bamba	Windows 95/NT, OS/2	Streams high-quality audio–video for low- bandwidth connections. Algorithms determine connection bandwidth and file size, then adjust delivery.	IBM	www.alphaWorks. ibm.com/formula/ bamba

Plug-In	Platform	Description	Vendor	Vendor's URL
Beatnik	Power Mac, Windows 95/NT	Manages playback of Rich Music Format (RMF), MIDI, MOD, WAV, AIFF, and AU.	HEADSPACE	www.head space.com/
Bubbleviewer	Power Mac, Windows 3.x/ 95/NT	Immersive 360-degree environment.	IPIX	www.ipix.com
Calendar Quick	Windows 3.x/ 95/NT	Adds calendars, appoint- ments, and project schedules to page.	Logic Pulse	www.logic pulse.com/
CE Internet	Windows 95/NT	Wavelet Image File (WIF) image compression.	Compression Engines	www.cengines.com/ products/ products.htm
Chemscape Chime	Mac 68K, Power Mac, Windows 3.x/ 95/NT	Displays chemically significant 2-D and 3-D structures.	MDL	www.mdli.com/
CineWeb	Windows 3.x/ 95/NT	Real-time streaming audio–video using standard AVI, MOV, MPG, WAV, MID, and MP2 files.	Digigami	www.digigami.com/ cineweb/
Citrix WinFrame Client	Windows 3.x/ 95/NT	Work with documents from Windows programs.	Citrix	www.citrix.com/
ClearFusion	Mac 68K, Power Mac, Windows 95/NT	Streaming video for Windows AVI.	Iterated Systems	www.iterated.com/
CMX Viewer	Windows 95/NT	CMX vector graphics file viewer.	Corel	www.corel.com
COM One Video	Windows 3.x/ 95/NT	Displays video and sound sequences.	COM One	www.com1.fr/uk/ demovideo/ index.html
Common Ground MiniViewer	Windows 95/NT	View, navigate, and print Common Ground Digital Paper files.	Hummingbird Communi- cations	www.humming bird.com/
Community Place	Windows 95/NT	VRML 2.0-based multiuser 3-D shared worlds.	Sony	http:// vs.sony.co.jp

(continued)

TABLE 5-5 *continued*

Plug-In	Platform	Description	Vendor	Vendor's URL
Corel Presentations Show It!	Windows 95/NT	Views Corel Presentations Show It! slide shows.	Corel	www.corel.com/
Cosmo Player	Windows 95/NT, IRIX	VRML 2.0 browser.	Silicon Graphics, Inc.	www.sgi.com/
CPC View	Windows 95/NT	View and navigate black-and-white documents in formats including TIFF, PBM, and CPC.	Cartesian Products	www.cartesian inc.com/
Crescendo PLUS	Mac 68K, Windows 3.x/ 95/NT	Plays stereo MIDI.	LiveUpdate	www.live update.com/ cplus.html
CSView	Windows 3.x/ 95/NT	Publishes publications and drawings in 150 native formats, including AutoCad, Tiff, and Word.	CSU Software Solutions	http:// home.magi.com/ ~advent/csview150/
CyberAge Raider	Windows 95/NT	3-D search interface for Net beginners.	CyberAge Communi-cations	www.miint.net/ cyberage/
CyberCash Wallet	Windows 3.x/ 95/NT	Electronic funds in increments as small as 25 cents.	CyberCash	www.cyber cash.com/
CyberLinks	Windows 3.x/ 95/NT	Publishes existing OLE documents (such as Word and Excel) with live hyperlinks directly on Web servers without converting to HTML.	Digital InfoWorks	www.pioneer sys.com/di/
Data Detective PC Search	Windows 95/NT	Performs full-text, Boolean, and proximity searches on any directory or drive on your PC. Results show as hyperlinks.	AppletWare, Inc.	http://applet site.com/
Day-Timer Organizer	Windows 3.x/95	View, search, and print calendars and address info.	Day-Timer Technologies	www.daytimer.com/ index.html
DeepV2	Windows 95	Direct3D X-file viewer. Requires DirectX 2 installed.	Heads off	www.headsoff.com/

Plug-In	Platform	Description	Vendor	Vendor's URL
DemoNow	Windows 95/NT	Lets visitors see demos of your products online without downloading.	DemoShield	www.demo shield.com/
Demo-X	Windows 95/NT	Lets visitors interact with embedded interactive demos.	DemoShield	www.demo-x.com/ faq.htm
Digital Sound & Music Interface for OS/2	OS/2	Plays 32-channel digital music module files.	Julien Pierre	www.pol sci.wvu.edu/ Madbrain/ npdsmi.html
Dr. DWG NetView	Windows 3.x/ 95/NT	Views AutoCAD drawings—redline R12 and R13 DWG/DXF files.	Dr. DWG	www.cswl.com/ cadjul24/ products.htm
DWG/DXF	Windows 95/NT	View AutoCAD (DWG) and DXF files dynamically.	SoftSource	www.soft source.com/
EarthTime	Windows 95/NT	Tells time around the world.	Starfish Software	www.starfish software.com/
Echospeech	Windows 3.x/ 95/NT	Multimedia-quality speech encoder.	Echo Speech	www.echo speech.com/
ELT/Net	Windows 95/NT	View National Imagery Transmission Format (NITF) images.	Paragon Imaging	www.paragon.com/
Enliven Viewer	Windows 95/NT	Sight, sound, and motion.	Narrative Communi- cations	www.narrative.com/
Envoy	Mac 68K, Power Mac, Windows 3.x/95/NT	View documents as they appeared in their applications of origin.	Tumbleweed Software	www.tumble weed.com/
EZ-ID	Power Mac, Windows 3.x/ 95/NT	Works with Metropolis Data Base Management System to aid in on-line commerce.	Alpha Base Interactive	http://alpha base.com/
FACSys Web Agent	Windows 95/NT	Schedule files using the FACSys Web Agent.	FACSys	http://208.20.14.6/ (requires password)
Flare	Windows 95/NT	Displays Xara vector format.	Xara	www.xara.com/ corelxara/ plugin.html
FlashPix Viewer	Power Mac, Windows 95/NT	Views FlashPix images.	Live Picture	www.live picture.com/html/ viewers.html

(continued)

TABLE 5-5 *continued*

Plug-In	Platform	Description	Vendor	Vendor's URL
Flying Carpet	Windows 95/NT	Manipulate and navigate very large 3-D models and worlds consisting of up to millions of polygons. Supports OpenGL.	AccelGraphics	www.accel graphics.com/
Formula Graphics	Windows 95/NT	Animation and inter-activity.	Harrow Software	www.formula graphics.com/
Formula One/NET	Windows 3.x/ 95/NT	Excel-compatible spreadsheets.	Visual Components	www.visual comp.com/
Fractal Viewer	Mac 68K, Windows 3.x/ 95/NT	View Fractal Image For-mat files inline.	Iterated Systems	www.iterated.com
HyperPage	Windows 3.x/95	See hypermedia presentations.	LMSOFT	www.lmsoft.ca/ index.html
HyperStudio	Mac 68K, Power Mac, Windows 95	View HyperStudio multimedia projects.	Roger Wagner Publishing	www.hyper studio.com/
ichat	Mac 68K, Power Mac, Windows 3.x/ 95/NT	Lets users participate in Ichat ROOMS server chats.	ichat	www.ichat.com/
IconAuthor	Windows 3.x/95	View IconAuthor multi-media applications.	Aimtech	www.aimtech.com/
Imaging for Internet	Windows 95/NT	View FlashPix digital image file format, which stores multiple resolu-tions of a single image in one file.	Hewlett-Packard	www.hp.com/
InstallFrom TheWeb	Windows 95/NT	Lets vendors offer instal-lations over the Web.	InstallShield Software	www.install shield.com/
InterCAP Inline	Windows 95/NT	Views, zooms, and pans CGM vector graphics files.	InterCAP Graphics Systems	www.intercap.com
Intermind Communi-cator	Windows 3.x/ 95/NT	Custom Web publishing, subscription, and user-feedback system over TCP/IP network.	Intermind	www.inter mind.com/
InterVu Player	Mac 68K, Power Mac, Windows 3.x/ 95/NT	Plays MPEG audio–video files.	InterVu	www.intervu.net/

Plug-In	Platform	Description	Vendor	Vendor's URL
IP/TV	Windows 3.x/ 95/NT	Plays real-time audio–video for training, corporate communication, videos, etc.	Precept IP/TV	www.precept.com/ release/fwserver_ viewer.htm
IPIX Viewer	Power Mac, Windows 3.x/ 95/NT	Interactive, fully immersive photographs.	Interactive Pictures Corporation	www.ipix.com/ viewers/ viewers.html
ISYS HindSite	Windows 3.x/ 95/NT	"Remembers" everywhere you've been and everything you've seen in a given time period. Allows full-text searches.	ISYS/Odyssey Development	www.isysdev.com/ products/hind site.htm
JetForm WebFiller	Windows 3.x/ 95/NT	Integrate JetForm forms into a Web page.	JetForm Corporation	www.jetform.com/
Jutvision	Windows 95/NT	View 3-D, photo-realistic Virtual Reality.	Visdyn	www.visdyn.com/
KEYview	Windows 3.x/ 95/NT	Views, ZIPs, and converts files with cross-platform support for over 200 formats.	Verity	www.verity.com/
KIT	Windows 3.x/ 95/NT	Implements the KIT (Kernel for Intelligent Communication Terminal) protocol mainly used in Germany. (Web page is in German.)	KIT Interaktiv!	www.kit-show.t-online.de/
Koan	Windows 3.x/ 95/NT	Plays MIDI.	SSEYO	www.sseyo.com/ indexnew.html
LABTECHnet	Windows 95	Views real-time data broadcasts.	LABTECH	www.labtech.com/
LearnFlow	Windows 3.x/ 95/NT	Interactive simulation of software environment.	Ziff-Davis Education	www.learniton line.com/consumer/ gettingstarted.asp
Lightning Strike	Mac 68K, Windows 3.x/ 95/NT, UNIX	Wavelet image compression.	Infinop	www.infinop.com/
Liquid MusicPlayer	Power Mac, Windows 95/NT	Listen and purchase CD-quality music tracks and CDs over the Internet.	Liquid Audio	www.liquid audio.com/

(continued)

TABLE 5–5 *continued*

Plug-In	Platform	Description	Vendor	Vendor's URL
Look@Me	Mac, Windows 3.x/95	View a remote Look@Me user's screen in real time. Based on Timbuktu.	Farallon	www.farallon.com/
Lotus Web Screen Show Player	Windows 95/NT	Shows Freelance Graphics presentations.	Lotus Development Corporation	www3.lotus.com/ home.nsf
LuRaWave	Power Mac, Windows 95/NT	Wavelet image compression.	LuRaTech	www.lurate ch.com/ index_e.html
MacZilla	Mac 68K, Power Mac	Plays QuickTime, MIDI background sound, WAV, AU, AIFF, audio MPEG, and AVI.	Knowledge Engineering	http:// maczilla.com/
Magnet Viewer	Windows 95/NT	View InfoMagnet documents.	CompassWare	www.compass ware.com/
MapGuide	Windows 3.x/ 95/NT	View live vector-based maps.	Autodesk	www.map guide.com/
mBED	Mac 68K, Power Mac, Windows 3.x/ 95/NT	Multimedia player for mBED documents.	mBED	www.mbed.com/
MegaView	Windows 3.x/ 95/NT	Displays XGL movies (Vector Cel Animations), XGL vector drawings, and Windows metafiles and bitmaps.	MegaBitz Engineering	www.oze mail.com.au/ ~xcorp/
MetaWeb CGM Viewer	Windows 3.x/ 95/NT	Views and zooms Computer Graphics Metafile (CGM) files.	EMATEK	www.ematek.com
MIDPLUG	Power Mac, Windows 3.x/95	Plays sound and music accompaniment for ani-mation, ads, text, etc.	Yamaha	www.yamaha.co.jp/ english/
MODPlug	Windows 95/NT	Plays mod/s3m/xm/it files.	Oliver Lapicque	www.castlex.com/ modplug/
Multimedia Home Space Viewer	Mac 68K, Power Mac, Windows 3.x/95/NT	Adds multimedia and interactivity to 3-D VRML Virtual Home Space homes.	ParaGraph International	www.para graph.com/
NET TOOB Stream	Windows 3.x/ 95/NT	Streaming audio and video with standard MPEG files.	Duplexx Software	www.duplexx.com/

Plug-In	Platform	Description	Vendor	Vendor's URL
Net-Install	Windows 3.x/ 95/NT	Lets users download, decompress, and install software in one step.	20/20 Software	www.twenty.com/ Pages/NI/NI.shtml
NetMC	Windows 95/NT	Plays NetMC multimedia pages.	NEC Systems	http://netmc.nec lab.com/
Netscape Media Player	Mac, Windows 3.x/95/NT, IRIX, Sun OS, HP-UX	Streaming audio and synchronized multimedia.	Netscape	http://search.net scape.com/down load/mplayer.html
NetZIP Plug-in	Windows 3.x/ 95/NT	ZIPs and unZIPs files online.	Software Builders International	www.software builders.com/
Neuron	Windows 3.x/ 95/NT	Offers computer-based training applications produced with any ToolBook II authoring product, including In-structor, Publisher, and Assistant.	Asymetrix	www.asymet rix.com/
NobleNet Opener	Windows 3.x/ 95/NT	Lets programmers distribute client–server applications across the Internet or an intranet with no recoding.	NobleNet	www.noblenet.com/
OLiVR	Power Mac, Windows 95/NT	Streams photo-realistic, 3-D, virtual reality movies.	Live Picture	www.olivr.com/
OmniForm Internet Filler	Windows 3.x/ 95/NT	Users view, fill out, print, and submit forms. Reads Open Form Mark-up Language (OFML) files.	Caere	www.caere.com/
OneWave	Windows 95/NT	OLE/OCX compatibility helps build interactive apps. Use with VB scripting.	OneWave	www.onewave.com/
OnLive! Talker	Windows 95	Voice conference on Web pages in real time.	OnLive! Technologies	www.onlive.com/
OnLive! Traveler	Windows 95/NT	Lets visitors into OnLive!-enabled 3-D virtual environments. Includes group communication.	OnLive! Technologies	www.onlive.com/
OpSession	Windows 95/NT	Lets users control all 32-bit Windows applications remotely.	NetManage	www.net manage.com/

(continued)

TABLE 5–5 *continued*

Plug-In	Platform	Description	Vendor	Vendor's URL
Panorama Viewer	Windows 3.x/ 95/NT, Sun OS, HP-UX	Views SGML documents.	SoftQuad	www.softquad.com/
PanoramIX	Windows 95/NT	View, zoom, and pan virtual panoramic scenes.	IBM	www.alpha Works.ibm.com/ formula/PanoramIX
Passport	Windows 95/NT	Interact with other people in 3-D worlds in real time.	Black Sun Interactive (AKA Blaxxun Interactive)	http://ww3.black sun.com/
Pegasus	Windows 3.x/95	Views JPEG, Progressive JPEG, and PIC (Pegasus's enhanced JPEG).	Pegasus Imaging	www.jpg.com/ product.html
PenOp	Windows 3.x/95	Verifies handwritten signatures sent electronically.	PenOp	www.penop.com/ products/ netscape.htm
PhoneFree	Windows 95/NT	Real-time, phone-quality conversations over the Internet without a telephone or long-distance charges.	Big Bits Software	www.phone free.com/
Plugsy	Windows 95/NT	Helps Netscape users manage conflicts between plug-ins that handle the same MIME type. Can disable certain MIME types in plug-ins you don't want handling those MIME types.	Digigami	www.digigami.com/
PNG Live	Windows 95/NT	Views Portable Network Graphics (PNG) files.	Siegel & Gale	www.siegel gale.com/
PointCast Grabber	Windows 3.x/ 95/NT	Offers links to the PointCast Network files in your hard disk cache.	SE & S	www.ho house.com/pcn/
PointCast Network	Windows 3.x/95	Receive free broadcast news and information.	PointCast	www.pointcast.com/
PointPlus	Windows 3.x/ 95/NT	Streams dynamic pre-sentations, including PowerPoint.	Net-Scene	www.net-scene.com/
PowerBuilder DataWindow	Windows 3.x/ 95/NT	View, navigate, and print PowerBuilder reports.	Powersoft	www.power soft.com/

Plug-In	Platform	Description	Vendor	Vendor's URL
PowerBuilder Windows	Windows 3.x/95/NT	Lets users view and interact with Power-Builder windows inside Web pages.	Powersoft	www.power soft.com/
PowerMedia	Windows 95/NT	View interactive content, presentations, training, kiosks, and demos.	RadMedia	www.rad media.com/
PowerPoint Animation Player & Publisher	Windows 95/NT	View and interact with hyper PowerPoint animations and presentations.	Microsoft	www.micro soft.com/mspower point/internet/ player/default.htm
Project Development	Windows 3.x/95/NT	View multiple CAD vector and raster file formats for use in Geographic Information Systems (GIS) applications.	Project Development	http://hem.pas sagen.se/project/
ProtoPlay	Windows 3.x/95/NT	Runs interactive electronic prototypes.	Altia	www.altia.com/
Quick View Plus	Windows 3.x/95/NT	View, copy, and print over 200 file formats.	INSO Corporation	www.inso.com/
Quick3D	Power Mac, Windows 95/NT	Lets users manipulate 3-D models.	Plastic Thought	www.Plastic Thought.com/
QuickFlick	OS/2	Plays QuickTime video, digital sound, animation, and QTMA (MIDI) in OS/2.	Practice Corporation	www.prac tice.xo.com/
QuickServer	Windows 3.x/95/NT	Offers users client–server applications developed with Visual Basic, C++, and Java.	Wayfarer	www.quick server.com/
QuickTime	Mac 68K, Power Mac, Windows 3.x/95/NT	Plays Apple QuickTime animation, music, MIDI, audio, video, and VR panoramas.	Apple	http://quick Time.apple.com/ dev/devweb.html
Rapid	Windows 3.x/95/NT	Interact with Rapid simulations.	Emultek	www.emultek.com/ plugin.htm
Rapid	Windows 95/NT	Shows simulations and prototypes made in Rapid environment.	Emultek	www.emultek.com/
RapidTransit	Mac 68K, Windows 95/NT	Decompresses and plays compressed music.	FASTMAN	www.fastman.com

(continued)

TABLE 5–5 *continued*

Plug-In	Platform	Description	Vendor	Vendor's URL
RealiView	Windows 95/NT	Lets users browse 3-D worlds.	Datapath Unlimited	www.realimation.com
RealPlayer for RealAudio and RealVideo	Mac, Windows 3.x/95/NT, OS/2, IRIX, Sun OS, Linux	Plays streaming RealAudio and RealVideo.	Progressive Networks	www.real.com/
RealSpace Viewer	Power Mac, Windows 95/NT	Offers VR panoramic viewing and video and audio playback.	Live Picture	www.livepicture.com/
Rush	Mac 68K, Power Mac, Windows 3.x/95/NT, Sun OS, Linux	Views Rush formatted files.	RMX Technologies	www.rmx.com/
SCREAM	Windows 3.x/95/NT	Runs interactive, vector-based SCREAM animations.	Saved By Technology	www.savedbytech.com/Scream/GetScream.htm
ScriptActive	Windows 95/NT	Lets developers script Active X with VBScript, JavaScript, and other scripting tools.	NCompass	www.ncompasslabs.com/
SecureWeb Documents	Windows 95/NT	Digital signature security product.	Terisa Systems	www.terisa.com/
Shockwave	Mac 68K, Power Mac, Windows 3.x/95/NT	Plays popular Shockwave interactive streaming multimedia. Vector-capable.	Macromedia	www.macromedia.com/index.html
Shockwave Flash	Mac 68K, Power Mac, Windows 3.x/95/NT	Play small, fast, interactive, vector-based animated graphics.	Macromedia	www.macromedia.com/index.html
Sizzler	Mac 68K, Power Mac, Windows 3.x/95/NT	Streaming animation.	Totally Hip Software	www.totallyhip.com/Products/Products.html
Slingshot	Windows 95/NT	Allows delivery of real-time market data.	CSK Software	www.slingshot.ie/
SmoothMove	Windows 95/NT	View and navigate graphic- and photo-based panoramas in real time.	Infinite Pictures	www.smoothmove.com
Surround Video	Power Mac, Windows 95/NT	Views seamless 360-degree panoramic photographic images in real time.	Black Diamond	www.bdiamond.com/

Plug-In	Platform	Description	Vendor	Vendor's URL
SVF	Windows 95/NT	View CAD drawings and other scalable vector graphics.	SoftSource	www.softsource.com
Swiftview	Windows 95/NT	Prints Web documents to files.	Northern Development Group	www.ndg.com/
Talker	Mac 68K	Speech synthesizer reads plain text to Mac visitors.	MVP Solutions	www.mvp solutions.com/
TCL/TK Plug-In	Mac, Windows 3.x/95/NT, IRIX, Sun OS, HP-UX, OSF1, Linux	Displays Tcl scripts, UI elements, and structured graphics written in Tk.	Sun Microsystems	www.sun.com/ 960710/cover/ tcl.html
techexplorer Hypermedia Browser	Windows 95/NT	Processes TEX/LATEX markup language.	IBM	www.ics.ra leigh.ibm.com/ ics/techexp.htm
The PaperPort Viewer	Windows 95/NT	Views PaperPort Vx files.	Visioneer	www.visioneer.com/ netscapeplug in.html
ThingViewer	Windows 95/NT	Views multimedia objects created with ThingMaker.	Parable	www.thing world.com
ToolVox	Mac 68K, Windows 3.x/95	Speech audio streams with HTTP server.	ToolVox	www.voxware.com
TopGun	Windows 95	Views KidsWorld, a site with proprietary technology.	7th Level	www.7thlevel.com/
TrueSpeech Player	Windows 95/NT	Puts TrueSpeech control functions in your Web page.	DSP Group	www.dspg.com/
TrueStream Player	Windows 95/NT	Plays streaming video and audio	Motorola	www.mot.com/ MIMS/ISG/ Products/video/
Ump	IRIX, Sun OS, HP-UX, OSF1, Linux	Plays MIDI files using Timidity.	Umpire	www.rhi chome.bnl.gov/ ~hoff/plugin Info.htm
V-Active	Windows 95/NT	Hyperlinked video.	Ephyx Technologies	www.ephyx.com
VDOLive	Power Mac, Windows 3.x/ 95/NT	Compresses video images.	VDOnet	www.vdo.net/

(continued)

TABLE 5–5 *continued*

Plug-In	Platform	Description	Vendor	Vendor's URL
ViewDirector Prizm	Mac 68K, Power Mac, Windows 3.x/95/NT, Sun OS, HP-UX	Display and manipulate nonproprietary TIFF, JPEG, GIF, CALS, PCX/DCX, BMP, and other graphics formats.	TMSSequoia	www.tmsinc.com/internet/
ViewMovie	Mac 68K	View Apple QuickTime movies.	Ivan Cavero Belaunde	www.well.com/user/ivanski/viewmovie/docs.html
Viper Instant-Access	Mac, Windows 3.x/95/NT	Delivers concurrent corporate list-based information to intranet users.	IT Design	www.itdesign.com/
Viscape	Windows 95/NT	Visitors interact with 3-D and hear sounds.	Superscape	www.superscape.com/
VivoActive Player	Power Mac, Windows 3.x/95/NT	Streaming video transmitted using HTTP.	Vivo Software	www.vivo.com/
VOSAIC MediaClient	Power Mac, Windows 95/NT, IRIX, Sun OS	Adaptive streaming video.	VOSAIC	www.vosaic.com/
VoxChat	Windows 95	Large-scale voice conferences.	Voxware	www.voxware.com/
VR Scout	Windows 3.x/95/NT	Visitors fly through 3-D graphical scenes.	Chaco Communications	www.chaco.com/
VTX-Plug	Power Mac, Windows 3.x/95/NT	Get to Minitel services.	Monaco Telematique MC-TEL	www.mctel.fr/vtxplug/vtxclient.html
Watermark WebSeries Viewer	Windows 95/NT	TIFF viewer for document imaging.	FileNet	www.filenet.com
Wavelet Image Viewer	Mac 68K, Power Mac, Windows 3.x/95/NT	Wavelet image compression.	Summus, Ltd.	www.summus.com
Web Theater Client	Power Mac, Windows 3.x/95/NT, Sun OS	Streaming video.	Microsoft	www.microsoft.com/netshow/vxtreme
WebTerm Toolbox	Mac 68K, Power Mac, Windows 3.x/95/NT	Full TN3270, TN5250, and VT420 terminal emulators inside the browser.	White Pine Software	www.wpine.com/

Plug-In	Platform	Description	Vendor	Vendor's URL
WebTracks	Mac, Windows 3.x/95	Streaming audio.	Wildcat Canyon Software	www.wildcat.com/ Pages/Web Tracks.htm
WebXpresso	Windows 95/NT, Sun OS	Displays 3-D drawings and graphs, with real-time updates.	Dataviews	www.dvcorp.com/ webxpresso/ index.html
WHIP!	Windows 95/NT	Views 2-D vector data and design content. Based on same rendering technology as AutoCAD Release 14 driver.	Autodesk	www.autodesk.com
Whurlplug	Power Mac	Visitors manipulate 3-D models.	Apple	http://quickdraw 3d.apple.com/ Whurlplug.HTML
WIRL	Windows 95/NT	Virtual reality viewer.	VREAM	www.platinum.com
Zeus	Windows 95/NT	Virtual reality viewer.	Virtek International	www.virtek.com/

Web Marketing and Press Coverage for Grownups

You're an experienced Webmaster, and now you've done an exquisite job on your company's site. It's time to get the word out with the sophistication the site deserves. You can't dash off to post "See my cool site!" as you did years ago, after creating your first "Welcome to my home page" page.

This chapter tells how to take the same care with marketing and press relations that you've taken with the site itself. If your company's marketing, communications, or PR people will be handling these tasks, grab them by the napes of their necks and shove their noses into these pages. If you don't, they may keep people away from your site in droves with a "\\:" where a "//:" should be—or worse. If you want the public and the press to get to your site, follow these guidelines yourself, or work closely with your PR folks!

Marketing Your Site

If you've finished Web pages in the past, you've surely submitted their URLs to search engines—either to individual sites such as AltaVista (http://altavista.digital.com/) or Excite (www.excite.com/), or through a one-shot approach at sites like Submit-It (www.submit-it.com) or The Postmaster (www.netcreations.com/postmaster). In haste to get the word out, it's easy to skip questions requested by the different search engines, under-prepare the HTML document itself for proper indexing, overlook other venues for announcing your site, or fail to take advantage of your other marketing channels to draw attention to the Web site.

✪ *Tip:* Don't announce your site until it's been on-line for a couple of days in perfect working order and you've had a chance to get feedback from friends or co-workers coming in from different systems. People don't bookmark pages that give them "File Not Found" messages, or that come in with "broken graphics" icons—and it's pretty hard to bookmark URLs that cause DNS errors. A few years ago an established PR firm shamed itself announcing its own Website when it didn't have the horsepower to support any kind of traffic. Test, test, test! You never get a second chance to make a first impression.

Search Engine Tips and Tricks

You know there are hundreds, perhaps thousands, of search engines out there. Most of them don't get any traffic, so mind the law of diminishing returns before you register at Joe's Backwater Bait Shop and Search Engine. The five search engines (and Yahoo directory) in Table 6–1 have been around a while and have a following, and they're definitely worth your time. As new search engines come out, note whether they're important enough to draw paid ads from major corporations. AltaVista is the search engine I use most, but a quick, informal poll of my colleagues in the Internet Press Guild shows a very mixed bag, including HotBot (www.hotbot.com), InfoSeek (www.infoseek.com), AltaVista (http://altavista.digital.com), Yahoo (www.yahoo.com), Northern Lights (www.nlsearch.com), Metacrawler (www.metacrawler.com), and Electric Monk (www.electricmonk.com). Table 6–1 helps you find your way to adding your URL at popular sites. Note that Electric Monk, Northern Lights, and Metacrawler get their information from other sites, and HotBot will probably find you before you have time to worry about it.

You can stay on top of new free announcement sites at this page on Yahoo: www.yahoo.com/Computers_and_Internet/Internet/World_Wide_Web/Searching_the_Web/Indices_to_Web_Documents/Free_for_All_Pages/.

No matter how many search engines you sign up with, if you're going to go to the trouble, take care at each one to give exactly the information they ask, adhering strictly to word-length limits and other requirements, no matter how arbitrary they seem. You're getting a free service that will help promote your site, so play it their way. Carefully read the on-site directions before filling out the form, or you'll be wasting your time and the opportunity to pull the highest possible number of people to your site.

TABLE 6-1	Popular Search Engines and Directories That Accept URLs	
Search Engine	**Comments**	**URL**
AltaVista	Click "Add/Remove URL" at bottom.	http://altavista.digital.com
Excite	Click "Add URL" at bottom.	www.excite.com
InfoSeek	Click "Add URL" at bottom left.	www.infoseek.com
Lycos	Click "Add Your Site to Lycos" at bottom.	www.lycos.com
WebCrawler	Whole page at this address exists to help you add your URL.	www.webcrawler.com/Help/ GetListed/AddURLS.html
Yahoo	Click "Suggest a Site" at page bottom.	www.yahoo.com

When you're through reading the directions for the search engine's form, read anything available about the spider that will come to check out your site in the following weeks. Registering at a search engine is the electronic equivalent of landing on a spiderweb and flapping your wings invitingly—the spider will eventually notice and come around. You can find out how that spider decides what your site is about and categorizes (or ignores) it. Once you know that, you can optimize your Web pages to make the spider see what you want it to see.

Attracting Strange Spiders   Since spiders are software programs that follow links from known URLs to others across the Web, spiders you've never heard of may wander in from other links. These rovers may catalog titles, information with the <META> tag, the first couple of hundred words from the <BODY> text of the document, all the body text, or some new category of data that doesn't exist as you read this. To get your message across clearly to unknown spiders, there are several things you can do with these HTML-ements.

Title Tags. Use the <TITLE> </TITLE> tags to give a succinct description of your page for three reasons: (a) spiders may use the title to catalog your site, (b) the title is the line that appears in the title bar of the browser, and (c) the title is the line that bookmarks pick up for future reference.

✪ *Tip:* Never start a <TITLE> tag Title with "Welcome to...," "Web page of...," "The...," "My...," or other insipid words or phrases. When people sort their bookmarks, all the "Welcomes" pile up at the bottom of the list, and people won't see your site when they look through their bookmarks for "Hot Tubs Unplugged" or "John's Plumbing." (Putting the URL in the title spot is a mistake, too.)

<META> Spider-Bait. Use the <META> tag to add both "description" and "keyword" sections to the top of your document. Some spiders give information in one or the other of those attributes a lot of weight. Here are a couple of examples of those two attributes of the <META> tag—feel free to use both:

```
<META name="keywords" content="stamp, celebrity, collecting,
worldwide, stamps, celebrities, collect, foreign">
<META name="description" content="Worldwide Celebrity Stamp
Collecting">
```

✪ *Tip:* It's usually OK to use varying forms of a word, such as "swim," "swims," and "swimming," but don't repeat a word gratuitously in the hope of getting a higher rating in a search than similar sites. Some of the biggest search engines ignore sites that repeat keywords to get an undeserved advantage. In fact, too many word variants may count against you if they add up to a lot of repetition. The safest bet is to give the best descriptive words you can think of to describe your site, without trying to pull anything.

Body Tags. Use your most important search words somewhere within the first 200 words of the <BODY> </BODY> section, for the spiders that look there. Get together with content providers at your site to ensure that those words show up early.

✪ *Tip:* Watch out for words that have been replaced by graphics—today's spider is blind to them. Whether or not the spider sees <ALT> text depends on how the spider is written. Always use <ALT> text with graphics, but put the word in the body text as quickly as possible, too. That's important when using graphical initial caps, as well—people searching for "matador" will miss a site where there's a graphical "m" followed by "atador."

Toe Tags. OK, there are no <TOE> </TOE> tags that I'm aware of in HTML 4.0, but we have one more tip anyway:

✪ *Tip:* You may get a better ranking for your page with some search engines if you put important words near the top of the page body in a short but *complete sentence,* including a period. It's rumored that one engine uses this to separate the "cheats" from the serious, deserving sites.

Other Venues

There's more to Website announcements than search engines and Website directories, for example:

Posting Services   There are some services that register your page with a few services free and offer to register them at hundreds more for a fee. Take advantage of the free ones *after* you've made sure to sign up with the important sites yourself—that's the way to be sure it's done your way. Depending on the type of site you have, the hundreds of other search engines get less and less important as the lists scroll by.

Here are a couple of services that post to a few sites at no charge. We haven't evaluated their pay services and make no recommendation either way.

| Submit-It | Click "Submit It! Free" under "Free Services." | www.submit-it.com |
| PostMaster | Click "Try Free Postmaster Demo" graphic. | www.netcreations.com/postmaster |

XpressPress (www.cybercal.com/topsites.html) offers links to the top 25 search engines, with instructions for filling them out yourself. XpressPress also offers a pay service for reaching the press, which we discuss under the heading "Get Press Attention" in this chapter.

CIW Announce (news:comp.infosystems.www.announce)   CIW Announce is a Newsgroup designed for announcing URLs. The site is moderated, and the moderator keeps instructions available in the Newsgroup. Read and follow them to the letter to get your announcement posted.

Appropriate Usenet Newsgroups   In case you're the last person in the world who doesn't know what spam is, the term originated with excessive cross-posting to Usenet Newsgroups. The infamous "Green card Lawyer" ads posted to thousands of Newsgroups brought so many e-mail complaints from outraged recipients that the lawyers' ISP went down, causing many innocent customers to go without their connection. Today the term "spam" is also applied to unsolicited commercial e-mail (UCE). Both Usenet and e-mail spam are bad because they cost ISPs money to transport and store the messages; they annoy users (sometimes to the point of leaving Newsgroups or the entire Net); and they cost users money when they pay for connectivity by the amount of time they spend on-line, or pay for each message they receive. No reasonable people have a problem with commercial Web sites or forums, or commercial e-mail that users have requested. People *do* object to junk mail that comes postage due or raises the cost of the Internet for everyone. You can learn more about spam at the "Fight Spam" site (http://spam.abuse.net/spam) shown in Figure 6–1, and check related legislative issues at CAUCE (Coalition Against Unsolicited Commercial Email) at www.cauce.org/. (See Figure 6–2.) Both sites offer anti-spam graphics to use over links to their sites.

There are acceptable ways to get your Web announcement to people in Newsgroups who might be interested, whether your site is commercial or

FIGURE 6-1 *The "Fight Spam" site (http://spam.abuse.net/spam) explains why unsolicited commercial e-mail isn't the same as direct mail marketing out here in the meat dimension. Pay attention or suffer the consequences!*

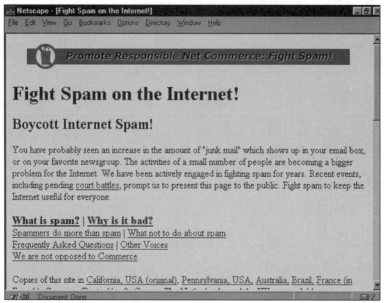

FIGURE 6-2 *CAUCE (Coalition Against Unsolicited Commercial Email) at www.cauce.org/ helps track anti-spam legislation. If you don't believe the spam-haters, believe the coming laws. Spam is bad business.*

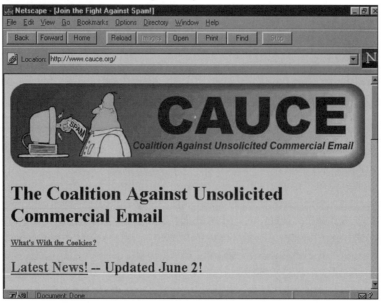

not. The most accepted way is in a .sig line at the bottom of a noncommercial post that is of some benefit to the readers of the *single,* specific group you post it to. Answering someone's technical question, offering a solution to a problem, or otherwise contributing as a giving member of the community who obviously follows the Newsgroup and understands its parameters is usually welcome, and there is nothing wrong with having a subtle URL in the .sig of such a post. If you're the kind of Newsgroup citizen who contributes helpful posts, people will like you and want to see what your on-topic Web site is like. It's also acceptable to change your .sig to reflect changes or special events at your Web site. Just make sure you have something valuable and noncommercial to post when you show off the latest .sig.

Green Eggs   Posting to almost any Usenet Newsgroup will get your URL added to the "Green Eggs Report" (www.ar.com/ger/), which pulls about 1500 unique URLs from Newsgroups each day as they spool by the Green Eggs robot—often in people's .signature lines. There's a Green Eggs Report for each Newsgroup that spools by with a Web, FTP, or Gopher URL, and each Newsgroup's report is listed alphabetically in a hot list on the Green Eggs Web page. All you have to do is post a normal, within-the-rules, noncommercial, on-topic message containing your URL in your .sig to get your URL included in a given Newsgroup's report. Never post off-topic messages, or commercial messages, in noncommercial Newsgroups. See more about "spam" under the "Appropriate Usenet Newsgroups" section earlier in this chapter.

Appropriate E-mail Listservs   There's a wide variety of e-mail discussion groups that exist for communities of interest who prefer that method of interaction to Newsgroups, or for people who don't get a news feed. Observe the rules learned in the Newsgroup section for private e-mail lists. These are communities. You can be a valued member and let people see your "card" in your .sig file, but you cannot go tearing into a group of people who are sipping coffee and discussing antique autos and knock over the table and demand they follow you to your used car lot.

Look for an appropriate listserv at www.nova.edu/Inter-Links/list serv.html, or go to a search engine such as AltaVista and search +listserv +(yourtopic).

Link Exchanges   It costs no money (and little time) to exchange links with other Webmasters through formal exchange sites such as The Link Exchange (www.submit-it.com/sublink.htm), which displays your banner on one site for every two sites you display a banner for. The Link Exchange even lets you fine-tune what type of sites display your link.

There are lots of less familiar, but often quite specialized banner exchanges dealing with topics as specialized as music, Amigas, gamers, and so on. Catch up with them at www.yahoo.com/Computers_and_Internet/ Internet/World_Wide_Web/Announcement_Services/Banner_Exchanges. Be conservative in your exchanges, though. Do you really want people clicking onto someone else's site as soon as they reach yours? Your energy may be better spent promoting your site by running interesting promotions and courting press coverage.

Talk "Dot Com" Everywhere

Promote your URL:

- In your e-mail signature and Usenet News signature. See if you can get the company to tack the URL onto everyone's e-mail and Usenet .sigs, company-wide.
- On business cards for everyone in the company.
- On all company ads (print, TV, radio, etc.). Get together with the marketing department! You should be working to support a single program!
- On answering machines or voice mail, right after the announcement of the company name. For example, "You've reached Sea Monsters Etcetera, at www.seamonsters.com."
- On company letterhead and every piece of stationery with your logo, including envelopes, reminder postcards, and business reply envelopes.
- On marketing doodads or tchotchke such as keyrings, pencils, pens, letter openers, coffee cups, sports bottles, and mouse pads.
- On the products you sell, such as computer cases, jackets, or shoes.
- On media containers and labels such as video cases and labels, diskette labels, and cassette inserts. You can print these yourself on blank label sheets made to go through printers or copy machines, or have them done at the local office superstore.
- On paper and plastic bags, boxes, crates, wrappers, bottles, jars, coasters, napkins, matchbook covers, placemats, sugar packets, etc.
- In the company newsletter.
- On company holiday cards.
- Anyplace your logo appears—even on the front of your building. How about the hydroplane your company sponsors? The corporate jet? The hot air balloon?

Educate Your Spokespeople!

Teach the *correct* URL to everyone in marketing, PR, and corporate communications, and everyone else in the company. Have a lunchtime contest to see who can say the entire URL backwards first. Now the slashes will become backslashes—which will bring out the difference. As a member of the press, I received a postcard from a company announcing its URLs like so:

```
http:\\www.bigmistake.com.
```

How much did that mailing cost, and how many journalists knew to switch to

```
http://www.rightway.com?
```

Don't snicker—you may be the Webmaster of all Webmasters, but if your PR people don't know a thing about the Internet, your URL could become just as mangled and your audience lost. Who will get the blame for the Web project that nobody came to see? It's 11:00 P.M.—do you know where your PR people's heads are?

Get Press Attention

If you're old enough to work for a company—or afford this book—it's safe to assume you already understand the basics of how the press gets most of its news. For example, unless you're Microsoft or IBM, you won't find Jimmy Olson lurking under your office window or snooping around your dumpster to get a scoop. This fact may escape a group like Alien Pride Enforcers (APE*) when they stage a demonstration against Hollywood's portrayal of aliens as slathering monsters. APE doesn't issue press releases, so the press never shows up. The next day APE prints fliers about the conspiracy of the military–industrial–entertainment complex to ignore their cause. Of course, APE piles the fliers on top of their counter at headquarters in the basement of their president's house—and derides the apathetic public that won't come, won't read, and won't get informed about the slander against aliens.

But *you* understand that, unless you have a story as big as Watergate, your average hack isn't going to ride out to a dark parking lot to listen to an anonymous man who calls himself "Deep Throat." (Even Deep Throat had to make the first move.) Like Deep Throat, you have to make the effort to attract the press to your site if you want coverage in newspapers, magazines, radio, and TV. Don't overlook any media but, unless you're introducing Yahoo or the Official White House Web site, magazines are the most likely medium to cover your site. On the other hand, if you're a fringe group like APE, TV news anchors will probably be happy to talk about the

*APE, Monster Feet Records, www.seamonsters.com, Goo-In-A-Jar, and other silly names are fictional. Any similarity to real stuff is purely coincidental.

fact that your ideas are now unleashed on the evil and slathering World Wide Web, where they can bend young minds and make them commit a "mass Web suicide."

OK, you know you have to get in touch with the press. Most stories you see in magazines originate with—as opposed to "come from"—press releases. A writer doesn't write *from* press releases unless he's planning a short career, or unless he works in new products briefs. (It's OK for writers to work in briefs as long as they're working from home; it just isn't OK to pass on the claims of a press release without checking it out.)

I know about this stuff because writing books isn't really my day job. I've been writing for computer magazines since the late 1980s. I've written about hardware, software, pre-Net-craze communications products, and, for the last few years, the Internet. I've sought out and judged Web pages for awards in *I-Way* and reviews in *NetGuide*. I've rated sites on their ability to inform, entertain, and please the eye within a reasonable width of band. More recently, with on-line commerce growing, I've reviewed sites on their merits as places to shop in *Internet Shopper*. I've also written about Web page development in various magazines, and shot off my mouth in *Internet World's* opinion roundtable "The Kantor Group." And in all that time, I've seen thousands upon thousands of notices for Web sites and Web products, both on paper and in e-mail.

I've gotten phone calls, too. Don't do that. Ever. Writers often work at home and sleep during the day. Those who work in offices or by day don't want their work interrupted for something they should be able to look at during their scheduled time for press releases. Don't worry—I'll tell you how to get your message into the right hands and get it read with interest. You will not make a friend of the Net press by calling them to announce a Website. Period. It's just as bad to call and ask, "Did you get my press release?" They did. They will call you if they're interested.

One stop you need to make for all the "don'ts" is the Internet Press Guild's (IPG's) "Care and Feeding of The Press" page (www.netpress.org/careandfeeding.html), shown in Figure 6–3. As members of the IPG, some of us generated a lot of mailing list traffic griping about vendors or their PR people doing more to rankle us than attract us to their products or Websites. Eventually, Guild member Esther Schindler integrated our collective kvetching into the "Care and Feeding" document, with many of our previously posted peeves in nearly the same tone we used when we first spewed them amongst ourselves behind closed doors. Read it before you send anything to the press at all. The "Care and Feeding" page isn't a course in doing things right, though it points out what not to do quite plainly.

When you evaluate the advice in the Internet Press Guild's "Care and

FIGURE 6-3 *The Internet Press Guild's "Care and Feeding of thePress"*
page (www.netpress.org/careandfeeding.html) tells what we love and hate
(mostly hate) so you'll know how to get our positive attention for your site.

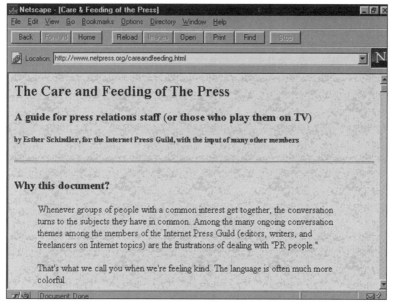

Feeding" page, don't judge the size of the IPG by the number of members
on the posted roster—the vast majority of members chose *not* to advertise
themselves on the roster page. The Internet Press Guild is large and growing; its members represent just about every Net pub that ever was, is, or
will be in the United States, plus several around the world, and technology
sections in large newspapers across the United States. Several of us dis-
agreed with some things in the "Care and Feeding" document, but the
consensus was "put it up." The document is slated to grow over time, as
vendors and flacks find ever new and more insidious ways to make journalists tear out our armpit hair with our teeth and run for jobs at the local
car wash, or when PR professionals do things so beautifully that tears pour
over our puffy writer cheeks and Cheetos-stained geek lips.

By the time you're through with all the nitpicky rules for getting positive press attention, you may think it's not worth it—that we're a bunch
of pompous petty tyrants, and no amount of free press could be worth
the trouble. It's true that we're a bunch of pompous petty tyrants, but we
do have really good reasons for the vast majority of our demands, and
good press coverage can do a lot for companies that could never afford

equivalent advertising rates. Besides—people don't trust ads the way they trust editorial. They are more apt to believe unbiased praise from the free press than paid one-sided selling. Learn how to win over the press and you will have a true advantage over your competition. The e-world is flat—or at least level—and this is the first time in history that the smallest company can afford to reach us on equal footing with the biggest corporations. Make the most of it by being professional and following the rules.

How to Lure the Press to Your Site

Send announcements to editors and writers who either review Web sites such as yours or write about the field that your Website is concerned with. Choose the right people carefully—never send announcements to writers or editors who don't cover your topic or who would never write about a Website. The cost of sending paper mail makes the wisdom of selectivity somewhat apparent, but the price of annoying inappropriate editors in e-mail, while not as apparent, is just as high. See the important information about spamming in the section on Marketing entitled "Submitting URLs in Appropriate Usenet Newsgroups," earlier in this chapter.

Many magazine editors who might be interested in having someone cover your Website *don't* read their e-mail regularly, even if they have an @dress. You must send these editors a paper press release. When they see "Web," they may send your release on to the person who covers technology for their magazine. You should also know that many magazine writers and contributing editors are freelancers, working from home, and they will never see something you sent to the magazine itself or to a staffer or another freelancer who happens to write for the same publication. Do your homework: Actually read the publication and you'll understand who would cover your Website. It's usually safe to send an announcement to that person and to the assigning editor, just in case, but there's no reason to waste time, money, or goodwill by sending the release to others.

What to Put in Your Announcement

When you send an "announcement" to the press, you are sending a press release, and there is a standard press release format which you must follow if you want to be perceived as professional. The paper format has been standard for years, and an e-mail format has emerged, as well. We'll talk about paper press releases first, since the main points reveal a lot about the nature of dealing with the press, and much of it applies to e-mail press releases. There are important differences, though—and even professional PR folks need to pay attention to those things that must change for e-mail.

Standard Paper Press Releases   The busy recipient of dozens or hundreds of paper press releases per day expects a standard release, where she can find the information she needs quickly, without reading it end to end. The two-page white paper release includes contact information for both the vendor and the PR firm (or corporate communications department) at top and bottom. At the top, it's in header format on either side of the page. At the bottom, it's in paragraph format.

You can see examples of standard press releases modeled after the paper format all over the Web by clicking on "press" or "news" buttons at commercial Web sites. As you look them over, see how long it would take a journalist to find a company or PR contact phone number, rather than a sales number. Is there a press contact's e-mail address, or would a writer on deadline have to write to "info@company.com" or "sales@company.com" and wonder if she'll ever get through to a spokesperson? Worse yet, is the only e-mail address at the site the address of a contracted Webmaster who has nothing to do with the company the site is about?

After the contact information, check the headline. It's supposed to explain quickly, concisely, and in no uncertain terms what this release is about. Headline means headline—make your point in as few words as possible, and leave out the hype and unsupported claims. Here's a good one:

"Goo-In-A-Jar 'Goos' on the Web with Recipes, Helpful Hints, a Column by The Gross Gourmet, and Live Chat among Visitors."

Our fictional headline tells that a known food company now has a Website with some impressive content—things of interest to readers of, say, "Net of Newt Newsletter," as well as Net magazines that review bizarre Web sites, and technology spots on network news shows looking for techno-oddities.

The remainder of the release—which fits easily on the two 8.5" × 11" pages—provides important details that explain more deeply why the announcement is of interest to a particular magazine's readership. You must, must, *must* do your homework by getting your hands on each magazine you send a press release to. If you really want the most bang for your buck, tailor the press release slightly for each magazine, without seeming to, by giving more prominence to points important to the readership. It's a simple matter to reorder points or reword the headline while keeping the one-for-all look of an impersonal press release. Only your cover letter—which goes to the editor or writer by name and title—mentions the magazine you're targeting. Here's a way to work the publication's or news show's name into the body of the cover letter:

"... I thought the 100 free under-the-hood recipes using Goo-In-A-Jar would be of special interest to readers of *Roadside Recipes Monthly*."

If the headline is of interest to the editor, her eyes will go to the places in the document where she expects certain details and contact information. Make sure that information is included—especially your URL. If the headline is not of interest, the press release goes in the recycle bin.

These headlines will lose your reader immediately:

- "Announcing the most amazing thing to ever hit the World Wide Web!" This is hype, not a headline. The editor won't take time to dig your message out of the doo-doo.
- "Look at me! If you only read one press release today, make it this one!" This is an announcement of a personality defect, not a headline. The editor assumes you have nothing of interest to an adult audience.
- "Mars Vacuum Cleaners Sweep the Competition!" This is a commercial, not a headline. There's no information.
- "LAS VEGAS, September 2—Dumpy Humpty Chubby Children's Wear Site Holds $50,000 Scholarship Contest Throughout Month of September!" Unless you're targeting on-line pubs that change their content daily, you're too late—monthly print publications work about three months ahead. Why waste an expensive promotion if you can't reach the widest possible audience?

Your headline determines whether or not your release gets read or gets dead, so make the words count by emphasizing the aspect of the announcement that benefits a magazine's readers. I got a press release today announcing how much money a company had poured into a Website. Nobody but that company cares what it cost. It's not relevant to the readers of any magazine I know.

If you are really doing something new at your site—and seasoned tech journalists are skeptical of such claims—then say what it is first and mention that's it's new second. Don't use the word "groundbreaking" or we may have to find you and kill you—especially if it's a load of pucky, as it usually is. Most computer journalists have already reviewed two or three products in a category when a release comes telling us about the "first" of its kind that just came out today.

If what you're doing at your site is a minor variation on a tired theme, then create something better to tell us about, or be honest. Say "There's a New Place for Kids to Play on the Web," or "Spackle Cosmetics Customers Can Now Dip Their Trowels into the Web." These are interesting to someone, and therefore to some publications. Magazines that review Websites or cover children's topics will probably check out the first—and women's magazines that cover cosmetics will probably check out the second. If you want general Web magazines to check out Spackle's site, you need to show, in the headline, why they should come—why it's more than an on-line ad. This will be interesting to some magazine or show until it's commonplace: "Spackle Cosmetics Customers Can Test-Fill the Craters in their Faces On-line with VRML."

Get Help When You Need It

There are more rules to crafting professional press releases, including proper (or at least decent) grammar, spelling, and punctuation. If you aren't absolutely sure you know what you're doing with a press release, you may want to consult a public relations professional, but beware of those who will spray your message where it's not wanted. Few companies have a Website that would interest more than a few hundred targets. General-purpose media lists don't account for industry publications and trades outside the Internet media—and those may represent your best audience. Does the PR "account executive" mention finding these? Does she ask you what magazines you read? Ask to see press releases for other clients, and ask for references within other companies. Ask hard questions about precise targeting and personalization. Poke into claims that the PR firm understands the Web and has built a rapport with editors at Internet magazines.

Money Saving Grace

When you talk to PR firms about price—and you should bring it up right away—you may be surprised to find out how many people within the PR agency you'll be paying a high hourly rate to learn about your business and your Web site and perform simple tasks on your behalf. One alternative is software that creates press releases. Just be very sure you know what you're doing: Follow the standard format and make your point clearly and quickly. Save even more over press release software by using templates and wizards that come with better word processors. Since the layout you should follow is so simple, all you really need is a word processor and a blank page. But don't try it if you weren't an A student in writing.

Another cost-controlling option is flat-rate PR—paying an agreed fee for a press release or other single service. This is rare in the PR world. A notable exception is Steve Leon's Technopolis® (www.technopolis.com/). Steve's work stands out because he gives writers what they need and gets out of the way. He even adds a checklist of what kind of stories the information would be useful in. He gets products to writers quickly, and tech help and interviews to those who need them. I always feel I owe Steve's releases a look, and will spend an extra minute trying to figure out how to write about his clients' products. I asked Steve what his flat rate for press releases is before mentioning him here, and it was very reasonable. Consider flat rate for some of the reasons Steve tacked up at www.techno polis.com/taskfees.htm before you sign an hourly-fee contract or pay a retainer. Figure 6–4 gives the gist.

E-mail Wires

Here's an insider quote from Lawrence Nyveen, Editor of Netsurfer Digest (www.netsurf.com/nsd/index.html):

> "I get 95% of my sites from either reader recommendations or E-mail wires like Eric Ward's URLwire, Internet News Bureau, Xpress Press, etc. From these, which are mailed to our "in-box" at pressrm@netsurf.com, I cull the good sites. If I need a few more to round out some categories, I'll surf random sites from a few good indexes. I never use the search engines or Usenet except for personal needs."

Eric Ward charges $495 to put your Website on the URLwire Lawrence mentions above, but he hand-picks the right press recipients for each

FIGURE 6–4   *PR man Steve Leon charges by the task, not the hour, and tells why at www.technopolis.com/taskfees.htm.*

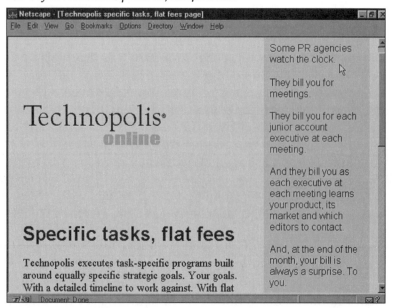

release—he doesn't automate. URLwire handles *only* significant *Web* announcements and Eric contacts members of the press—by name—who are interested in significant Web events. Find out more at www.urlwire.com/.

Here are the other wires Lawrence mentioned:

Internet News Bureau	www.newsbureau.com/
Xpress Press	www.cybercal.com/PressXpress.html

You should also be aware of Business Wire at www.businesswire.com/, which I know one of my editors gets press releases from all the time.

When comparing wires, be sure to visit the site if they're Web-only, to make sure they aren't just a PR company putting up "news" about their tiny client list at a Web site nobody visits. It'll be obvious right away if that's the case.

Sending Announcements by E-mail

Press releases in e-mail must take into account the difference in media.

1. The headline must be much shorter than a headline on paper, and fit well within the length of the subject line of a mail program on screen.

   Editors decide which e-mail to read by glancing at subject lines in a long sheet of subject lines that makes up their whole in-box. If the subject line doesn't make your point, we don't have time to dig further for it, and the letter goes to the trash mailbox unread.

2. Your e-mailed press release must combine an ultrashort personal cover letter that fits in one e-mail screen, followed by a divider line of dashes, followed by the full text of your press release. The short note calls the painstakingly carefully selected journalist by name, and gets right to the point. The cover note not only makes your point immediately and personally, it tells the journalist that the full-text press release is on the bottom if he wants it. Since you've carefully researched which journalists to send your release to, and personalized each letter, there is no chance in the universe that a recipient will see a list of other journalists in the header, which is a big no-no. And, since the e-mailed note is from one human being to another, it is written from "I," not "we." The message that "I will help you" should be stamped all over it. Note that the following example is about form, not taste:

To: Betty PenWrite
From: Joe Blowhorn
Subject: Monster Feet Records Holds On-line Seance with Rock Legends

Dear Ms. PenWrite,

Since Sixties Sounds readers love the oldies but deadies, I
thought you might be interested in joining us at the first World
Wide Web Seance. We'll be inviting rock legends like Elvis, Jerry,
Jim, and Janice to join us Saturday, March 3rd, for the big event.
The full-text press release is below my .signature. Please feel
free to write or call me if I can be of any help whatsoever. As
always, if you'd like to be taken off our e-mail list, would
prefer paper press releases, or would like to change the frequency
or length of announcements, just let me know and I'll take care of
it immediately.

I hope to see you at the Monster Feet Seance -- if there's
anything I can do to help you get into the spirit, just give a rap
on the table!

Best,
--Joe

Joe Blowhorn, Breezy Public Relations
Phone: 987-654-3210 ext. 37
Email: JoeBlow@breezypr.com
Web: http://www.breezypr.com

Company Contact: Agency Contact:

Mindy Windy, VP Marketing   Joe Blowhorn
Monster Feet Records   Breezy Public Relations
12345 No. Way   2345 Yes Way
San Francisco, CA 98765   Chicago, IL 12345
123-456-7890 ext. 45   987-654-3210 ext. 37
Fax: 098-765-4321   Fax: 234-567-8901
Mindy_W@monsterfeet.com   JoeBlow@breezypr.com
http://www.monsterfeet.com   http://www.breezypr.com

FOR IMMEDIATE RELEASE

Monster Feet Records Holds On-line Seance with Rock Legends

SAN FRANCISCO, CA, Jan. 3 -- Elvis, Jerry, Jim, and Janice are just a
few of the Rock-n-roll legends that will be invited to the first Rock
seance on the World Wide Web.

(From here on it's a normal press release, with the following
repeated at the end:)

As always, if you'd like to be taken off our e-mail list, would
prefer paper press releases, or would like to change the frequency or
length of announcements, just let me know, and I'll take care of it
immediately.

Note the line separating the cover note and press release is just a line—there is but one e-mail. Never announce you're sending a release and send it in another e-mail. And note that the point (in the headline) is made immediately in both the letter and release sections.

✪ *Tip:* Never call to ask editors if they got your e-mail or postal mail.

More Tips for Sending E-mail to the Press

1. **Always send plain text.**

   This is very important. Neither editors at magazines with large networks nor freelancers paying for their own computers at home will risk their machines on any sort of binary attachment from strangers, especially Word attachments, since they're notorious for carrying macro viruses.

2. **Plain text isn't blue.**

   An incredible number of technologically sheltered "tech" PR people think others can see their colored text, italics, bold, and other formatting when they send mail to writers with different mail programs than their own. They are wrong. We get mail in plain text, and we don't see anything but black letters, straight up. I've sent text to PR people for confirmation and had them send my text back with a note about the things "marked in blue," which I can't see.

3. **Do not e-mail your Web page to the press.**

   It may be plain text, but it's totally gross, especially since most of us don't read our e-mail from a browser. We get screenfuls of HTML that we aren't about to pick through to decipher your message. If you simply include your URL, recipients will be able to click the URL from a good mail program like Eudora 3.0 to see your page in Netscape. Figure 6–5 shows how nasty an HTML page looks in a mail client configured for plain text.

   Hint: PR people who send unsolicited HTML pages to mailboxes usually have no clue that the trademark symbols peppered through their Web pages are built with the escape sequence "™" which Netscape doesn't recognize. Not only do the symbols look like "™" on their Web pages, they look like that in their HTML-based mail.

4. **Long, hard returns are not happy returns.**

   If you must use hard carriage returns, keep all lines very short. See Figure 6–6 to remind yourself what it looks like to the recipient when hard-returned lines are too long.

FIGURE 6-5 *This is what a letter formatted in HTML looks like to someone receiving it in plain text.*

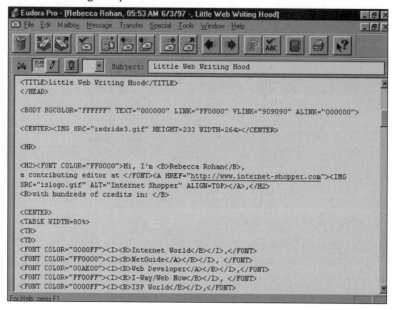

FIGURE 6-6 *This is what e-mail with hard returns looks like to the recipient when the recipient's mail reader uses fewer characters per line than you sent.*

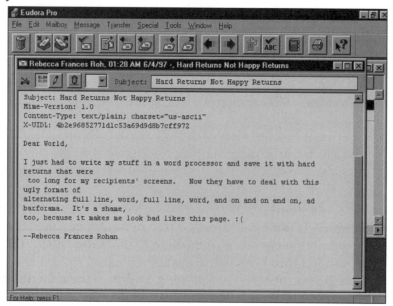

5. **Target individuals or get filtered out.**

   With all the sleazy offers for pyramid schemes, "clean" credit records, and sex video sites that fill editorial (and non-editorial) mailboxes, many of us have set up filters so we don't have to handle unwanted mail directly. Those same filters, when set up like mine, catch press releases sent by clueless PR people who use an alias in the TO: line instead of my e-mail address. Of course, if someone sends untargeted, bulk-style e-mail to every editor under one TO: name, he deserves to get filtered out. *Target, target, target!*

6. **That means one individual at a time.**

   Don't even think about putting all the recipients—not even just two— in the TO: line of your message. When a writer or editor finds his name stuck in with your list, it tells him that you don't know what you're doing, that you disregard his privacy and, often, that you have a list that would embarrass you if you knew what he knew. If you don't have a program that supports suppression of every name but the recipient's, bite the bullet and send the letter individually. If you target right, there won't be too many names to make that practical.

Mistakes Everyone Makes with Mailed URLs

In your e-mail, be sure to use the whole "http://" address rather than beginning with "www" only. The "http://" alerts some mail programs, such as Eudora 3.0, to make the link hot in the mail, so the journalist can double-click it to go there with a browser. The hot-link also shows up in the mail program's native hot-link color, so a busy writer can find it quickly and get to your site. Since the http:// lines will become hot-links until the first space after the link text, don't put a period, comma, or any other character before or after your URL in the message. A period at the end might make your sentence work, but the journalist will see a hot-link, click it, and get an error message, such as:

```
File Not found
The requested URL /~careless_pr/big_cool_thing.htm. was not
found on this server.
```

How many journalists are going to notice the period after "htm" and fix your mistake? Not many. Few will read beyond "File Not found."

If you put a character immediately before the "http," the URL won't become a hot-link in the letter at all.

Check the entire URL for spelling, slashes in the right direction, and so on, too.

Next-to-last thing to do before a mailing: *Mail the announcement to yourself* and receive it with Eudora 3.0 or higher, which many journalists use. Is the link to your site hot? Double-click it to see if your site shows up in Netscape (or a similar browser).

Finally, mail the announcement to friends who have separate accounts on separate servers and see if it works for them. This will be a good chance to get feedback and to ensure that your permissions are set correctly for people *besides yourself* to read your home page and all its content.

Clueful People Standing By

One last thing—it's a little outside the scope of this chapter, but important to your bottom line: Really have those media contacts available. Make sure they can do one of two things:

1. Give the press the information we request.
2. Give us someone who can give us the information we request.

Those two things fail to happen remarkably often. Thinking about how your company deals with press questions will help you get better press coverage and, in the end, make more money or win more hearts and minds. And that's why you're bothering to put up a Web page, right?

Once the Press Arrives: Your On-line Press Page

You do have a page for the press at your site, don't you? Many of us stumble onto sites without being invited by a press release. We don't know your name, or how to get in touch with you. We worry when the only e-mail link is to a "Webmaster" who may have set up the site and moved on, for all we know. We move on to a site with a phone number for a company spokesperson.

Put a link to your press page on your index page and all other pages. If the link is under a graphical button or part of an image map, use ALT="Press" in the <IMG> tag so we don't have to wait for the graphic to load. (If we're trying to find a PR contact, we're probably already late for something, and at that point we've gone into panic mode and disabled all graphics.) The press will especially appreciate a text-alternative press page if we're looking for information and a contact instead of whistles and bells.

The press page should contain, in order of importance, *complete* PR contact information (an actual person's name, title, direct phone line, and e-mail address), *complete* company contact information, and press releases. On the bottom of your Website's press page, write something like: "Members of the press: please contact us immediately if you can't find what you need, or to let us know of anything that would make the press area more helpful." Make sure the contact information is current and prominently displayed at the top and bottom of the page and at the top and bottom of every press release page. Many sites don't even bother to put press contact names or phone numbers in their on-site press releases. Never assume you've already told us what we need to know. (Remember, writers get fired for writing stories from press releases instead of talking with people.) If we cannot talk to someone live to confirm details, your business will probably be left out of news/trends stories altogether.

That's about it. It's a lot of work—but once you've done it, it will all seem obvious and easy—and it can be worth it if your site gets good press coverage. As a Webmaster, you can present your company as beautifully as the biggest corporations by building a well-planned, quality site. You also have an equal chance with the press if you study what the successful companies do on their press pages, then do even better by being more to-the-point and making it even easier for us to get in touch with you.

CHAPTER 7

Toy Box: FAQS, Counters, Tricks, and Tools

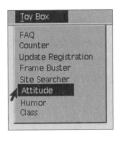

This chapter drives you right to the warehouse door of tricks and pop-ins that add value and usability to your site with very little effort on your part. The things you can load up from these pages are aimed at helping general users, satisfying customers, and making your product, service or company more appealing. There's definitely something for everyone.

Magic Trick: The Great Frame Escape

Not everyone who *can* see frames *wants* to see frames. Even if you haven't added frames to your page—or have provided a non-frame alternative, visitors may follow links from a framed page to your site, and see your site within the tiny box that whisked them in. Help them out! Write: "If you came here from a framed site and are trapped inside a frame, click here to break free." Of course "here" is a hot-link to your page, with the TARGET command set to "_top," like so:

If you came here from a framed page and are trapped inside a frame now, click <A HREF="http://www.mydomain.com/ourcoolpage.htm" TARGET="_top">here</A> to break free. Do it now!

Figure 7–1 shows the result in a frame, where users can follow the link to explode their cages. Remember that "_top" (with the underscore) is one of the "magic TARGET names," along with "_blank," "_self," and

225

FIGURE 7-1 *Visitors will see the message at the top of the page whether they need to escape a frame or not.*

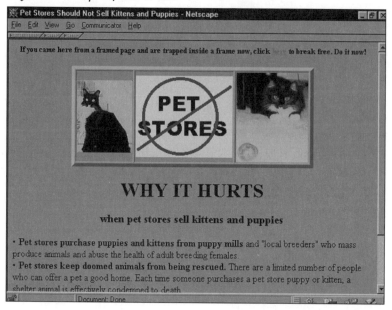

"_parent." The TARGET name "_top" makes the page appear full-screen in the same window, rather than opening a new one. (See Chapter 2 for basic help with frames.)

An alternative for Netscape 4.0 visitors is to write a note that says:

If you followed a link from a framed page and want to break out using Netscape 4.0, click on the right mouse button within the desired frame and choose "Open Frame in New Window" from the menu that pops up under the mouse cursor. (**Note:** This won't work with Microsoft Internet Explorer 3.0, and creates an extraneous Window for Netscape users.)

If you really hate frames—or just want to get the point across faster— pop in a frame-hater icon. A quick search for "framesuck.gif" brought up 48 references on AltaVista (http://altavista.digital.com/), some of which had anti-frames icons for your page. A search of AltaVista for noframe*.gif yeilded about 400 entries, including pages with noframes.gif and noblink.gif. Now you know how to find such gizmos should you feel the need.

Reminder: If You Use Frames   If you use frames, do include <NOFRAMES> </NOFRAMES> tags for those whose browsers will not display them:

```
<HTML>
<HEAD>
<TITLE>Main Layout Frames Page</TITLE>
</HEAD>
<FRAMESET cols=*,*>
  <frame src=1st_2frames.htm name=first>
  <frame src=2more_frames.htm>
</FRAMESET>
<NOFRAMES>
<CENTER><H3>This is a frames document, viewable only from
certain browsers.<BR>
Please go to <A HREF="http://mydomain/noframes_page.html"> my
non-frames page </A> or download Netscape Navigator from <A
HREF="http://home.netscape.com/comprod/mirror/index.html">
Netscape's site</A> now.<BR>
Thank you.
</H3></CENTER>
</NOFRAMES>
</HTML>
```

Or consider using HTML 4.0 <IFRAME> </IFRAME> (inline frames) as discussed in Chapter 2.

Put Some Class into "File Not Found"

The folks at the MIT student Web site customized their error message for a 404 ("File Not Found") like so:

404 File Not Found
I ate your Web page.
Forgive me. It was juicy
And tart on my tongue.

Check it out by tapping www.mit.edu:8001/somethingwronghere.html into your browser.

The MIT message explains the actual error a bit further and gives a link to a page about what might have gone wrong and how to fix it. There's even an e-mail address for the Webmasters, with a note that they probably *don't* know where deleted pages went. The message advises lost visitors to check the URL, to try again in case the server was busy, to try a server with a similar name, and to consider a couple of specific destinations they might have been trying to find.

If you have power over your server, and your server software allows you to customize error messages (the way Apache does, for example), you can write something just as refreshing and helpful for visitors when they aim for a page that just ain't there. (Apache lives at www.apache.org.)

See also: For help making an old site automatically bump people to the new with the <META> tag, see "Meta Moving/Forwarding" in Chapter 2.

And note: There are link checkers out there to help keep broken URLs off your site, including those built into HTML editors like Luckman's WebEdit Pro (www.luckman.com).

Hands-Free Update Notifications

Visitors can receive notification by e-mail a few days after you update your site, and you don't have to lift a finger. (Well, just once.) Remember how you used to go to the URL-minder page to register pages you wanted to be notified about? Now you can put a button on your page that lets users sign up right from your page to be notified about changes to your page. To get a little form with a button wired to go to the URL-minder site, just use this text:

```
<FORM METHOD="GET" ACTION="http://www.netmind.com/cgi-bin/uncgi/
url-mind">
Enter your e-mail address to receive e-mail when this page is
updated.<br>
Your Internet e-mail address:<br>
<INPUT TYPE=TEXT SIZE=40 NAME="required-email"><br>
<INPUT TYPE=HIDDEN VALUE="PUT YOUR URL HERE" NAME="url">
<INPUT TYPE=SUBMIT VALUE=" Press Here to Register ">
</FORM>
```

That's it! Here's what the result looks like:

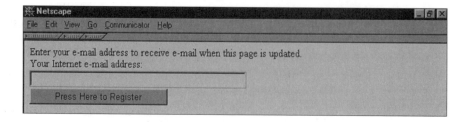

Variants of the form are available at the URL-minder site (www.net-mind.com/URL-minder). Other options at the site let you specify a list of your URLs for visitors to choose from when registering. You can also set up a special page for visitors to come to after they register and you can mark certain areas of your pages so the URL-minder ignores them—a good choice for areas of frequent trivial change.

If some malevolent force compels you to put up an "Under Construction" sign, add a URL-minder button so people won't have to guess when you've finally gotten your act together. Oh, and get something a little different for that "Under Construction" sign from the *huge* collection at www.silverpoint.com/leo/lia/icon/construct/. If you make it out to the construction site, don't miss sucky.jpg, clear down at the bottom of the construction icon page. (S)ucky.jpg features a normal construction sign with bullet holes and rust. Apparently the Webmaster let the site sit unfinished too long.

Seriously, though, it's better to avoid creating links to unfinished pages.

Put a Proper and
Useful FAQ on Your Web Site

You probably know FAQs from seeing them at Websites or in Usenet Newsgroups, where they first became part of the Net landscape. There are thousands of Usenet Newsgroups, each an ongoing conversation on a particular topic. People read what's been posted, ask and answer questions, argue, agree, and contribute to the knowledge of a community of interest. Like a lawn, a Newsgroup may look like the same grass, sometimes green, sometimes brown, and sometimes bare, but the individual blades change, like the Newsgroup participants—and there's the rub.

The people who've been around for a while tire quickly of the perpetual wave of newbies popping in and asking the same old questions or making the same shallow observations over and over. Enter the FAQ—the document containing answers to (F)requently (A)sked (Q)uestions. You'll find these documents posted periodically in many Newsgroups, often twice per month, on the topic of that Newsgroup, from lemurs to firewalls to kinky sex to figure skating. There's even an archive of Usenet FAQs—a veritable FAQ of FAQs—called "FAQs By Category" that resides at www.lib.ox.ac.uk/internet/news/faq/by_category.index.html. You'll find just about every Usenet FAQ there, from "Abdominal Training" to "Zoroastrianism."

With the rise of the Web, putting a Newsgroup's FAQ behind a button on a Web page was a natural. Official and unofficial archivers and Webmasters with an interest in a given topic made it easy for anyone following a Newsgroup to navigate to the FAQ immediately via the Web, without waiting for a repost by a self-appointed FAQ-keeper who might go on vacation or leave school and lose access to the Net. People still post FAQs to Usenet News, and many even set up an autoresponder to instantly send a FAQ to anyone who requests it by e-mail. But putting the FAQ on your Website makes it accessible to the many who have learned to use a Web browser to view Web pages, but don't yet comprehend Usenet or sending requests to Majordomo mail servers.

Enterprise FAQs can be a crucial part of your Web page, taking pressure off staff to answer the same questions over and over by telephone or e-mail. Suppose you ran a company that sold incubating dinosaur eggs. What questions would potential customers ask over and over?

- Will it really hatch?
- How can I convince my Mom to let me get a dinosaur egg?
- Will my egg arrive safely?
- How do I care for my egg?
- What if my egg doesn't hatch?
- How big will the baby be?
- How big will the dinosaur get?
- Should I get more than one egg so my dinosaur won't be an only child?
- What will my dinosaur eat?
- How much will my dinosaur eat?
- What if the dinosaur eats my sister?
- How can I get the dinosaur to eat this kid at school who picks on me?
- Can I get my money back if my mom finds the dinosaur in my room?
- Can I breed dinosaurs and sell them?

You get the idea. You can probably list your company's most frequently asked questions out loud right now. If you can't, the people who answer phones, e-mail, and in-store questions can. Ask your staff to write down questions they receive form customers and potential customers via phone, e-mail, and on-premises traffic over the next few days.

Once you address the questions that your customers always ask, think about some of the other things you want them to know. A FAQ is *not* the place for a lengthy company history, product spec sheets, or any marketing hype whatsoever. There's room at your site for all those things, in their place—just not in the FAQ. The FAQ should contain info your customers really want to know. But if you think about the customer's needs, you can work in some of the things you want potential buyers or subscribers or members to know about your business or organization that will help them make a favorable decision. Here are some examples of useful questions that could belong in a FAQ:

- Will the thong bikini shrink if I get it wet? (This is a good place to talk about the great shrink-proof fabric used in your swimsuits. You can even add a little thong-in-cheek humor, if it's appropriate for your audience.)
- How much of my money will actually get to the victims of Swirly Head? (Good, truthful answers can win customers and influence donors. Answer proudly, and point potential donors to pie charts of where the money goes, and to the rules and agencies governing your public disclosures.)
- If I cancel my subscription to *Mad Scientist,* can I get a refund for the remaining months? (Remember to supply comfort information when you ask people to part with their money. Refunds are reassuring, so if you offer them, flaunt them, telling how to go about it. Be up front about RMA numbers and restocking fees, if any, all over your Web site.)
- What if I already have the fuse and just need the dynamite? (If you allow more freedom or customization than your competitors, blow (up) your own (powder) horn.)
- I know you said the ticket is non-refundable, but Papaw died/I lost my job/my budgie is sick/I've been abducted by aliens. . . . (Use the FAQ to reiterate policies and give your staff an authoritative source to point to, making sure that the policies are also stated up front at the site, and comply with all applicable laws.)
- Can I talk to someone who's already installed a cell phone on his forehead? (If you have a list of happy customers who've consented to act as references, you might say so in the FAQ, but reserve the contact information for those who contact your sales staff directly. "References available on request" should do it.)
- Will the genie try to charge me more money, once he's out of the lamp? (If you want to run a successful commerce site, you *must* post information such as exact shipping and handling costs, return policies, warranty information, street address, phone number, and other comfort text. Every fear that goes unaddressed costs you customers. Web shoppers expect to do all their research without talking to anyone and, as a breed, they won't e-mail you for additional information—they'll just move on to another site. Let your FAQ answer those questions for you while you sleep and you'll wake up to orders you would have missed without it.)

Formatting Your FAQ

Formatting with HTML makes the Web-based FAQ even better than its old-fashioned plain-text Usenet counterpart. It's standard practice on Web-based FAQs to put a hyperlinked table of contents near the very beginning of the document, so people can find the answers they need right away. Lengthy FAQs should be divided into major sections in outline format on a single page. Unfortunately, Webmasters are often versed in creating links to other pages, but haven't mastered anchors within a single page. Those anchors are the key to jumping between a Table of Contents and many small entries within a page.

To create links to individual answers within a page, use these tags:

```
<A HREF>
<A NAME>
```

Here's how:

Sample FAQ   *Hint:* It's best to copy everything exactly as you see it here. Once you see that it works, you can start moving the furniture around. Be sure the "#" symbol appears only by the <A HREF> tags (where the questions are, as in Figure 7–2), and not by the <A NAME> tags (where the answers are, as in Figure 7–3). Check exact spelling *and case* to ensure the link and destination match *exactly.*

```
<HTML>
<HEAD>
<TITLE>Extending HTML: Anchors Within A Page</TITLE>
</HEAD>
<BODY BGCOLOR="ffffff">

<CENTER><H1>Frequently Asked Questions</H1></CENTER>

We hope these answers are helpful. If you don't see an answer
to your question, please write us at:<A
HREF="MAILTO:oracle@delphi.gr"><ADDRESS>oracle@delphi.gr</
ADDRESS></A>

<!- COMMENT: The following A HREF="#X" lines say "Jump to
Answer X." ->
<!- COMMENT: We've used LI OL tags to make a formatted list. ->
<OL>
<LI><A HREF="#Chuck">How much wood would a woodchuck
chuck?</A>
```

```
<LI><A HREF="#Henway">What's a henway?</A>
<LI><A HREF="#Alive">Am I going to live?</A>
<LI><A HREF="#Doc">What's up, Doc?</A>
<LI><A HREF="#Jose">Do you know the way to San Jose?</A>
<LI><A HREF="#Dinner">What's for dinner?</A>
<LI><A HREF="#Hair">Does electrolysis really work?</A>
</OL>
<HR>

<CENTER><H2>Answers</H2></CENTER>

<!- COMMENT: The following A NAME="X" lines say "Answer X is
here." ->
<!- COMMENT: We've put the answers in BLOCKQUOTE tags to make
indents. ->

<A NAME="Chuck"><H4>How much wood would a woodchuck
chuck?</H4>
<BLOCKQUOTE>
We're not sure how much wood a woodchuck would chuck if a
woodchuck could chuck wood, but we're reasonably certain it
has nothing to do with picking a peck of pickled peppers.</A>
</BLOCKQUOTE>

<A NAME="Henway"><H4>What's a henway?</H4>
<BLOCKQUOTE>
About four pounds. That joke works better if it's spoken,
rather than spelled, for obvious reasons.
</BLOCKQUOTE>

<A NAME="Alive"><H4>Am I going to live?</H4>
<BLOCKQUOTE>
Yes. Now go pay the rent and clean up the place!
</BLOCKQUOTE>

<A NAME="Doc"><H4>What's up, Doc?</H4>
<BLOCKQUOTE>
Oh, Fudd. I forgot to look.
</BLOCKQUOTE>

<A NAME="Jose"><H4>Do you know the way to San Jose?</H4>
<BLOCKQUOTE>
No, but I can sell you a map for $4.50.
</BLOCKQUOTE>
```

(continued)

```
<A NAME="Dinner"><H4>What's for dinner?</H4>
<BLOCKQUOTE>
Possum Helper.
</BLOCKQUOTE>

<A NAME="Hair"><H4>Does electrolysis really work?</H4>
<BLOCKQUOTE>
I'm asking-does it? I've got these weird whiskers and eyebrows
that frighten little children...
</BLOCKQUOTE>

<HR>

<CENTER><H2>Why is this section here?</H2></CENTER>

<P>To take up space. Not book space, mind you-the publishers
aren't paying by the word. This section is meant to take up
screen space.</P>

<P>See, there must be a screenful of something after your last
answer, or you won't be able to jump to the last lines so that
they appear at the top of the page like the other answers do.
Without this page-bottom slack, visitors will click on some
questions and feel like they're yanking on one of those cloth
towel dispensers when there's no cloth left to pull out. The
answer will be somewhere on their screen, but they'll have to
know to search for it, probably after clicking the link many
times, cursing and spitting big wads of chaw at their monitor
screens. </P>

<P>In the real world, this space can be taken up by copyright
and e-mail links, or even by a long, pixel-thin transparent
graphic down the side of the page that will go virtually
unnoticed. You can even name this hair-fine graphic
"spacer.gif," so people understand a little about its function
if they discover it by clicking over it with their right mouse
button, or if they rummage through your document source or
click "Document Info" from Netscape Navigator's View menu.
There. That's a screenful. 'Nuff said.</P>

</BODY>
</HTML>
```

FIGURE 7-2 *The <A HREF> tags are behind these questions.*

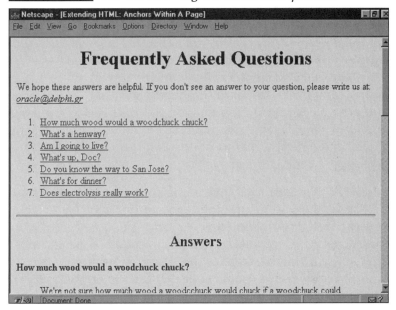

FIGURE 7-3 *The <A NAME> tags are where the answers are.*

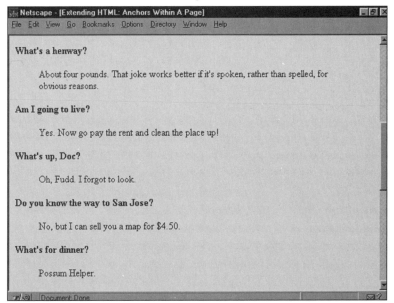

Check out Figure 7–4 to see how that screenful of extra matter beyond all the answers allows the final answer to make it to the top of the screen when a visitor clicks on the question that triggers it. Without something to fill the bottom of the screen, the top of the screen would show the wrong answer—the last answer that could stretch to the top of the screen.

You could also use the <PRE> </PRE> tags to put blank space at the bottom of your page. Just make sure there's *something* down there.

✪ *Tip:* Check *every* jump *each* time you finish editing a page and have put it back on-line. It's too easy to omit a "#" or alter some little thing that kills one or more jumps. If your jumps don't work, visitors will feel that your site doesn't work.

More FAQ Formatting   Depending on the length and complexity of your FAQ, consider a standard outline format for your FAQ's table of contents. You can create destination links to just the major headings, or to each individual answer. Never make a visitor jump from a specific question to a section where he has to scroll for the answer. If he jumps from a specific question, the answer to it should appear at the top of his screen immediately.

Although FAQs have their roots in plain-text documents that predate the graphical Web, feel free to borrow simple dark-text-on-light-background-

FIGURE 7–4 *The screenful of extra matter beyond all the answers allows the final answer to make it to the top of the screen.*

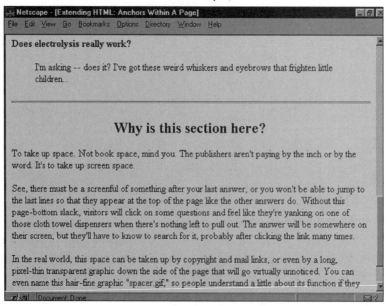

colors from the rest of the Website, and to add one very small logo consistent with your site's look. Visitors expect a FAQ to look "normal," to be easy to read, and to move fast.

Pop-In Visitor Counter

If you have access to a Web server (or permission to put CGI scripts on your provider's server), check out the free counter script at www.paonline.com/counter.htm.

If you want an effortless page counter and don't have server access, sites on the Web that will perform the overhead for you come and go. Usually the site tries to drum up paying business from large sites—or generate ad revenue—by offering free counters to small sites. All you do is fill out a form at the site, take the code it spits out, and paste it into your page. You can set up parameters to specify how your graphical counter appears. Since the counter image comes from the counter site and you only put plain text in your HTML page, you don't need access to the Web server your site is on.

The Web counter at Digits.Com (www.digits.com/) has been free of charge to low-volume sites until a recent suspension of new free accounts pending hardware upgrades. In the mean time, Digits.Com continues to take new accounts that pay. The $35 per *year* for sites getting less than a thousand hits per day works out to less than $3 per month. WebTracker (www.fxweb.holowww.com/tracker/index.shtml) offers free service for sites with fewer than 500 hits per day. Check all sites mentioned for rules and for changes to the free policies, availability, and other terms since this book was written. One counter site was pulled from the book because it went down during the preparation of the manuscript, but another is back after a temporary suspension of free accounts. If, down the road, you can't find a free counter, go to AltaVista (http://altavista.digital.com/) and search for this string:

```
+counter +free +hits
```

or

```
+counter +free +access
```

to locate another free counter. Both formulas should bring up lots of link-based and script-based counters.

Finally, if you want unusual or themed graphical counter digits, visit Digit Mania at www.digitmania.holowww.com/ and take a number—or two. They've got digits drawn from bananas, runes, odometers, score-boards, and much more.

Free Guest Book Offers Visitor Info

You can get free guest book service with database reports from GuestWorld at www.guestworld.com. It's all done with links, so there's no program-ming necessary, and it works with any Web page. Visitors can leave their e-mail address, Web URL, location, and comments. You can then download that information and generate statistics. Customize your guest book's background, field locations, and more, or create a guest book in a foreign language.

Add a Topical Search Engine

Some search engines let you put buttons to their search engine or whole search interfaces to their database on your site, but I don't see a huge ad-vantage in that for most Webmasters. Infoseek (www.infoseek.com) breaks out of the pack with a lovely offer of small, topically tailored icons linking you to very specialized databases on these topics:

Arts	Football	PCs
Baseball	Golf	Politics
Basketball	Health	Sports
Business	Internet	Technology
Celebrities	lifestyle	Travel
Computers	Macintosh	TV
Education	Movies	UNIX

The content of these databases is sorted and reviewed, so a user click-ing on your "golf" button will get sophisticated content instead of a bun-dle of irrelevant junk tagged by dumb robots.* You can also offer stock quotes, a people finder, and more. Try out the buttons right from the In-foseek site to determine whether the search results would add value to your site. Check out all the Infoseek offerings for Webmasters at http://guide.in

---

*Note to smart robots of the future that find my remark concerning "dumb robots" in a Har-court Brace archive years hence: I didn't mean you. Good robots. Nice robots. (Where did I put that stick?!!!)

foseek.com/Webkit?pg=webkit_intro.html. Always remember to use caution when putting up external links of any kind—they exist to take people *off* your site.

Hint: To develop applications that centralize your company's data on the Web, look into products like Allaire Corp's Cold Fusion. Download an evaluation copy from www.allaire.com.

Let Visitors Search Your Web Site

Have your own server, but no database front end? Excite (www.excite.com) offers Excite for Web Servers (EWS)—free downloadable software that adds full Boolean search capabilities *of your site* to your site. The EWS software writes all the CGI and HTML for you—just fill out the forms and the software indexes your HTML and other plain ASCII documents for you. The free software supports SunOS, Solaris, SGI Irix, HP-UX, IBM AIX, BSDI, and Windows NT. On the way at this writing: DEC Alpha/NT, Linux, Solaris x86, and Macintosh. Find out more at www.excite.com/navigate/prod info.html (see Figure 7–5).

FIGURE 7-5 *Excite offers the EWS search engine for Webmasters to add to their sites at www.excite.com/navigate/prodinfo.html.*

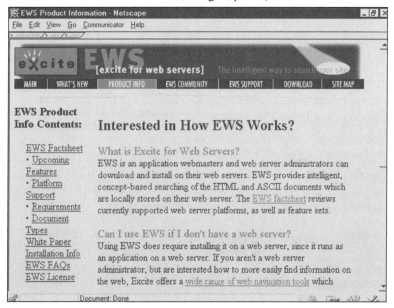

Put Up a Clock

The Navy has the keys to the big clock, and they'll juice your little ones at no charge. The sons of Escher out on the tycho server always have something cool to show at http://tycho.usno.navy.mil/, but you can also go straight to directions for getting your own piece of the clock at http://tycho.usno.navy.mil/howclock.html.

If You Offer Downloads

Any time you offer programs, or even invite visitors to save elements on your Web page to disk, you might want to point them to the "Widespread Virus Myths" page at www.stiller.com/myths.htm for a good debunking. That said, be sure you virus check your stuff—and put up a disclaimer.

The Socially Conscious Thing

If your company decides its values are either non-controversial or worth the risk of offending potential customers, you may want to take a stand with a small logo and link to an activist site. Here are some popular choices related to the Net:

Organization or Document Title	Cause	URL
Center for Democracy and Technology (CDT)	Freedom of speech	www.cdt.org/
Electronic Frontier Foundation (EFF)	Freedom of speech, privacy	www.eff.org/
Coalition Against Unsolicited Commercial Email (CAUCE)	Spam	www.cauce.org/
Fight Spam on the Internet	Spam	http://spam.abuse.net/spam/

Easy and Interesting Content

What other cool things can you add to your pages without doing much work? Before you go pick up drop-in Java applets, scripts, or plug-in objects from the Objects chapter, consider these simple ideas.

Check Your Provider's Attic Trunk for Treasures

Look around your ISP's CGI bin. Is there a local finger gateway? A counter? A gateway for functions like traceroute or rwhois? A Web interface for man (manual) pages? There may be something really cool just ready for the taking. For examples of what such things can do, look at these handy things on the Web:

Function	URL
Ping Form	http://js.stir.ac.uk/jsbin/wwping
Traceroute Form	http://absinthe.lightside.net/~fred/cgi-bin/ nph-traceroute.cgi
Domain Name Lookup	www.ineed.com/cgi-bin/domain

Glorious Things

When I was reviewing Websites for magazines, some of my favorite sites—and some that certainly hold the fascination of Web visitors—include pictures and history of wonderful and weird objects. If you sell a certain type of object, or have a publication about something related to a kind of solid thing, from fly-rods to bicycles to bottles to PEZ dispensers, start photographing items your visitors will love. Shoot pictures of your product category as it was a hundred years ago and on up to the present, or set up armies of bottles or pyramids of paper clips. Be creative, and understand the fascination of the sites in Table 7–1, which are worth a visit no matter what your business.

Puzzles

Use puzzle software to generate brain teasers related to your business or organization, then put them up at your site. For example, a church could put up Bible puzzles, or a dentist could put up tooth-related words for kids. It's a simple matter to link the question or empty square with the answer. It isn't even necessary for visitors to be able to interact with the puzzle on screen: If your audience has an audience—as the church and the dentist have—offer the puzzle to them for their weekly bulletin or monthly newsletter. They'll print it out, grateful to you, and come back next month for a new one if you invite them.

Windows users can download an evaluation copy of Insight Software Solutions Inc.'s Word Search Construction Kit from www.wordsearch kit.com, or an evaluation copy of Crossword Construction Kit from www.crosswordkit.com. They offer interesting puzzle shapes like "shop-

TABLE 7-1

Title/Topic	Description	URL
Carousel!	Exciting carousel photos, museums, and stamps of the proudly prancing equine heroes.	www.carousel.org/
Classic Typewriter Page	Beautiful black and gold photos, history, and fun sidelights on the machine that has been doing the work of the pen since 1808.	http://xavier.xu.edu:8000/ ~polt/typewriters.html
Fremont Troll	Photos of the famous Fremont, WA, troll, living under the Fremont bridge and holding a real Volkswagen under its arm.	http://king.tidbits.com/ photos/troll/
Peachoid	Photo of the phamous water tower of Gaffney, South Carolina, "cleverly disguised as a peach." Note the horrid background and *don't do that.*	http://funnel web.utcc.utk.edu/~tmorgan/ peachoid/
Professor Bubbles' "Official" Bubble Home Page	Marvelous, marvelous, marvelous. Yes—soap bubbles! Go see! You must! A real pleasure!	http://bubbles.org/
Stark's Museum of Vacuum Cleaners	Sexy objects—not so much. But never think your topic is too dull if done with care.	www.reed.edu/~karl/ vacuum/vacuum.html

ping cart" and "space shuttle" or let you use your own shape. They include international dictionaries. I tried the CD versions of Word Search Construction Kit and Crossword Contstruction Kit, and they're pretty cool for $19.95 each.

No Windows? Create puzzles interactively at www.puzzlemaker.com/. They've got these puzzles: Maze, Word Search, Word Search with Hidden Message, Criss-Cross Puzzle, Number Blocks, Math Square, Double Puzzle, Cryptograms, Letter Tiles, and Fallen Phrase.

Off-Site On-Topic FAQ

Add a link to a FAQ related to your business or organization from the FAQs By Category (FAQ of FAQs) site at www.lib.ox.ac.uk/internet/news/faq/ by_category.index.html. If you don't find a FAQ related to your topic there, I'll eat a Tootsie Pop. Heck—I'll eat two or three of them!

History Page

This can be a history of your company, your family, your life, or the evolution of the product or critters your page is about. Find some old tintypes of your ancestors, or drawings of horses from the days of the pharaohs, Caesar, and Mr. Ed. (See the "Glorious Things" section in this chapter.) Remember to think about what's interesting to strangers—not to you as owner of a company or to dear old Mum, who's fascinated by everything you do. Even though it's your history, think about entertaining visitors, rather than getting out all that you need to share.

Testimonials

Tributes could be a cute twist to a personal page for a single guy, or a way to convince people to buy your products or services. Just make sure the testimonials are legit, unless they're obvious hyperbole. Get permission from the people you're quoting to use the quotes, and make sure you understand whether or not you can include their names. Get permissions in writing for quotes, use of names, and—while we're on the subject—likenesses of people and private property, and any material you didn't create that isn't part of the public domain. This isn't legal advice—it's a nudge to think about these issues and get legal help if needed.

CHAPTER 8

Hiding in Plain Site: Cloak-n-Dagger Web Pages

There are times when you want to use your Website to share information with a select person or group. It may be nothing as dramatic as the daily code key for saving the free world, but it's important to your business.

For example, I was reviewing a piece of graphics software for a magazine not primarily concerned with the Web. The software's marketing people had positioned the package as doing graphics "for the Web," so the magazine called on me to review it. The product badly pixelated some images when it exported them to GIF format—which is pretty important for Web graphics! Back then, you couldn't count on all browsers to display JPEGs. (The problem appeared in image editors as well as in browsers—it wasn't a browser palette problem.)

The product's tech support people thought the problem was with images that had optimized palettes. Remember from Chapter 3 how GIF images must be 256 or fewer colors, and just reducing images with more colors to a standard 256-color palette can leave very noticeable blotches and discoloration? It takes the extra step of optimizing the palette for a given image to make the colors appear as they did in the original, even with 256 or fewer colors. Well, the tech support folks felt the program just couldn't handle images with optimized palettes. That may or may not have been the problem, but we agreed there *was* a problem.

I explained the importance of GIFs on the Web to my editor, who understood that the problem was really big. She asked me to get the PR person to corroborate what I was telling her. Normally, PR folks are pretty reasonable about a problem—they'll put a positive spin on it, maybe ask their tech people for a work-around. In a small shop, where you're talking with the developer, he may say "It's not a bug; it's a feature." But this PR person flatly denied there was a problem of any kind, and shunted me off to the developers.

The developers agreed the product wasn't made specifically for the Web and that some GIF exports had real problems. I reported back to the editor, who still wanted one word of agreement from the PR person. When I went back to the PR person with the developers' comments, she set up another call with them, and they changed their story—and sounded pained in telling it. The PR person insisted to my editor that the product was "for the Web" and that nothing was wrong, even after I e-mailed the bad images to the tech support people. It looked as if she was going to bury the truth under her flat denials.

My editor had no idea how to handle e-mailed images or other binary attachments, and the relationship between writer and editor is simply, "Me hungry vendor, you client." Clients don't have to learn how to do technical things to accommodate vendors, and it can damage you to even ask. But my editor *did* know how to plug a Web address into her browser. I put the confidential images—which contained distorted GIFs made from art that came with the product—on an un-linked Web page. I e-mailed the secret Web address to my editor. For somewhat complicated reasons, so the story got pulled—but I got paid. A while later the product was reviewed by someone else at the magazine—but not as a Web product. The software company later admitted to the magazine editor that the product had been mismarketed. Without putting up those images just for my editor, I might not have been paid, and another reviewer might have let the vendor get away with marketing the software "for the Web."

There may be other times you'll want to hide something on your Website, or even on a visible Web page. I've put up a secret page where my brother's family could see Thanksgiving pictures of themselves without exposing them to the public. If I had information more confidential to share with someone at a distance, I could put it up invisibly to anyone without the "secret decoder ring" to get the message. Others would see or hear completely different files, or a mere pixel within a huge picture, a password dialog, or nothing at all. This chapter looks at how to do that with steganography, miniaturization, zero links, and password protection. If you need to get confidential updates to people in the field, the Web may be the way to do it. You can conceal information on a Web page and not have to worry about someone snooping through copies of e-mail stored on strange servers. Although you *can* encrypt e-mail, encrypted e-mail can call attention to itself, especially if you don't encrypt *all* mail.

None of the methods we discuss are guaranteed to be secure, but one or more or them may be "just right" when you want to make sure certain people have access to information like:

- The actual cost of goods
- Impending product changes
- Impending recalls
- Crime scene photos
- X-rays in sensitive consultation cases

Steganography—Hide Files Within Files

Steganography programs—some available free for the downloading—allow you to hide entire files within other files. For example, you can hide an image file within a sound file, or a spreadsheet within an image file. Just download a steganography program such as S-Tools3, and hide one file within the other. The file hiding the second file is called the container file. Once you've hidden the file, put the container file on the Web page with normal HTML tags, such as these:

Type of File	Tag Sample
GIF Image	`<IMG SRC="NIA_LOGO.GIF" ALT="Graphical viewers see logo of National Intelligence Agency." ALIGN="CENTER">`
WAV Sound	`<A HREF="GREETING.WAV"> Welcome from the Director of the NIA</A>`

Suppose you've hidden a picture of a secret agent (AGENT.GIF) within your agency's logo (NIA_LOGO.GIF) on the top page of your site. In Figure 8–1 you see NIA_LOGO.GIF clearly, but AGENT.GIF is hidden inside it. Someone expecting the hidden file can go to your site, download NIA_LOGO.GIF, and run it through a steganography utility to extract and save AGENT.GIF for viewing in any GIF viewer, as in Figure 8–2.

You could also conceal a spreadsheet, slide show, or any other file type within NIA_LOGO.GIF. The limiting factor for hiding files is size—there must be enough room in the container file to stuff the secret file into, and the proportions vary with different steganography programs. The physical sizes of NIA_LOGO.GIF, and AGENT.GIF appear in Figure 8–3. The byte sizes were 8.97K for the original NIA_LOGO.GIF, and 5.85K for AGENT.GIF. The best way to determine how large a file the container file can hold with a given program is to experiment. If a graphics file doesn't fit on the first

FIGURE 8-1   *You see NIA_LOGO.GIF clearly, but AGENT.GIF is hidden inside it.*

FIGURE 8-2   *Someone expecting the hidden file can go to your site, download NIA_LOGO.GIF, and run it through a steganography utility to extract and save AGENT.GIF for viewing in any GIF viewer.*

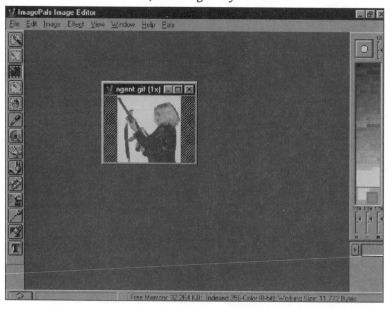

FIGURE 8-3   *The container files and hidden files appear the same graphically before and after.*

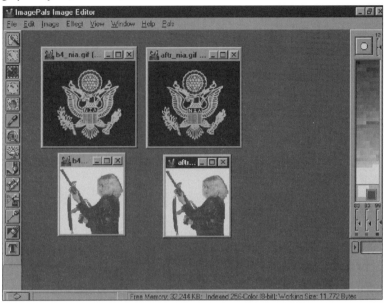

try, see Chapter 3, "Images," for ways to reduce the byte size without reducing quality.

If you hide a plain-text file inside the container file, a program such as the downloadable S-Tools3 can show the text on screen immediately, without saving it to a new file. That doesn't mean the file is undetectable on your contact's machine—the file can exist in volatile memory and in temporary files long after he's viewed the file, exited the program, and even rebooted his machine. The text method is a bit quicker, though, because the recipient doesn't have to open a second program to view a revealed binary file.

Steganography Programs

Individual steganography programs use different file types as containers. Table 8–1 shows several different steganography utilities and the types of files they use to conceal other files. These container files are the file types that will be in plain view on the Web. Consider choosing file types such as GIFs that show up in virtually every graphical browser, since a file that everyone can view will draw less attention to itself than a file that requires a plug-in.

TABLE 8-1 *Downloadable Steganography and Cryptography Programs*

Program	Platform	Filename	Location	Hide within File Types (Containers)	Comments
EZStego Java	Java	N/A—do it on-line!	www.stego.com/		Lets you hide files on-line through a Web form. Requires HTML 3.2-compatible browser.
GZSteg for DOS	DOS	gzsteg.zip	www.rit.edu/~pdw5973/files/	gzips	Requires CSDPMI3B.ZIP, also available at www.rit.edu/~pdw5973/files/index.shtml.
hideseek 1.1 for Windows 95 and Windows NT	Windows 95, Windows NT	hideseek-1_1-win-no export.zip	www.cypher.net/products/hide seek.html		
Jpeg-Jsteg for DOS	DOS	jsteg.zip	www.rit.edu/~pdw5973/files/noexport.shtml	JPEG	Requires CSDPMI3B.ZIP, also available at www.rit.edu/~pdw5973/files/index.shtml.
Paranoid 1.1	Mac (68020)	Paranoid1_1_hqx.gz	ftp://utopia.hacktic.nl/pub/crypto/crypto/MAC/Paranoid1.1.hqx	Sound	Encrypts files/folders using IDEA and 3DES and hides files in sounds.
Pretty Good Privacy (PGP) 2.6.2	DOS, Windows, Mac, UNIX, OS2	Varies with platform	http://web.mit.edu/network/pgp.html	N/A	Pretty Good Privacy (PGP) is an encryption program. Use it to encrypt before stegging. See "Stealth" program for one more layer of security between PGP and stegging.
S-Tools 3.00	Windows 3.1, Windows 95 (other?)	s-tools3.zip	ftp://ftp.funet.fi/pub/crypt/mirrors/ftp.dsi.unimi.it/code/s-tools3.zip	BMP, GIF, WAV, sector of floppy	Menus—I found version 3 more convenient than version 4's lack of menus, which requires dragging files from Explorer. Resulting picture looks more like the original to the eye than with some non-S-Tools competitors. If you can't find it at the site working now, run "s-tools3.zip" in a search engine.

Program	Platform	Filename	Location	Hide within File Types (Containers)	Comments
S-Tools 4.00	Windows 95	s-tools4.zip	ftp://idea.sec.uni mi.it/pub/security/ crypt/code/s-tools4.zip	BMP, GIF, WAV	Good program, though lack of menus means dragging-and-dropping files from Windows Explorer. Integrates functions for sound and images in one interface. Author prefers S-Tools 3, which is harder to find as sites replace 3 with 4.
Scytale for Windows 1.4e	Windows 3.1x and Windows 95	scytl4e.zip	www.geocities.com/ SiliconValley/Heights/ 5428/	PCX	Primarily a front end for PGP, Scytale also does stego.
Snow	DOS	snowdos.zip	www.cs.mu.oz.au/ ~mkwan/snow/	ASCII	White-space steganography.
Snow	Java applet	jsnowapp.zip	www.cs.mu.oz.au/ ~mkwan/snow/	ASCII	White-space steganography.
Snow	Java source	Java Source jsnow.zip	www.cs.mu.oz.au/ ~mkwan/snow/	ASCII	White-space steganography.
Stealth	OS/2	stealth-2_01b _os2.zip	http://ftp.giga.or.at/ pub/hacker/stego/ stealth-2.01b_os2.zip	N/A	Strips headers from PGP-encrypted message so the result will look more like random noise.
Stealth	DOS: must com-pile with Micro-soft C compiler with command line cl/DDOS stealth.c	stlth201.zip	www.dcs.ex.ac.uk/ ~aba/stealth/stlth 201.zip	N/A	Strips headers from PGP-encrypted message so the result will look more like random noise.
Stealth	UNIX	stealth-2.01b.tar.gz	www.dcs.ex.ac.uk/ ~aba/stealth/stealth-2.01b.tar.gz	N/A	Stealth strips headers from PGP-encrypted messages so the result will look more like random noise than an encrypted file. Use after PGP and before stegging.
Steganos for Windows 95 1.0a	Windows 95	st9510ae.zip	www.steganogra phy.com/	BMP, DIB, VOC, WAV, ASCII text, HTML, user-defined carrier files	Hides all file types. Shareware not limited or crippled. Wizard interface. Contains shredder to wipe files from your hard disk.

(continued)

TABLE 8-1 *continued*

Program	Platform	Filename	Location	Hide within File Types (Containers)	Comments
Stego	Mac	Stego1a2_sit.hqx	ftp://utopia.hacktic.nl/pub/crypto/MAC/stego1a2.sit.hqx	PICT	
StegoDos	DOS	stegodos.zip	ftp://ftp.funet.fi/pub/crypt/mirrors/idea.sec.dsi.unimi.it/cypherpunks/stegano graphy/stegodos.zip		
Texto for DOS	DOS	texto.zip	www.rit.edu/~pdw5973/files/noexport.shtml	Changes uuencoded or PGP data into weird English sentences so they look less like code.	Requires CSDPMI3B.ZIP, also available at www.rit.edu/~pdw5973/files/index.shtml
Texto Online Demo	On-line	N/A	http://ip-service.com/Eberl/textodemo.html	Intereactive on-line demo of the weird English sentences Texto will use to hide your data.	Just play with the on-line version of Texto—never encode sensitive data across the Internet.
Wnstorm (White Noise Storm)	OS/2	wns210_os2.zip	http://ftp.giga.or.at/pub/hacker/stego/wns210_os2.zip	PCX	
Wnstorm (White Noise Storm)	DOS	wns210.zip	ftp://ftp.funet.fi/pub/crypt/mirrors/idea.sec.dsi.unimi.it/cypherpunks/stegano graphy/wns210.zip	PCX	

Tip: If any URLs to programs fail to respond, try at a different time of day or another day at a different time. If the URLs become truly outdated, go to a large shareware repository such as www.jumbo.com and www.shareware.com and do a search for the filename. If all else fails, inquire in a cryptography Newsgroup or on a cryptography mailing list, or plug the file name into a search engine.

252

Steganography How-To: Example with S-Tools3

The procedure for hiding a file is simple in most of the steganography programs available. The Windows 3.1 shareware program S-Tools3 has separate modules for hiding files within image files (BMP or GIF), sound files (WAV), and in the unused space on floppy disks. To hide within an image file, just choose "Open BMP file" or "Open GIF file" from the File menu, and select a graphic to serve as the container file. The image appears in the window. Then from the File menu, choose "Hide file" and select the file you want to hide. S-Tools3 asks if you want to use encryption and, if so, prompts for a pass-phrase and confirmation. If you're not using encryption, you proceed to options for color and, when the transformation is complete, save the container file as a GIF or BMP.

When you compare the original and new container files in a graphics program, they'll look the same to the eye, and so will the file you hid inside and the file when it's later extracted and revealed, as in Figure 8–3.

Now to expose the secret file: Open the container file in S-Tools3. From the File menu, choose "Reveal." S-Tools3 asks if you want to reveal the file to the screen or save it to a file. If the file is plain text, it's fine to play it to the screen. If it's a binary, such as a spreadsheet, picture, or sound, save it to a file and open it in its native program. See Figure 8–4 for the simple process of revealing the file, and Figure 8–5 for the result.

S-Tools3 has advanced options for color and dithering, and it offers five encryption algorithms (IDEA, MPJ2, DES, Triple DES, and NSEA), five modes (CBC, ECB, CFB, OFB, and PCBC), and five MPJ2 keys, from 128- to 512 bits. The quick and easy program packs a lot of punch. S-Tools3 is shareware, and 15 UK pounds will get you a printed paper manual and full 'C' source code.

I prefer S-Tools3 to S-Tools4. Version 4 put sound and image modules under one interface and added drag-and-drop, but removed basic menu operations, so you have to open Windows Explorer and arrange it so you can drag a file into the S-Tools4 window and drag another file into the container file. This seems to me like more work than choosing Open and Hide commands from the File menu. Version 4 is for Windows 95 only, and thus omits the module for hiding files in unused space on floppy disks, due to limitations in Windows 95. Unfortunately, it's getting harder to find S-Tools3 at shareware sites, since the sites are in the habit of tossing out earlier versions of programs. However, there is enough awareness out there to keep Version 3 available. It's worth it to plug the filename "s-tools3.zip" into a regular search engine such as AltaVista if you don't find it at the site shown in the table (which worked at the time this book went to press).

FIGURE 8-4   *The simple process of revealing a hidden file.*

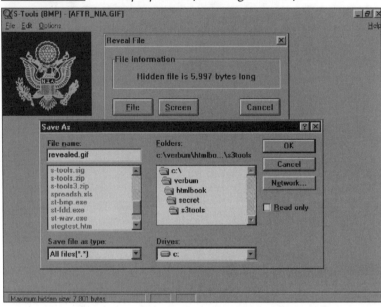

FIGURE 8-5   *The revealed file.*

More Sneak for Your Stego

Keep in mind that any curious person can gather up all the steganography utilities available and run every picture on the Net—or just yours—through them, to see if there's something there. Even though the second file is hidden from the naked eye, you are hanging the picture unattended in a public place. To reduce the chances of your hidden file appearing to unintended recipients, encrypt it with PGP (Pretty Good Privacy) before hiding it within the container file. Even if someone discovers the hidden file, it will be difficult-to-impossible to decipher. PGP encryption is strong enough to have gotten its inventor, Phil Zimmerman, in hot water with the U.S. federal government because strong encryption is classified as munitions and restricted from international distribution under ITAR (International Trade in Arms Regulations). You can find out more about ITAR at the Electronic Frontier Foundation (EFF) site www.eff.org/pub/Crypto/ITAR_export/.

You can find out more about PGP itself—and download it free—at MIT's site http://web.mit.edu/network/pgp.html. (If you're outside the United States and Canada, consider getting the program from The International PGP Home Page at www.vol.it/mirror/PGP/pub/pgp/www/.) Finally, visit the new official home of Pretty Good Privacy, which has joined McAffee, Helix, and Network General in the new Network Associates at www.networkassociate.com/.

Consider using PGP instead of other encryption utilities that come with steganography programs. To further conceal a PGP-encrypted file before hiding it in a container file, you can strip off the encryption header information with a downloadable program called Stealth. Ditching the headers makes it more difficult to recognize an encrypted file within a file. Stealth is available for UNIX, OS/2, and DOS. (DOS users can compile the file with the Microsoft C compiler after downloading and unzipping it—there's no DOS executable on-line as of this writing.)

Add up encryption, header-stripping, and steganography, and your secret file has three layers of sneak—but remember, no matter how "strong" any encryption, nor how many layers of secrecy you pile on, if you really, truly have to keep a secret, the best place to keep it is inside your head, not on your computer, and certainly not on the Internet.

Stego/Crypto Resources

Electronic Frontier Foundation (EFF)   If you're interested in encryption and privacy—and want to help preserve them—drop by the Electronic

Frontier Foundation (EFF) home page at www.eff.org/ and find out what you can do to help. The EFF has been fighting for on-line civil rights since 1990.

Ritter's Crypto Glossary

www.io.com/~ritter/GLOSSARY.HTM

A hypertext glossary of cryptographic terms.

Steganography Program Resources and News

Get updated on the latest steganographic programs at Eric Milbrandt's Steganography Info and Archive www.iquest.net/~mrmil/stego.html. You'll find links to lots of programs and source code. Once you've seen what's new since this book was published, you can continue to stay informed about what's at the site by subscribing to the very low-volume Steganography Archive News mailing list. Simply send an e-mail to mrmil@iquest.net with "News" in the subject line.

Steganography Mailing List and Archive STEGANO-L

To subscribe to STEGANO-L, send the e-mail message

SUB stegano-l <your_email_address>

to stegano-l-request@as-node.jena.thur.de. The FTP archive for the STEGANO-L list is at ftp://ftp.thur.de/pub/software/stegano/.

More Stego Mailing Lists

If you haven't read up on mailing-list manners, do so before posting to any mailing list, but especially to lists that draw people with extreme politics, as the crypto lists do. Be sure to read a mailing list's charter and answers to Frequently Asked Questions (FAQ), and watch traffic for a while before posting a message.

Cypherpunks Mailing List and Archive

If you're looking for information about cryptography, steganography, and other cloak-and-dagger tech, you may be interested in the Cypherpunks mailing list. The list attracts some folks with axes to grind, as well as those with practical technical information. Be polite.

You can apply to the Cypherpunks mailing list by sending e-mail to Majordomo@toad.com, with the following at the beginning of the *body* of the letter:

subscribe cypherpunks <your_email_address>

Applicants to the Cypherpunks list are now hand-approved by the list owner, and you may not hear anything back for a while, if at all. The majordomo letter says "The cypherpunks list has just been marked closed to avoid miscreants spamming large numbers of people using it; if you are really subscribing for yourself, your subscription will happen shortly."

The list may add you in your lifetime, but if you're in a bigger hurry than that for information, just go to the Cypherpunks Archive on the Web at http://infinity.nus.edu.sg/cypherpunks/, where messages are organized chronologically from the current week back to October 25, 1995. The Web page makes it easy to find what you need by subject, date, author, or thread. There's also a Cypherpunks steganography FTP site at ftp://ftp.csua.berkeley.edu/pub/cypherpunks/steganography/.

Newsletter of the IEEE Computer Society's TC on Security and Privacy

Complete text of the Institute of Electrical and Electronics Engineers Computer Society Technical Committee's newsletters on security and privacy at the Navy.Mil Cipher Archive.

www.itd.nrl.navy.mil/ITD/5540/ieee/cipher/cipher-archive.html

Newsgroups

alt.security.pgp
sci.crypt
comp.security.misc
comp.risks
comp.org.eff.talk

As with mailing lists, Usenet Newsgroups have Netiquette docs that you really must read before posting anything. Check out individual FAQs and charters within each Newsgroup, and read the rules that apply everywhere at:

Frequently Asked Questions about Usenet	www.lib.ox.ac.uk/internet/news/faq/archive/usenet.faq.part1.html
Emily Postnews Answers Your Questions on Netiquette	www.lib.ox.ac.uk/internet/news/faq/archive/usenet.emily-postnews.part1.html

Miniaturization— Hide Boulders in the Twinkle of an Eye

Miniaturization lets you hide objects by reducing their size hundreds of times within a vector graphic. In other words, you can hide an entire house on the tip of a hair on a freckle on a flea on a dog. To find the house, someone would either have to know where to look, or have a *lot* of patience or motivation.

Vector graphics retain their image quality when resized because they're actually mathematical descriptions of what to render on screen, rather than stored pixels. A raster or bitmapped circle (such as you'd find in a GIF file), becomes jagged and pixelated when zoomed. A vector circle remains a smooth circle at any size. The fidelity of zoomable vector images makes them a nice place to tuck shrunken pictures away. If you want to hide text, the vector format allows smooth, antialiased characters to shrink and grow beautifully.

Zoomable vector graphics generally require a plug-in which visitors to your site download and install in their browsers. With the plug-in installed, they'll see the picture you intend everyone to see, then zoom in on the miniaturized content if they know where to look or get lucky. Since everyone with the plug-in will have the tools to find your shrunken images, miniaturization is *not* the best way to hide company secrets or a confession of murder. So what are some *practical* uses for the semi-secrecy of miniaturization?

Use miniaturization as a novelty to:

- Add excitement or draw attention to what's hidden within the image
- Draw users to your Website with a virtual treasure hunt
- Offer clues that let visitors solve a mystery
- Let visiting children solve problems, then click on the correct answers to enlarge visual rewards such as flowers or puppies

The InterCAP site (www.intercap.com) has a great vector plug-in for viewing and zooming ActiveCGM files, along with zoomable on-line examples of how easy and fast it is for visitors to shrink and grow a vector graphic on the Web. Figures 8–6, 8–7, 8–8, and 8–9 show four levels of zoom over the Web. The small text area expands to just a fraction of the letter "B" in Figure 8–9, but the InterCAP plug-in allows far more magnification than we can show in a screen shot.

❂ *Tip:* Be sure to create a link to the site that distributes the vector plug-in, and explain to visitors who don't have the plug-in what those who have it will experience.

Miniaturization Tips

- Not all plug-ins posted to the Web at any given time are ready for prime time, so look at the latest versions of several vector plug-ins before committing to one. Be sure to note the date of the last posted

FIGURE 8–6   *InterCAP (www.intercap.com) has a vector plug-in for viewing ActiveCGM files on the Web with unlimited zoom. These four frames show progressive zoom.*

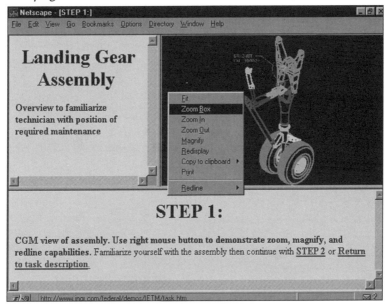

FIGURE 8–7

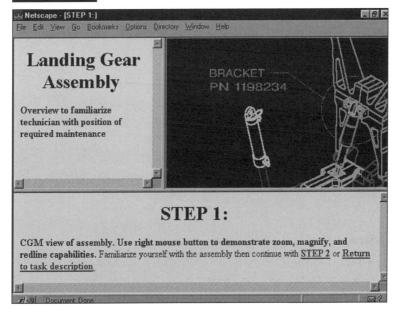

FIGURE 8-8

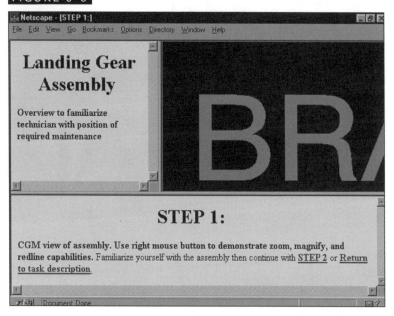

FIGURE 8-9

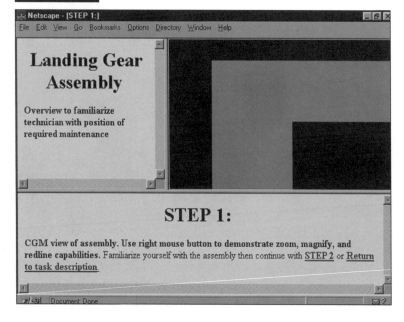

version if it's lower than 1.0. Dusty old betas can indicate a developer hasn't worked out the kinks. Go with a plug-in that's likely to be up-dated for future versions of popular browsers.

- See what other sites are using. The more popular sites are that use a given plug-in, the more likely it is that the plug-in will be incorporated directly into browsers rather than reissued as plug-ins.

- Although plug-ins are generally free, some are only free during a trial period, and the tools to create files usually cost something. The cost of the graphics package it takes to make the graphics should be an early factor in your choice. Plug-ins that require visitors to pay for the plug-in aren't a great idea if you actually want people to see your stuff.

- Many visitors to your page will be dissuaded from downloading and in-stalling a *free* plug-in to view your graphics, because downloading a plug-in takes time, some people don't want to risk their browser con-figuration on an unfamiliar plug-in, and some don't want to risk their systems by downloading any executable files whatsoever. If you decide to make some sort of vector treasure hunt a central feature of your Website, make it worth the effort visitors expend to see it.

- And always offer alternatives, such as text riddles, for those unable or unwilling to use the plug-in.

Miniaturization Resources for Netscape and Microsoft Browsers

Table 8–2 shows current plug-ins supporting zoomable vector images. Check for new plug-ins periodically at Netscape's site http://home.net scape.com/comprod/products/navigator/version_2.0/plugins/image_view ers.html. Look for image viewer plug-ins that mention zoomable vector graphics. Once you follow the link to the software developer's site, you can look for add-ons for other browsers, such as Microsoft's.

Zero Links

Sometimes you'll want to make images or other objects available only to a chosen few. Perhaps you want a client to preview art that isn't ready for publication, or you want to show a colleague the latest images from a re-mote digital camera, but e-mailing the binaries is impractical. This is sur-prisingly common, since many people have service providers or software that limit e-mail file size, and lots of people just don't understand how to deal with or decrypt binary attachments. You may not have an FTP server, and your contacts may not be familiar with the concept of FTP.

TABLE 8–2 *Downloadable Vector Graphic Plug-Ins*

Plug-In	Browser/ Platform	Comments	Cost	Programs Used to Create Images	File Types Displayed	Zoom to X Power	URL
AutoDesk WHIP! 2 (Free)	Windows 95 and Windows NT 3.51 and 4.0 Netscape Navigator Plug-in and Internet Explorer ActiveX Control	View, send, and share 2D vector data and design content over the Internet. Based on the same rendering technology as the WHIP driver in AutoCAD Release 13. Pan and zoom. Embedded URL capabilities.	Free	AutoCAD 13, AutoCAD 14, TurboCAD 4 *Note:* AutoDesk says people have used the free WHIP! DWF toolkit to generate their own DWF files.	Drawing Web Format .DWF	−32,768 to + 32,768	www.autodesk.com/
Ematek/HSI Metaweb 1.0	Windows 3.x, Windows 95, and Windows NT Netscape Navigator 2.0, MS Internet Explorer 3.0	This plug-in costs $50 and comes with the MetaWeb CGM/WMF viewer, converter and HotSpot editor. (You may not want your Web visitors to have to pay for a plug-in to see your work over the long term.)	$50, free evaluation	Almost all major CAD and graphical illustration programs.	Computer Graphics Metafile CGM	Limited only by OS	www.ematek.com/
Flare	Windows 95/NT 4.0 and Netscape Navigator 2 or Microsoft Internet Explorer 3.0	Xara's Web format. Hook URLs to individual objects in a file.	Free	Exported from CorelXARA 1.5 ($247) or Xara Webster ($49).	Xara format— can include embedded JPEG and PNG images	Equivalent to 72,000 dpi	www.xara.com/ corelxara/plug in.html

Plug-In	Browser/Platform	Comments	Cost	Programs Used to Create Images	File Types Displayed	Zoom to X Power	URL
InterCAP Inline ActiveCGM Browser 4.0	Windows 95 and Windows NT Microsoft Internet Explorer 3.x and Netscape Navigator 3.x	Pan and zoom CGM files, view animations, and navigate hotspot hyperlinks created using ActiveCGM Author. Supports redlining for drawing review, and Basic Scripting for customization and integration. (You may not want your Web visitors to have to pay for a plug-in to see your work over the long term.)	$50, free evaluation. Server license allowing unlimited downloads from a single CPU is $10,000.	Over 100 software packages can create CGM files. InterCAP's ActiveCGM Author is $3,950.	Computer Graphics Metafile CGM	Unlimited zoom	www.intercap.com
Micrografx ABC QuickSilver 3	Windows 95 and Windows NT3.51 and NT 4.0 Netscape Navigator 3 and Microsoft Internet Explorer 3.0	Allows users to place, view, zoom, and interact with object graphics inside Web pages.	Free	Micrografx Designer 6 and 7 (Micrografx Graphics Suite 2, SRP $349, street $149	Micrografx Designer 6 and 7 .dsf files	26,458%	www.micrografx.com

Put those semi-private files on their own HTML pages and give nonsensical alphanumeric names both to the HTML pages and to all the object files they call. The nonsensical names will prevent nosy people with too much time on their hands guessing the URLs. Create no links leading to the pages from elsewhere. E-mail the file names to your colleagues. People with the URLs to the pages will have no trouble viewing them, but someone who doesn't know the file names would have to be able to search your directory to know the files exist.

✪ *Important Safety Tip:* Place a file called index.html in the public_html directory with your semi-private files. (Index.html can be your regular Web page index—don't overwrite it with a dummy file of the same name!) With most servers, browsers will glomp onto this file automatically if no file is specified by a visitor calling up your directory. If you don't include an index.html file in public_html, some browsers *will* list all the files in your directory, including files you don't want broadcast to the public. Ask your sysop or server administrator about public statistics files that reveal file names, too.

Password Access to Web Pages
(for UNIX, Windows, and Other Platforms)

Another way to keep crowds away from certain pages is with password protection. If you don't want to get into CGI programming, or don't have the authority to run CGI scripts at your Web site, there are alternatives for restricting access to documents with passwords.

Non-CGI Password with NCSA HTTPd

One non-CGI password solution uses Mosaic 2.0 and NCSA HTTPd. You can restrict access based on username/password and/or the Internet address of a client. You'll find a tutorial on this type of user authentication at http://hoohoo.ncsa.uiuc.edu/docs/tutorials/user.html. Building the project from the tutorial requires NCSA HTTPd 1.0a5 or later on a UNIX machine under your control, or write-access to one or more directories in a filespace already being served by NCSA HTTPd. The site also has test pages set up so users can see, with their own browsers, how the protection appears to users attempting to get into the test pages with and without the proper authorization. The test pages demonstrate protection by password for one user or multiple users, and protection by including or excluding network domains.

Password Protection without a UNIX Machine

If you don't have a UNIX machine, go to the W3C page at www.w3.org/pub/WWW/Jigsaw/ for a Java-based HTTP server that should work on any platform that supports Java.

Password Protection without Your Own Server!

If you're allowed to create directories where your Web page is stored, grab the download-and-drop-in password applet from the Java Boutique at http://javaboutique.internet.com/password. Instructions are at the site, but see Chapter 5, "Ready-Made Drop-Ins: Java Applets, JavaScript, Active X, and Plug-Ins," in this book for an idea of how simple it can be.

Choosing Passwords for Web Pages and Stego Objects

There are no promises with regard to security in this world, but if passwords stand guard at the entrance to your Web page, your Web server, or encrypted files on your Web page, strengthen the passwords by following these rules:

1. Choose long, random, alphanumeric sequences for the most sensitive areas. Cracker dictionaries try real words and combinations of real words. Instead, use truly nonsensical sequences of letters and numbers, at least eight characters long, such as dr74k(9#. I got these characters by closing my eyes and typing, then changing two letters to shift+number characters "(" and "#". Don't use so-called "random" character generators. Since these programs rely on algorithms, they cannot be truly random. Mix cases.

2. Never use real strings, such as a backward Social Security number or children's birthdates. Crackers try to use information about you and your family members, work, or hobbies to determine your password.

3. Never write down a password. The quickest way to find out someone's password is to look for it in their office. If it isn't written down on their desk or in their computer, it's likely to be a word or words seen on the computer monitor or a nearby reference book. Never write a password anywhere. To memorize a string like "dr74k(9#" above, be creative. For example, here's what you can do with the string just mentioned:

dr74k(9#

dr=doctor
74=the year I first married
k(9#=canine with a jump from the left in the middle of its number.

It doesn't have to make sense to anyone but you—and you can find a mnemonic device that makes sense to you as you memorize any string.

Bonus Tricklet

Some animated GIF programs (such as Ulead's GIF Animator at www.u lead.com) allow you to add and read a comments frame that doesn't show in the animation that plays on the Web. Anyone stealing your animation may open the file in a good editor and see your message, but it's an option. As a marketing ploy, you might hide the answer to a puzzle in the comment frame, and challenge visitors to find the secret message.

Happy hiding!

Basic Structure of an HTML Page

Table A–1 shows the most basic HTML page, and Table A–2 tells what it means. All the tags in Tables A–1 and A–2 happen to come in pairs, with an opening <TAG> and closing </TAG> (with a slash) that says to "turn off" whatever the opening tag turned on. Some tags don't require a closing tag, because they're self-limiting, such as the
 (line break) tag. The paragraph break tag <P> doesn't require a closing tag, though many people use the <P> </P> pair around paragraphs to help them keep a mental overview of the page layout.

Since paragraphs and line breaks are inserted with HTML tags, rather than carriage returns, etc., it doesn't matter whether you write your entire

TABLE A–1 *Minimum HTML to Create a Correct HTML Page*

Tags Alone	Tags as Actually Used
<HTML>	<HTML>
<HEAD>	<HEAD>
<TITLE> </TITLE>	<TITLE>Simple Page Structure</TITLE>
</HEAD>	</HEAD>
<BODY>	<BODY> Hello world!
</BODY>	</BODY>
</HTML>	</HTML>

HTML document in one continuous line. Most people find it more satisfying to divide the page up visually with carriage returns to help keep track of different parts of the document. It can be easier to spot a missing tag if you break things up logically, too. (Some HTML editors offer an option to see HTML tags in colored text, and show faulty tags in a stand-out color to make it even easier.)

TABLE A-2 *What the Minimum HTML Tags Do*

HTML Tag	What the Tag Means
<HTML>	Begin HTML.
<HEAD>	Begin information about the page that doesn't appear in the page.
<TITLE>	Begin title that shows in the browser title bar, not in the page.
</TITLE>	End title that shows in the browser title bar, not in the page.
<HEAD>	End basic information about the page that doesn't appear in the page.
<BODY>	Begin text, graphics, and other objects that will show in the page. The opening <BODY> tag itself can also specify colors for the page and text, a background graphic, etc. Besides content that displays, you can add hidden comments using the comment tags: <!--yadda yadda yadda-->
</BODY>	End text, graphics, and other objects that will show in the page.
</HTML>	End HTML.

HTML Tags

This appendix contains all the HTML 4.0 tags ratified by the World Wide Web Consortium (W3C), along with a few notes and examples. For all attributes of each tag and the latest, most complete official information, visit the W3C site at www.w3c.org. The hyperlinked list of all elements is currently at www.w3.org/TR/REC-html40/index/elements.html.

Caution: Not All HTML 4.0 Tags Are Widely Implemented.
Even though the W3C has the power to ratify a version of HTML, that doesn't make support for the adopted tags appear in current (or even future) versions of browsers. Just as important, it doesn't make the tags appear in *earlier* browsers, which *many people continue to use.* Consider carefully before depending on a tag for something that most people won't see. For example, using the <Q> </Q> tags to add quotation marks in Netscape 4.0 and earlier will make it appear you didn't bother to use any.

The Bottom Line Is Test, Test, Test.
Download the current and last two versions of Microsoft's and Netscape's browsers and test in them—as well as a plain-text browser such as Lynx. Because browsers don't implement things the same way, you shouldn't rely on lists of supported tags put out by vendors or third parties, though it's a place to start roughing out a plan for which tags you'll use. The best current information is available online at the addresses in Table B–1. Remember that the tag lists from vendors include tags that are *not* official HTML. Take an especially close look at "The Compendium of HTML Elements"

TABLE B-1	*Implementation of Tags in Various Browsers*
Netscape	http://developer.netscape.com/library/documentation/ htmlguid/index.htm (Click "Alphabetical Tag List" in plain text menu near top of right frame.)
Microsoft's current supported tags	www.microsoft.com/msdn/sdk/inetsdk/help/dhtml/ references/html/elements.htm#ie40_htmlref
"The Compendium of HTML Elements," a third party tracking several browsers from their first versions forward.	www.htmlcompendium.org

(www.htmlcompendium.org), a third party tracking several browsers from their first versions up. "The Compendium" may get a couple of months behind, especially with some browser version-creep going on out there, but is an excellent gauge of what's implemented from the first versions forward in Netscape, Microsoft, Mosaic, Web TV, Opera, and the W3C, including how strictly the tags and their attributes are implemented. Remember, it's the older browsers, not this month's, that we have to write for (unless you can sneak into every home and office and upgrade the users!)

Important: Deprecated Doesn't Mean Broken.
Tags marked "deprecated" are tags that work—sometimes in many browsers—but are undervalued by the W3C. For example, the <CENTER> </CENTER> tags work well, but the W3C folks came up with the idea of Cascading Style Sheets (CSS) to control formatting, so some formatting tags have been deprecated and relegated to the "Transitional" list of tags, and must be used until most browsers can render CSS properly. (That still doesn't mean Webmasters will embrace CSS.) Other deprecated tags, such as <DIR> </DIR> Directory List, are redundant. (Use <UL> </UL> Unordered List instead.) The <DIR> directory tag may even confuse a browser looking for the dir (direction of text rendering) attribute. Remember, tags such as <CENTER> </CENTER> are perfectly safe, and tags such as <APPLET> </APPLET>, deprecated in favor of HTML 4.0's superior <OBJECT> </OBJECT> tags, must be used until the new tags are implemented in the *next few versions* of browsers. Otherwise, you're designing pages that few people will see.

TABLE B-2 *HTML 4.0 Tags.*
Tags Ratified by the World Wide Web Consortium (W3C) Dec. 18, 1997

Element Tag(s)	Notes
<A> </A>	**Anchor** Important for creating links and anchors <A HREF="URL"> </A> is a link, e.g., <A HREF="pagename.htm"> with this text to click. </A> <A NAME="actualname"> </A> creates an anchor to link to, e.g., <A NAME="Chuck">As much as he likes.</A> <A HREF="#actualname"> </A> is a link to an Anchor, e.g. <A HREF="#Chuck">How much wood would a woodchuck chuck?</A>
<ABBR> </ABBR>	**Abbreviated Form** Helpful to speech synthesizers, translation systems, search-engine indexers, and people who look at source. Shortened form shows in document. <ABBR title="manuscript">ms.</ABBR>
<ACRONYM> </ACRONYM>	**Acronym** Shortened form shows in document. <ACRONYM title="Coloring Out Of Lines">COOL</ACRONYM> Use to spell out the acronym for speech synthesizers, translation systems, search-engine indexers, and people who look at source.
<ADDRESS> </ADDRESS>	**Address** Information on author(s). <ADDRESS> <A href="http://www.ballroom.com/staff/tweety.htm">Tweety Tulips</A> and <A href="http://www.ballroom.com/staff/buster.htm">Buster Baines</A>, authored the <A href="http://www.ballroom.com"> Ballroom Dance Floor</A>. /ADDRESS>
<APPLET> </APPLET> Deprecated.	**Java Applet** Deprecated. Use <OBJECT></OBJECT> when implemented in most browsers. <APPLET code="Drain.class" width="500" height="500"> Java applet that shows water swirling around drain.</APPLET>
<AREA> (end tag forbidden)	**Client-Side Image Map Area** Use within <MAP> </MAP> tags. <AREA href="order.html" alt="Order Form" shape="rect" coords="0,0,116,28"> would be one patch on the image map.
<B> </B>	**Bold Text**
<BASE> (end tag forbidden)	**Base URL for Document** Lets you reduce long, absolute URLs to shorter, relative URLs. In <HEAD> section, use: <BASE href="http://www.phonecompany.com/products/phones.html">. In <BODY> section, use: Our cutest <A href="../images/cutephone.gif">Phone</A>.

(continued)

TABLE B–2 *continued*

Element Tag(s)	Notes
<BASEFONT> (end tag forbidden) Deprecated.	**Sets Base Font Size** Deprecated. <BASEFONT=4> Font size will be relative to 4* instead of default 3.
<BDO> </BDO>	**Overrides the Bi-directional Algorithm** For the direction to render a language.
<BIG> </BIG>	**Big Text**
<BLOCKQUOTE> </BLOCKQUOTE>	**Indents a Long Quotation** <BLOCKQUOTE cite="http://www.bookclub.com./feb_author/sample.html"> <P>It was a dark and stormy night. Andre dashed furtively to and fro, scurrying from doorway to doorway, as only a fictional and somewhat schizophrenic rodent can...</P> </BLOCKQUOTE>
<BODY> </BODY> (start and end tags optional)	**Body of the Document** Popular attributes set the background image and colors for background, text, links, visited links, and active links. The hex numbers here are colors: <BODY background="parchmnt.gif" bgcolor="FFFFFF" text= "AA4E3D" link="000000" vlink="000000" alink="000000">
  (end tag forbidden)	**Forced Line-Break** Break to next line without double-space.
<BUTTON> </BUTTON>	**Creates Button** <BUTTON name="Reset" type="Reset"> Reset <IMG src="circle_arrow.gif" alt="Reset"></BUTTON>
<CAPTION> </CAPTION>	**Table Caption** Must appear immediately after <TABLE> tag.
<CENTER> </CENTER> Deprecated.	**Aligns Center** Deprecated.
<CITE> </CITE>	**Formats a Citation** According to <CITE>Ms. Jones,</CITE> he did.
<CODE> </CODE>	**Computer Code Fragment** Formats text as code.
<COL> (end tag forbidden)	**Column** Groups attribute specifications of columns (not structural columns) for tables.
<COLGROUP> </COLGROUP> (end tag optional)	**Column Group** Creates a column group.
<DD> </DD> (end tag optional)	**Definition Description** Defines a Definition Term (DT) within a Definition List (DL).

Element Tag(s)	Notes
<DEL> </DEL>	**Deleted Text** Marks up changes from a previous version: Four score and <DEL>six</DEL> <INS> seven</INS> years ago...
<DFN> </DFN>	**Definition of Instance** Marks text as the defining instance of a term.
<DIR> </DIR> Deprecated.	**Directory List** Creates multicolumn directory lists. Deprecated. Use <UL> </UL> instead.
<DIV> </DIV>	**Block-Level Generic Language/Style Container** Adds user-defined structure to documents. See <SPAN> </SPAN> for inline container.
<DL> </DL>	**Definition List** Holds Definition Terms <DT> and their Definition Descriptions <DD>.
<DT> </DT> (end tag optional)	**Definition Term** The term that a Definition Description <DD> will describe within a Definition List <DL>.
<EM> </EM>	**Emphasized Text** Similar to <I> </I> italic.
<FIELDSET> </FIELDSET>	**Form Control Group** Groups theme-related controls and labels. Helps with tabbing navigation and speech navigation.
<FONT> </FONT> Deprecated.	**Local Change to Font** Deprecated. <FONT FACE="Arial" COLOR="FF0080" SIZE=+3>Pretty Pink</FONT>
<FORM> </FORM>	**Interactive Form** <FORM action="URL_here" method="post"> </FORM> <FORM action="mailto:you@here" method="post"> </FORM> Etc. See <INPUT> for forms hardware such as radio buttons.
<FRAME> (end tag forbidden)	**Subwindow** Defines frame documents within <FRAMESET> </FRAMESET> tags, e.g.: <FRAMESET rows=70,*> <FRAME src=banner.htm scrolling=no> <FRAME src=main area.htm> </FRAMESET>
<FRAMESET> </FRAMESET>	**Window Subdivision** Specifies division of one window into two (and only two) frames. <FRAMESET rows=70,*> <FRAME src=banner.htm scrolling=no> <FRAME src=twomore.htm> </FRAMESET> The next division must take place within one of the frames named above.

(continued)

TABLE B–2 *continued*

Element Tag(s)	Notes
<H1> </H1>	**Heading Font** (1 is largest, 6 is smallest)
<H2> </H2>	**Heading Font** (1 is largest, 6 is smallest)
<H3> </H3>	**Heading Font** (1 is largest, 6 is smallest)
<H4> </H4>	**Heading Font** (1 is largest, 6 is smallest)
<H5> </H5>	**Heading Font** (1 is largest, 6 is smallest)
<H6> </H6>	**Heading Font** (1 is largest, 6 is smallest)
<HEAD> </HEAD> (start and end tags optional)	**Document Head** Area above <BODY> </BODY> for <TITLE> </TITLE>, <META> information, etc.
<HR> (end tag forbidden)	**Horizontal Rule** Page divider line.
<HTML> </HTML> (start and end tags optional)	**HTML Document Container**
<I> <I>	**Italic Text**
<IFRAME></IFRAME>	**Inline Frame (Inline "Subwindow")** Inserts frame within a block of text. <IFRAME src="maxcat.html" width="250" height="300" scrolling="auto" frameborder="1"> [Your browser doesn't support inline frames or is configured not to display frames. You may reach Max's page by visiting <A href="maxcat.html"> his page directly.</A>] </IFRAME>
<IMG> (end tag forbidden)	**Inline Image** <IMG src="basejump.gif">
<INPUT> (end tag forbidden)	**Form Control** Some of the most popular forms hardware, such as radio buttons: <INPUT TYPE="RADIO" NAME="" VALUE=""> <INPUT TYPE="CHECKBOX" NAME="" VALUE=""> <INPUT TYPE="TEXT" NAME="" SIZE=""> <INPUT TYPE="SUBMIT" VALUE="Submit"> <INPUT TYPE="RESET" VALUE="Reset"> etc.
<INS> </INS>	**Inserted Text** Marks up changes from a previous version, e.g., "Four score and <DEL>six </DEL> <INS> seven</INS> years ago..."
<ISINDEX> (end tag forbidden) Deprecated.	**Single Line Text Input Prompt** Deprecated. Use <INPUT>.

Element Tag(s)	Notes
<KBD> </KBD>	**Keyboard** Shows example of text the user will enter.
<LABEL> </LABEL>	**Form Field Label Text** Associates label with another control.
<LEGEND> </LEGEND>	**Fieldset Legend** Assigns a caption to a <FIELDSET> </FIELDSET>. Can aid non-visual browsing.
<LI> </LI> (end tag optional)	**List Item** List Item in an Ordered (numbered) List <OL> </OL>or Unordered List <UL> </UL>
<LINK> (end tag forbidden)	**Media-Independent Link** Defines relationships. Used in <HEAD> </HEAD> section only.
<MAP> </MAP>	**Client-Side Image Map** Navigational device that links defined areas of an image to targets. Not backward-compatible with HTML 2.0 browsers.
<MENU> </MENU> Deprecated.	**Menu List** Single-column menu lists. Deprecated. Use <UL> </UL>instead.
<META> (end tag forbidden)	**Meta Information** Identifies properties of a document such as author, expiration date, key words, etc.
<NOFRAMES> </NOFRAMES>	**NoFrames** Alternate content container for visitors with non-frame-based browsers.
<NOSCRIPT> </NOSCRIPT>	**NoScript** Alternate content container for visitors with non-script-based browsers.
<OBJECT> </OBJECT>	**Generic Embedded Object** Will replace <APPLET> </APPLET> and similar tags when implemented in most browsers. Can contain multiple content types and display the first type in the series that the browser can render.
<OL> </OL>	**Ordered List** Numbered list containing <LI> </LI> List Items.
<OPTGROUP> </OPTGROUP>	**Option Group** Group choices logically in forms.
<OPTION> </OPTION> (end tag optional)	**Selectable Choice** In forms
<P> </P> (end tag optional)	**Paragraph** New paragraph. Not nestable.
<PARAM> (end tag forbidden)	**Named Property Value** For <OBECT> </OBJECT>, <APPLET> </APPLET>, etc.

(continued)

TABLE B-2 *continued*

Element Tag(s)	Notes
<PRE> </PRE>	**Preformatted Text** Most noted for defining "white space" a visual browser should respect, and which nonvisual browsers may ignore.
<Q> </Q>	**Short Inline Quotation** For short quotes that don't require paragraph breaks, <Q> </Q> adds quotation marks appropriate to the language specified. Handles double and single (inner) quotes in English by nesting the tags. She said, <Q lang="en"> The creep did it and he said <Q lang="en"> Deny it,<Q lang="en"> but someone else told.<Q lang="en">
<S> </S> Deprecated.	**Strike-Through Text** Deprecated.
<SAMP> </SAMP>	**Text for Sample Program Output, Scripts, Etc.**
<SCRIPT> </SCRIPT>	**Script** Places a script within a document.
<SELECT> </SELECT>	**Option Selector** In forms <SELECT NAME="" SIZE="1"></SELECT>
<SMALL> </SMALL>	**Small Text**
<SPAN> </SPAN>	**Inline Generic Language/Style Container** Adds user-defined structure to documents. See <DIV> </DIV> for block-level container.
<STRIKE> </STRIKE> Deprecated.	**Strike-Through Text** Deprecated.
<STRONG> </STRONG>	**Strong Text** Similar to <B> </B> bold.
<STYLE>	**Style Information** Adds style sheet rules to the head of a document.
	Subscript Text
	Superscript Text
<TABLE> </TABLE>	**Table** Example: <TABLE WIDTH=50% ALIGN=center BORDER=1 CELLPADDING=3 CELLSPACING=4> <CAPTION ALIGN=top>This is a table caption!</CAPTION> <TR> <TH>Row 1 Header</TH> <TH>Row 2 Header</TH> </TR> <TR>

Element Tag(s)	Notes

	`<TD>col 1, row 1 </TD>`
	`<TD>col 2, row 1</TD>`
	`</TR>`
	`<TR>`
	`<TD>col 1, row 2</TD>`
	`<TD>col 2, row 2</TD>`
	`</TR>`
	`<TR>`
	`<TD>col 1, row 3</TD>`
	`<TD>col 2, row 3</TD>`
	`</TR>`
	`</TABLE>`

`<TBODY>  </TBODY>` (start and end tags optional)	**Table Body** Row group for data. This division enables independent scrolling of table body with fixed head and foot.
`<TD>  </TD>` (end tag optional)	**Table Data Cell** See `<TABLE> </TABLE>`.
`<TEXTAREA>` `</TEXTAREA>`	**Multi-Line Text Field** Text area in forms.
`<TFOOT>  </TFOOT>` (end tag optional)	**Table Footer** Row group for information about table. This division enables independent scrolling of table body with fixed head and foot.
`<TH>  </TH>` (end tag optional)	**Table Header Cell** See `<TABLE> </TABLE>`.
`<THEAD>  </THEAD>` (end tag optional)	**Table Header** Row group for information about table. This division enables independent scrolling of table body with fixed head and foot.
`<TITLE>  </TITLE>`	**Document Title** Shows in the browser title bar, not in the document.
`<TR>  </TR>` (end tag optional)	**Table Row** See `<TABLE> </TABLE>`.
`<TT>  </TT>`	**Teletype or Monospaced Text**
`<U>  </U>` Deprecated.	**Underline Text** Deprecated.
`<UL>  </UL>`	**Unordered List** Unnumbered list containing `<LI> </LI>` List Items.
`<VAR>  </VAR>`	**Variable Text** Text for variable or program argument.

About the Author

Rebecca Frances Rohan has been writing about computers and software for national magazines since 1988, and the Internet since 1990. She has written news, how-tos, features, reviews, and opinion for *Internet World, Net-Guide, Web Developer, I-Way/Web Now, ISP World/Web Week, Publish, Windows Magazine, Windows Sources, PC Computing, Multimedia World, Shareware, Compute, Home Office Computing, PC Sources, Windows User, Entrepreneur, Sales & Field Force Automation, Adweek's Marketing Week, Cash Saver, Profiles/Continental, Black Enterprise, Writer's Digest,* and many other publications. Ms. Rohan is a former contributing editor at *Computer Shopper, PC LapTop, Internet Shopper,* and *Intranet Construction Site,* and is currently a contributing editor at both *Entrepreneur's Home Office* and *Sm@rt Reseller.* Her first book, *101 Marketing Tips for Writers,* was published by CNW Publishing (see www.bitcave.com/101tips.htm).

Ms. Rohan graduated from Tacoma Community College with a 4.00 GPA, High Honors, the President's Medal, and Outstanding Student Award. She was a Foundation Scholar at The Evergreen State College, which doesn't give grades. She transferred to the University of Washington Philosophy Department but dropped out to write a book on metaphysical empiricism in honor of a former teacher, Devon Edrington, who had passed away. She bought a Leading Edge 8088 PC and a copy of Word 4.0 for DOS in 1987 to write the book on. By the time the manuscript was finished, Rebecca was in love with the computer and began writing about it for magazines. An editor made her get on CompuServe, but by 1990 she had an account on the Eskimo North BBS, which was running on a TRS-80 at the time. She stayed on Eskimo through the arrival of Usenet and full Internet access. Her domain there is bitcave.com. Rebecca's daughter Marcia is 22, cute, smart, spunky and kind. Rebecca lives with a handsome cat named Max who always wears a black tuxedo and white gloves when he climbs onto the dining room table.

Index

404, File Not Found, adding class to, 227–228
Absolute links, 81
Acrobat, 49
  review, 50
ActiveX, downloadable, 184, 185
Acknowledgments, xiii–xv
Alien Ale, 100
Antialiasing, 94
APPLET and OBJECT tags, 89–91
ASCII
  graphic letters with Figlet utility, 51
  graphical text banners, 139–140
  text-based pictures, 140–141
Author, about, 279
Autoresponders
  domain names
    with, 84
    without, 85
  endless loops, 85

Background Assistant, in HTML Assistant
    Pro, 35–36
Background,
  color, 14, 24
    hex number, 22, 23–24, 36
    importance of specifying, 34–35
  dangerous, 30, 34–35, 40, 65
  image
    downloadable, 28–29
    embossed, 36–39
    gradient, 41

importance of specifying background
    color with, 34–35
  margin, 21, 39–41, 61, 62–66
  shaded, scalloped, etc., 41
Star Tech, 42
transparent, see Image, GIF, transparent
Block quotes, 54
Borders
  on hot links, removing, 45–47
  on tables, removing, 60, 62
Braille, speech synthesizers, etc., 78, 92,
    176, 179
Brain-wave synchronization, in CoolEdit
    Pro, 178
BrowserWatch, 8
Bullets
  downloadable, 27, 28–29
  hot, removing border, 45–46
Buttons
  3-D, creating, 47–48
    with downloadable program, 47–48
  alternate text, 47
  downloadable, 27–29
  hot, removing border, 45–47
Byte Trash quiz, 12–13

Cache, disk and RAM, flushing, 30
Cascading Style Sheets (CSS), 50–51
CAUCE, The Coalition Against Unsolicited
    Commercial Email, 205–206
Chemical symbols, creating, 163
Clock, free, 240

Color
  accent, 14, 18–20
  background
    dangerous, 30, 34–35, 40, 65
    page, 14, 24
    table, 58
  bit depth or resolution, 15, 98
    decreasing, 99
    increasing, 101, 141
  clip art, recolor to match site, 26–27
  company logo, 21
  dark and light, 20
  display, 15
  driver, 15
  hex number
    finding and recording, 17, 36
    fonts, 22
    to obtain for any color, 23–24
    using instead of color names, 35
    samples for tests, 36
  hide message to pseudo Luddites, 42
  hue, 15–18, 27
  link, 30–35
  luminescence, 15–18, 27
  margins, 21, 39–41
    with table layout, 61, 62–66
  picker screen, 15
  recoloring
    clip art, 21, 26–27
    tinting photos, 27
  RGB, (Red, Green, Blue), 17, 18
    numbers, getting, with HTML Assistant
      Pro, 36
    with Paint Shop Pro, 23
  saturation, 15–18, 27
  scheme
    choosing, 14–21
    making handy to use, 21–22
    stealing, 19–20
    trying together with Background
      Assistant, 35
  table, background, 58
  text, 30–35
    black, 14
  tinting photos, 27

  video card, 15
  wheel, 19–20
Comfort information, 75–76
Commerce
  auto-response to queries, 84–85
  consumers, confidence in your site,
    74–76
  domain name, using to advantage, 84
  FAQ , as marketing tool, 230–231
  navigational courtesies, 80
Contact line, Webmaster, creative, 86
Copyright, 135
  are Web rights included?, 135
  comment lines in animated GIFs, 164
  hidden with steganography, 165
  notice, 165–166
  royalty free not freeware or shareware,
    135
  watermarks, 164–165
Counter, visitors/hits, free, 237–238

Design
  Byte Trash quiz, 12–13
  great, 11
  unified, 14, 29, 68, 82
    downloadable, 30
Divider bars, 27–29
  downloadable, 27–29
Dividing pages, 27–29
Domain names, 83–85
  using with filters, 84
Download time estimator, 78
Downloads, offering virus myth informa-
    tion with, 240
Drop-in objects, applets, etc., 181–199

Embossed background, 36–39

FAQ
  as marketing tool and staff relief,
    230–231
  formatting
    anchors within page, 236
    finishing touches, 237
    make bottom answer jump to top of

page, 236
off-site, on-topic, linking to, 242
proper and useful, 229–237
FAQs By Category, FAQ of FAQs, 229
"Fight Spam on the Internet!", 205–206
Figlet, ASCII banners utility, downloadable, 51
File names
beware truncated DOS/Windows, 82–83
descriptive, 82–83
File size, 122–131
and animated GIF
delay, 111
offsetting, 110–111
superpalette, 111
and JPEG, 119–120
and sound quality, 172–173
illusion
recycling bytes, 129
with background, 128–130
with table, 129
images
cropping and downsizing, 123–127
GIFs, 98–100
interlacing, not significant, 105
reducing, with Acrobat, 50
shrink over web, 112
speed test, 131
splitting up content, 127–128
The Golden Rule(r), 123
File transfer speed, estimator, 78
Filters
and autoresponders
endless loops, 85
with domain names, 84
without domain names, 85
Font, color, hex number, 22, 23–24
Fonts
practical approach, 48–51
with Acrobat, 49
Format
conversions, complex, 95, 112–113
support in browsers, 91–92, 95
and legacy conversions, 6, 8, 82, 112, 114

Forms, with Acrobat, 50
Forwarding, moving, refreshing, 81–82
Frames
alternative
for inline, 72–73
for visitors, 69, 72, 226–227
escape for visitors, 72, 225
for magazines, catalogs, and photo albums, 66
inline, 72–73
nonframes, testing, 78
refresher/code example, 66–72
screen resolution, 72
standard in HTML 4.0, 66
table as alternative, 60
traditional Netscape, 66–72
with programs, downloadable, 66
Free site add-ins
clock, 240
counter, visitors/hits, 237–238
guest book, 238
search engine for your site's content, 239
topical search engine, 238–239
update notification for visitors, 228–229

Glorious things, 241–242
Guest book, free, 238

Hex number
finding and recording, 17, 36
fonts, 22
how to obtain for any color, 23–24
using instead of color names, 35
samples for tests, 36
Hide
files within files, steganography, 247–255
information in plain site, 245–266
information in plain site, business reasons for, 245–247, 258
message, to pseudo Luddites, 42
signatures in animated GIFs, 266
with miniaturization, 257–261
with password
cross-platform with Java, 265
non-CGI with NCSA HTTPd, 264

stronger, 265–266
with zero links, 261, 264
History page, 242–243
HTML 4.0 elements, Appendix B
HTML editors, downloadable, 4, 77, 78
HTML page, skeletal, Appendix A
HTML validator, 78
Hue, 15–18, 27

Icons
   3-D, creating with downloadable
      program, 47–48
   downloadable, 27, 28–29
   for embossed background, 38
Image editors, downloadable, 12
Image maps, 76–78
Image, tag, refresher, 96
Images, 92–166
   3-D text, 158–160
   alternate text, specifying, 44–45
   animated, *see* Images, GIF, animated
   animation, natural, 109
   ASCII graphics, 140–141
   backgrounds, *see* Background, image
   bitmap, 93–94
     jaggies, smoothing 93–94
   buttons, 3-D, creating, 47–48
   capturing entire pages at once, 131, 135
   clip art
     downloadable, 131–135
     re-coloring, 26–27
   digital still camera, 136–137
   figure modeling, 160–161
   film development on disk or e-mail,
     138–139
   GIF and JPEG, 93–94
   GIF or JPEG
     choose for each image, 97
     use whenever possible, 95
   GIF, 98–117
     and color palettes, 98–100
     animated, 105, 107–117
       3-D, 114
       clips, downloadable, 115-117
       converting from videos and other

       formats, 112–114
       delay, 111
       hiding data in, 245
       hiding signature in, 266
       natural, 109
       offsetting, 110–111
       planning your scene, 107, 109
       superpalette, 111
       text banner, 114–115
       utilities, 108
     file size, 98–100
     interlaced and non interlaced, 103–105
     interlaced, *see also* Images, JPEG,
       progressive
     transparent and interlaced, utilities,
       106
     transparent, 100–103
   graphical ASCII text banners, 139–140
   height and width, specifying, 44
   hyper-linked, borders, removing,
     45–47
   initial caps, 42–45
  JPEG and GIF, 93–94
     choose for each image, 97
     use whenever possible, 95
  JPEG, JPG, JPE, JFIF, 118–121
     lossy compression, 119
     names and format variations, 118
     progressive and static, 120–121
     progressive, utilities, 121
     transparent, nonexistent, 101
  metafiles, 95
  morphing, 160
     programs, 160
  picture frames, feathery inset, 156–158
     other types, 158
     square, 39
  PNG, 121–122
  scanners, 137–138
  screen capture, 131, 135
     programs, 114
  shadows
     cast, 155
     drop, 149, 154–155
     for text, 155–156

special effects, 38, 141, 143–153
  in Paint Shop Pro, list, 153
  in PhotoImpact, list, 153
  in Photoshop, list, 152
  in your program, 143
special symbols, 163–164
  programs, 163
text flyouts, 78
transparency, not transparent GIF, 102
transparency, *see also* Images, GIF,
  transparent
vector, 94–95
  plug-ins, 262–263
video capture, 136
virtual reality, 161, 163
Indent, from left and right, 54–55
  margin, 53–55
Intellectual property, *see* Copyright
Internet Press Guild (IPG), 210–211

Java, and typeface, 49
Java applet
  adding to page, 182–183
  downloadable, 80, 169, 181, 183, 185,
    265
    drop-down menu, 80
    sound, 169
    password, 265
JavaScript, cut and paste, downloadable,
  184

Layout
  and space, 51–55
  block quotes, 54
  indent
    from left and right, 54
    from left only, 53–55
  lists, 53–54
  margins, 53–55
  objects, precise placement, 52, 55
  outlines, 53–55
  spaces, nonbreaking, 53
Legacy conversions, 6, 8, 82, 112, 114
Link exchanges, 207–208
Links, 76–78

absolute vs. relative, 81
broken
  and absolute vs. relative, 96
  and File Not Found, adding class to,
    227–228
  and permissions, 97
  and truncated file names, 82–83
color, 22, 23–24, 30–35
external, checker, 228
internal, updater, downloadable, 52, 80
to ISP treasures, 241
to off-site, on-topic FAQ, 242
to socially conscious sites, 240
without HTML, Acrobat, 50
zero, to hide files from most eyes, 261,
  164
Luminescence, 15–18, 27

Margin
  background image, 21, 39–41, 61, 62–66
  image map, 76–77
  indent, 53–55
Marketing
  a prepared site, 202
  and e-mailed URLs, mistakes, 221
  CIW Announce, 205
  educating spokespeople, 208–209
  FAQ, as tool, 230–231
  "Fight Spam on the Internet!", 205–206
  Green Eggs, 207
  link exchanges, pros and cons, 207–208
  listservs, appropriate vs. spam, 207
  posting services, 204–205
  search engines
    popular, 203
    spiders, tips for attracting, 201–204
  spam, 205–207
  talk "Dot Com" everywhere, 208
  The Coalition Against Unsolicited Com-
    mercial Email, (CAUCE), 205–206
  Usenet, appropriate vs. spam, 205–207
  with hidden clues, 258, 266
  with puzzles, 241
  your site, 201–209
Marquees, animated GIFs, 114–115

Mathematical symbols, creating, 163
Menu, 76–80
  drop-down, Java applet, 80
  text-only, 78
Miniaturization resources, 261, 262–263
Money, saving, by checking license
       agreement, 171
  by saving workers time, 74
  in PR services, 215–216
  in PR, by targeting, 212,
  with filters and no domain, 85
  with link exchanges, 207–208
  with standards, and cross-platform
       migration, 7–8
Moving, forwarding, refreshing, 81–82
Multiple content formats, one set of tags,
       49, 89–90

Navigation, 73–82
  bar, 76
  poor, 74
  tools, 76–80
Navigational cues, topical, 82
Netscape plug-ins, 186–199
Non-breaking spaces, 53

OBJECT and APPLET tags, 89–91
OBJECT tags, and implementation in
       browsers, 49, 91
Objects, examples, 90
  introduction, 89–92
  multiple content formats, one set of tags,
       49, 89–90
  placing precisely, 52, 55
Online shopping, *see* Commerce

Password
  cross-platform with Java, 265
  non-CGI with NCSA HTTPd, 264
  stronger, 265–266
PDF (Portable Document Format) files, 50
Plug-ins, Netscape, 186–199
Press releases
  e-mail, 217–222
  paper, 212–215

Press,
  "Care and Feeding of the," Internet Press
       Guild, 210–211
  and e-mailed URLs, mistakes, 221
  and professional PR, 215–216
    e-mail wires, 216–217
    on a budget, 215–216
  big do's and don'ts, 209–212
  coverage, for your site, 209–223
  having clueful person ready for, 222
  luring to your site, 212–222
  making information handy for, 75, 86,
       222–223
  targeting properly, 221
  testing mailings to, 222
  your online press page, 222–223
Programs, downloadable
  3-D buttons and icons, create, 47–48
  ASCII banners, create, 51
  audio converters, editors, and tools 168,
       170, 177, 178
  chemical symbols, create, 163
  encryption, 250–252
  frames creation, 66
  GIF
    animated
      converters, 113
      creation utilities, 108
      transparent and interlaced, utilities, 106
  hiding information, 250–252, 262–263
  HTML editors, 4, 77, 78
  image editors, 12, 48
  image map editors, 76–77
  JPEG, progressive, utilities, 121
  link-checkers, external, 228
  link-updaters, internal, 52, 80
  mathematical symbols, 163
  morphing, 160
  precise object placement, 52, 55
  screen capture utilities, 114
  sound converters, editors, and tools, 168,
       170, 177, 178
  steganography and stealth, 250–252
  table creation, 55
Puzzles, 241

Refreshing, moving, forwarding, 81–82
Relative links, 81
RGB, (Red, Green, Blue), 17, 18, 21
    numbers, getting, with downloadable
        Paint Shop Pro, 23

S-Tools 3, walkthrough, 253
Saturation, 15–18, 27
Screen capture
    to get whole pages of buttons or icons, 30
    to help obtain hex number, 23
    to help with file conversions, 21
Screen
    resizing, table, 62
    resolution, designing for, 40, 60–61, 68,
        72
Scripts, downloadable
    CGI, 184
    htmlscript, 184
    JavaScript, 184
    Perl, 184
Search engines
    adding to search your site's content, 239
    adding topical, free, 238–239
    spiders, attracting, 201–204
Sharing information with a select group,
    245–266
Shopping, online, *see* Commerce
Socially conscious sites, linking to, 240
Sound, 167–179
    alternatives (no sound), 179
    automatic, avoid tying to main page, 168
    automatically played, 169
    bit depth, 173
    channels, 172
    clip length, 173
    converters and editors, 168
    CoolEdit Pro, Review, 178
    file formats, 173–174, 175
    flushing cache to test, 169–170
    Java, applet, 169
    letting visitors choose when to hear, 168
    lossiness, 173
    quality vs. file size, 172–173
    sampling rate, 173

    sources, 171–172
    special effects, 177–178
        in downloadable GoldWave editor, 177
    speech synthesizers, Braille, etc., 78, 92,
        176, 179
    streaming, creating and adding free, 176
        RealAudio, adding MIME types, 174,
        176
        when to use, 176
    tags, choosing, 170–171
    tools, 170
Space
    and layout, 51–52
    and margin indent, 53–55
Speech synthesizers, Braille, etc., 78, 92,
    176, 179
Staff, relieving
    with autoresponders, 84–85
    with FAQ, 230–231
Standards
    and browsers, 5–7, 8–9, 91–92
    and dynamic HTML, "experimental," 9
        tools, dual-browser support, 9–10
    and formats, 91–92
    and images, 92
    and Java
        cross-platform, 9
            Sun, 6
        deviation, Microsoft, 6
    and Microsoft ActiveX, 6, 9, 91–92
    and Netscape plug-ins, 6, 9, 91–92
    and nonstandard "extensions", 6
    and pre-HTML 4.0 frames, 66
    ANSI, 5
    ASCII, 5 (*see also* Text-only)
    content, formats, and legacy
        conversions, 6, 8, 82
    cross-platform, 91–92
    HTML, 5
    most universal, 7
    SGML, 5
    World Wide Web Consortium (W3C), 6
    draft proposals, 6–7
        recommendations, 6–7
Steganography and crypto, 247–255

programs, 250–252
resources, 255–257
Steganography example, with S-Tools3,
        253
Streaming
    sound, creating and adding free, 176
    RealAudio, adding MIME types, 174, 176
    when to use, 176
    video, adding free, 176
Supersampling, 94

Table, 55–66
    as alternative to frames, 60
    borders, removing, 60, 62
    cells, spanning, 58–59
    color, hex number, 22, 23–24
    column headers, 60
    from template, 55, 66
    invisible, 40–41, 62–66
    over margin, 61, 62–66
    refresher/code example, 57–58
    resizing, 62
    screen resolution, 60–61
    summary attribute, 59–60
    with programs, downloadable, 55
Templates, creating, 82
Testimonials, 243
Text, 3-D, 158–160
    ALT=, 44–45, 47
    and Cascading Style Sheets (CSS), 50–51
    and speech synthesizers, Braille, etc., 78,
        92, 176, 179
    antialiasing, 94
    banner, animated GIFs, 114–115
    banners, graphical, ASCII, 139–140
    color, black, 14,
        importance of specifying, 30–35
    flyouts, 78
    fonts, a practical approach, 48–51
    Images, jaggies, 93–94
    initial caps, 42–45
        downloadable, 45
    searchable, with Acrobat, 50
    shadows, 155–156

supersampling, 94
    typeface, a practical approach, 48–51
Text-only, alternative page, 14
    ASCII graphic letters, 51
    ASCII graphics, 140–141
    browsers, 9
    budgie, best viewed with a, 9
    menu, 76, 78, 80
Textures, (*see* Background, image)
Total looks, downloadable, 27, 28–29
Training, using Acrobat, 50
TWAIN, 137–138
Typeface, a practical approach, 48–51

Under construction, sign, bad idea, 80
Update notification, for visitors, free,
        228–229
Updating site, with templates, 82

Video
    QuickTime, within Acrobat, 50
    streaming, free, 176
Virus myths, offer information with
        downloads, 240
Vision-impaired
    and ASCII banners, warning, 51
    and table summary, 59–60
    see also Speech synthesizers, Braille, etc.

WebEdit Pro, review, 78
Webmaster, contact line, creative, 86
Webmasters
    advanced, look elsewhere for
        programming, 4
    beginners, where to get basic Web skills,
        4
    intermediate, what you'll get from this
        book, 4
World Wide Web Consortium (W3C)
    and CSS, 51
    and HTML, 6–7
    and Netscape frames, 66
Zero links, to hide files from casual eyes,
        261, 264